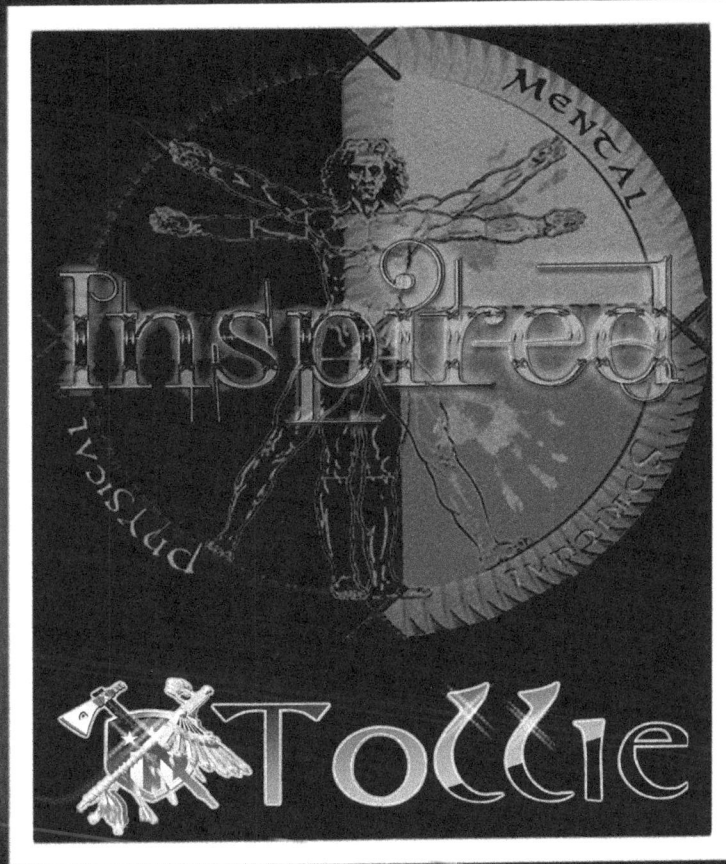

inspired

written by TOLLIE SCHMIDT

Inspired

Table of Contents

Table of Contents

Copyright

Copyright © 2013 by Tollie International Inc.

Cover design by Tollie Schmidt

Book design by Tollie International Inc.

All rights reserved.

No part of this publication may be reproduced, distributed, or transmitted in any form or by any means, including photocopying, recording, or other electronic or mechanical methods, without the prior written permission of the publisher, except in the case of brief quotations embodied in critical reviews and certain other noncommercial uses permitted by copyright law. For permission requests, write to the publisher, addressed "Attention: Permissions Coordinator:"

Crew@tollieinternational.com

www.tollieinternational.com

www.tollieschmidt.com

Schmidt, Tollie.

Inspired The Art & Science of Personal Transformation / Tollie Schmidt.

ISBN-978-0-9917121-3-7

First Printing/2013

Dedication

Inspired: The Art & Science of Personal Transformation is dedicated to the untapped potential of the human experience instilled in all of us by God, your power to love ALL and serve. To those who have hit rock bottom and decided right now to Rise Inspired!

Most of all for me, to God for my life's experiences giving me the family I love very much. My privilege to use life's challenges to open doors, hearts and minds so I can serve ALL. For the instilled the truth that nothing is impossible.

Inspired

The Art & Science of Personal Transformation

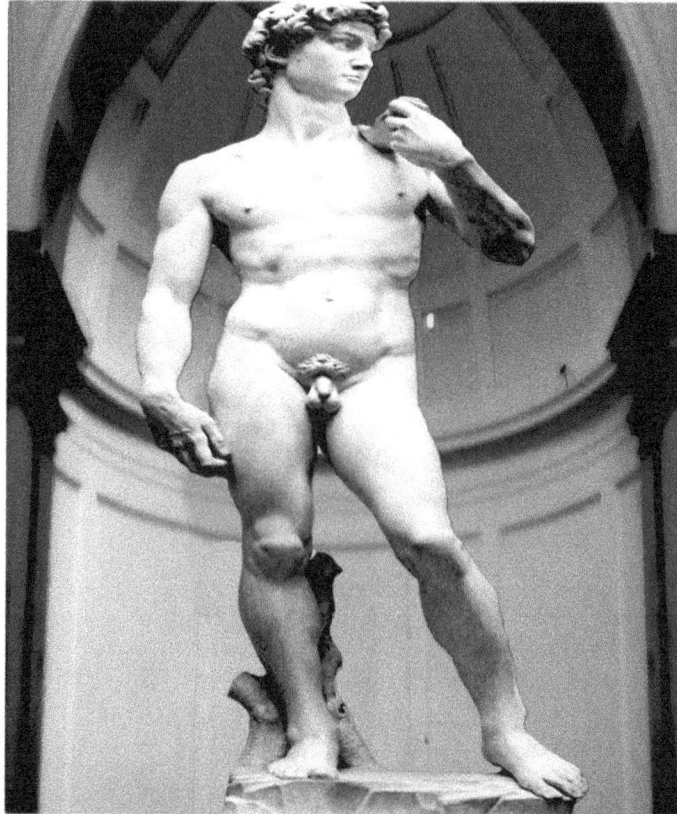

Foreword

Leonardo Da Vinci's "DAVID"

Foreword

It has been 653 years since Plato's dialogue of Timaeus dawning man's search for the lost city of Atlantis. A conscious quest to discover Plato's Republic a perfect utopian state. As human's we seek external forces to create a better life for ourselves. Why?

You already posses the ancient tools to create the life you want & deserve. You are the artist ready to stroke your own masterpiece. Leonardo Da Vinci's iconic Venturian Man, was cast in stone as a testament to the human body, propelling forth the human spirit. Rise UP, become Inspired and begin to sculpt your own personal "*David*"

With God all things are possible. Do not lay victim to circumstances, and in desperation call out in God's name as if prayer is nothing more than the crippled man's crutch. Do not shackle your days in the bonds of strain. I spent 22 years bound in self-pity, emboldened by my own self dictated script of blame and excuses. I've heard many stories, and witnessed their rouse played out in front of me…

Our country is at a cross roads. It is the individual human spirit within all of us, who has sat by and allowed the American Dream to be dictated to us, for far to long. Let the political parties and media focus on their, "*truths.*" Let them keep reinforcing their arguments by simply regurgitating the same talking points to their audiences, who tune in so they can have their own opinions be reinforced. What's the definition of insanity?

Our founding father's were humble enough to recognize their own fallacy as men, as they freely professed when they breathed life into the words we all know.

"*We hold these truths to be self-evident, that all men are created equal, that they are endowed by their Creator with certain unalienable Rights, that among these are Life, Liberty and the pursuit of Happiness.*"

The founding fathers infused a moral compass, divinely woven through their words to serve as an anchor for this, "*American Idea.*" Those words encompass what we now call the American Dream.

Powerful nations, kingdoms & dynasty's have come and gone, yet the American dream has endured. Political correctness can not tarnish the resiliency & power which can be found within the American dream. General George Washington in the midst of a blinding snowstorm on Christmas Day 1776 ordered his men across the Delaware river. A storm so violent even the British and Hessians were confident Washington would not attack. However, the snowstorm concealed the noise of Washington's movement and provided frozen roads that quickened the army's approach into Trenton. The battle of Trenton was a complete American victory, and turning point in the American Revolution. Washington did not have a collection of men who followed him by coercion or penalty. Washington had men who choose to believe in their Generals faith to a God unto which he pulled his strength, courage, it was his uncompromising belief in the human spirit within all of his soldiers. An army of good men, who did great things, and did so by their free will and choice.

Even in some of the darkest moments in our nations history, the American dream endured. Suffering and betrayal of the United States Government during the Indian Removal Act of 1830, is a testament to the perils of a few elite men attempting to create a nation forced through a collective vision, circumventing the free will of individuals. The Indian Removal Act cast a 1,200 mile sodden trail of tears, haunted by more than 4,000 spirits of my ancestors. The Cherokee, Muskogee (Creek), Seminole, Chickasaw, and Choctaw nations, integrity, pride, self dependance, slipped further and further with each mile, and the heart beat of these tribes symbolized through the ceremonial drum beat went still. Yet, the American dream was emboldened by Chief Crazy Horse of the Lakota nation in a vision to be foretold:

"*The Red Nation shall rise again and it shall be a blessing for a sick world. A world filled with broken promises, selfishness and separations, a world longing for light again.*"

America's dark past did not stop at the Trail of Tears, it continued on into Selma marching forth into Montgomery Alabama. A march led by a man who recognized the divine province guaranteed within the American dream. He vowed that no man, nor government, could ever impede on those unalienable rights, granted only through God. Martin Luther King Jr., slipped the surly bonds of earth prematurely, however, he found peace.

Dr. Martin Luther King Jr., steadfast and true, ascended upon his final mountain, April 4, 1968. As he touched the face of God, he heard the words, "*well done, good and faithful servant.*" In one shot, a coward, tried and failed to snuff out the dream Dr. King cast in Washington DC on August 28, 1963.

His dream continues to grow stronger, dawn to dusk, season by season, leaving footprints stretching through the sands of time for generations to come. Those footprints, bear witness to the unseen, a simple reminder, that on earth among men, Jesus still walks.

Become curious, Ask "*What Can Be*" rather than except status quo. Don't simply make choices, be steadfast and resolve to commit to making bold decisions. Think for yourself. Today, start by a commitment to serve yourself first. Only by serving yourself first will you create the excess and abundance to serve others in a deep and fulfilling manner. Stop the insanity of the quick fix, "*shot-gun*" approach to problem solving. Rather, seek the deeper underlining message, so you can **re**Build from a solid foundation.

Many times people blame events for how their lives turn out. However, what really shapes our lives is the meaning we attach to events.

How you interpret any event in life, the meaning you attach to the event, shapes who you are today, and who you will become tomorrow.

I'm reaching out to those who still dare to dream, more importantly those who want to achieve their dreams. How can you expect to change the world, when you can't change your personal situation? How can you tell others how to live based upon your personal belief system, when you, yourself have not achieved your desired goals? How can you fight for the right to Health Care without recognizing the contradiction of the term? Yes, health care is a human right, it is your personal responsibility to live a healthy life. As for "*Sick Care*" which is what the American health care system truly is. Perhaps you would better serve yourself and those around you by focusing on real health & vitality so you won't need to rely on a "*Sick Care*" system.

If your ready to gain the specialized knowledge and skills in order to succeed in every aspect of your life, then you have found the right place. **re**Connect with yourself at the deepest level, allowing you to give even more to all those around you. Experience a rich, meaningful happiness by discovering your purpose in life. Stop blaming, demonizing, making excuses, and telling yourself stories, using events, making disempowering choices and decisions to dictate your life. Rise Inspired and allow yourself to propel your life to a higher level.

Success leaves clues, and any great success story, innovator, leader, performer, and scientist will tell you that the first step to achieving your dream is personal responsibility. Any therapist will tell you that you are responsible for your happiness, no one can make you happy, they can only magnify that happiness. So it shouldn't be unreasonable to conclude that success must be earned it can never be given, and through freedom and personal responsibility is the path of least resistance to achieve your dreams. No Government can ever give you that which they do not take from another first.

Excuses are tools of the ignorant, do not use them. This is the time for the spirit of the individual to Rise and reestablish the American Dream, through achieving their own dreams. Let others sit around arguing and complaining, while you start doing and achieving. Let us together start the new era of enlightenment and reEducation, using the strategies of the most successful giants throughout history. Let us become the beacon of hope allowing light to pierce the darkest corners of the inner cities where hope has lay dormant long enough. Let our actions become the rallying call for the reEmergence of the American Dream giving momentum to ideas, innovations, culture, and empower, from within the human spirit, to proclaim this day and everyday after, our Carpe Scrotum. It's time to grab life by the balls and roll. Know this, who you are today will magnify in the future, so surround yourself with those who choose to dream, envision & create. It's time we stop playing by the rules. **re**Define how you will interpret the word "*NO*" will it be your *Alpha or Omega*… **You Decide!**

Tollie

About the Author: TOLLIE SCHMIDT

Author

ART OF INFLUENCE SPECIALIST | **ENTREPRENEUR** | BEHAVIORAL MODIFICATION SPECIALIST | **INTERPERSONAL COMMUNICATION GURU** | CERTIFIED PERSONAL TRAINER | **LIVE EVENT SPEAKER** | CHILDHOOD OBESITY EXPERT | **DREAM-INFUSED ENTERTAINMENT VIRTUOSO** | EATING DISORDER AUTHORITY | **PHILOSOPHY INFUSED EDUCATION ACTIVIST** | SELF-HELP AUTHOR | **VITAL RUSSIAN ELEVATION STRATEGIST**

Behavioral Modification Specialist

Tollie has proved to scores of people through his speaking engagements, media, and seminars that by exploiting the dominance of your mind you can do, have, achieve, and create anything you want for your life.

He has overcome morbid obesity, and shown others how to do the same. He hid his own personal eating disorder, he developed following his dramatic weight loss of over 300 pounds. He privately lived in darkness before excepting no more excuses for his self imposed prison of bulimia. He has worked with people all across the world, of every background and walk of life, his energy and passion for others is infectious and his methods achieve astounding results.

Tollie's story of growing up as the Fat Kid who ballooned to over 500 pounds before achieving an astounding weight loss of over 300 pounds has caught media attention. He Has been featured in many national publications, network talk shows, and radio programs across the U.S. He has been called the dreamer, the self-help guru, the Energizer Bunny, and his message and solutions have resonated with countless individuals worldwide.

Tollie is a sought after expert in childhood obesity, eating disorders, self-mutilation and depression. He has used his natural talents to create change for teens struggling with body image issues and is a voice for those living in a darkness of depression. Tollie has contributed to programs dealing with obesity, and eating disorders for major hospital groups, and physicians. His ideas and concepts have been considered cutting edge because of his link between obesity, eating disorders, self-mutilation etc., all stemming from a mind set stuck within a body image illusion.

Tollie's Out of the Darkness Project is a non-profit offering solutions and support to teens struggling with body image issues, eating disorders, depression and obesity.

Decisive Advisor to World Leaders

Tollie has met with, consulted, or advised international leaders including *Vladimir Putin*, *Boris Yeltsin*, *Queen Elizabeth II*, *Sergei Nikitich Khrushchev*, *James D. Wolfensohn*, and *Nikolai Lysenko*. He has consulted members of two Russian administrations, members of the U.S. Congress, the Russian Army, the U.S. Marines, the World Bank, the Russian Federal Space Agency and the son of former Soviet Premier *Nikita Khrushchev*. Tollie has had the unique opportunity to distinguish patterns and model the critical blueprint which brings about persistent habitual results for some of the most successful individuals in the world.

Engaging International Negotiations & Corporate Strategist

At only 16 years old; Tollie was flung into the world of International Business & Intercontinental Trade Negotiations.

The stigma of Tollie's age and obvious weight challenge could not overshadow his charisma and ability and he excelled to becoming the youngest international negotiator in Eastern Europe.

TOLLIE RECALLS THIS PERIOD IN HIS LIFE AS TRANSFORMATIONAL:

"You don't always get to choose your particular situation in life, yet what you decide to do in the situation is up to you. You may not be the most qualified, sought after, or revered in any particular situation. Nevertheless in that particular moment you ARE there, which makes you the most qualified, sought after, and revered. I chose to rise and stand in the gap, make mistakes, except failure, learn and grow till I finally succeeded."

At the age of 16 Tollie was apart of partnerships, negotiations, and Intercontinental Trade Contracts Arbitration with companies such as, McDonalds, Pizza Hut, BP, Mobil, IBM, The Boy Scouts of America and Stolichnaya. He was called on a daily basis to serve as a consultant with representatives from the United States, England, Ireland, Germany and Italy.

reStored Honor Leadership Development

Tollie has a vision to develop a community of leaders to strengthen and propel America into the future. His concept is to focus on **re**Building from within and instilling honor, values, ethics, drive, passion & creativity into our young future leaders. With the American Educational system in decline, the teaching of the values of service, citizenship, and free enterprise has become increasingly rare. Tollie has been a featured speaker at the American Leadership Academy in Cabo San Lucas, Mexico. ALA Founded by Entrepreneur *Jerry Nelson*, provides a unique and intimate venue through which successful leaders share their experiences and inspire the values, skills, habits and discipline needed to lead America.

TOLLIE HAS SPENT WEEKS SHARING IDEAS AND STORIES WITH OTHER SPEAKERS SUCH AS:

* Bob Barr - retired Congressman (R) Georgia; 2008 Libertarian Candidate for President

* Dan Cook – retired Partner, Goldman Sachs; Senior Advisor, National Center on Policy Analysis; Senior Advisor, MHT Partners

* Don Fites – retired Chairman and CEO, Caterpillar; Board Member, Exxon/Mobil, ATT Wireless, Georgia Pacific, Wolverine World Wide and others

* Hank Gatlin – retired CIA officer and member of Senior Intelligence Service

* Eric Greitens – Navy Seal, Rhodes Scholar, and many more.

When the *National Miss Teen USA Pageant* contacted Tollie to be a judge at their week long National competition, he jumped at the opportunity. Now this year will mark Tollie's second time spending time with contests from all 50 states for a weeklong event. For the first time a judge has helped to transform the traditional "beauty pageant" culture, and instill a deeper self-worth and value within these young women.

The Show Must Go On...

Just as *Temple Grandin*, was portrayed in the HBO movie about her life with autism. Words are like a second language to Tollie. He translates both spoken and written words into full-color movies, complete with sound, which run like a feature film in full surround sound in his head. When somebody speaks to him, their words are instantly translated into pictures. Language-based thinkers often find this phenomenon difficult to understand, but in entertainment & production, and even speaking, visual thinking is a tremendous advantage.. So entertainment and the possibilities to create change, effect emotions and influence an audience is in essence Tollie's natural state.

Growing up Tollie always felt at home on stage performing, always a audience favorite, he found that on stage his size and weight seemed to be neutralized. He produced, directed, and performed in many facets and has won critical acclaim and awards.

In a year Tollie went from over 500+ pounds to Under 200 and continues to create lasting empowering change in his mind, body and spirit daily. Tollie is known as a guy who does not believe in personal limits, his creative and artistic nature infused with his natural marketing ability charisma and charm has catapulted him into many new business opportunities.

To Learn More, Please Visit:

www.TollieSchmidt.com

www.TollieInternational.com

www.Facebook.com/TollieSchmidt

www.Twitter.com/TollieSchmidt

www.TollieSchmidt.com

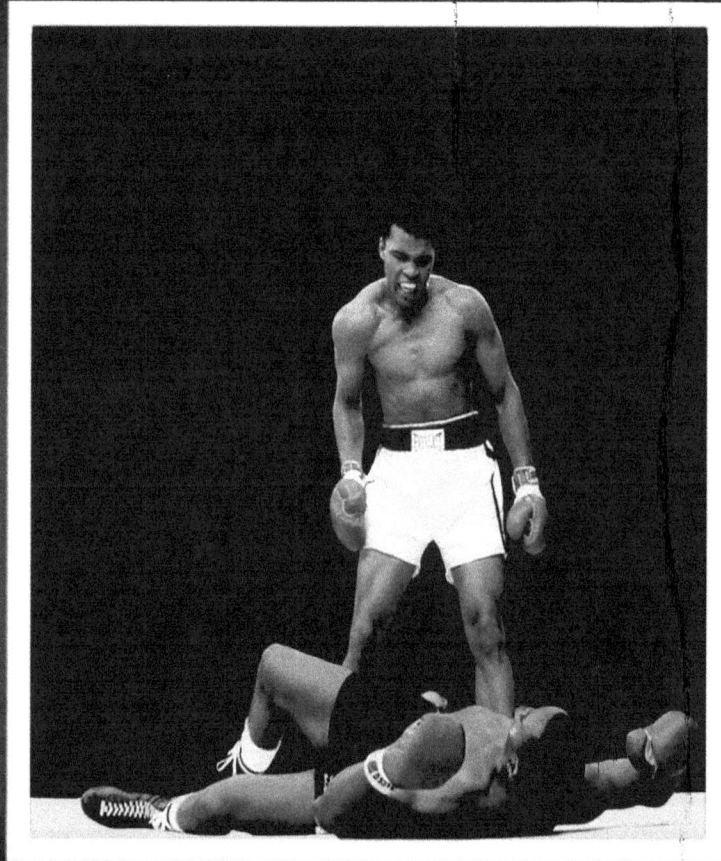

Chapter 1

I Am the Greatest!

I Am the Greatest

"I AM THE GREATEST, I SAID THAT EVEN BEFORE I KNEW I WAS." -
MUHAMMAD ALI

I have been hearing for months about the dire economic situation in Europe, then seeing America's own Nation Debt swelling to over $17-trillion dollars. A number so large and profound that its testing even comprehending what that number actually means. All the analysis of experts weighing in on our economy, state of unemployment without solutions to correct course, it became clear to me what we have actually lost. And by we I mean the people of America. We lost our mojo, our fighting spirit, the thirst to participate, our pride in success, we lost the independent spirit. Hard work, sweat, countless hours, education, and a healthy amount of stubbornness was a champion ready to respond.

We have gone from Robin Leach's Lifestyles of the Rich and Famous to how can we hide, a life of wealth, and achievement. We have gone from celebrating even a hillbilly named Jed Clampett striking it rich after an extraordinary lousy shot discovered oil under his swamp in the Ozarks.

Do you ever recall anyone watching The Beverly Hillbillies and while Granny was taking a dip in the cement pond, they would say:

"They don't deserve that money, they didn't earn it, are they paying their fair share?"

No, Even thru all their zany backwoods antics, we all recognized the simplicity and blessing we call The American Dream.

Some can scratch a lucky ticket; others by pure luck can be found swimming in cash. Others learn from those who succeed, work hard, take risks, face numerous rejections, knocking on one door after another, refusing to give up, they took their hits, until they picked themselves up off the mat, and proclaimed, "*I am the greatest; I am the champion!*" We would be inspired through the trials and tribulations as we witnessed one more American dream come true. Where did all of America's Muhammad Ali's go? More than a boxer, more than a champion, he not only embodied the American Dream, he embraced the Champion he was, and was not shy about expressing how passionate he was.

"This is the legend of Cassius Clay. The most beautiful Fighter in the world today. He talks a great deal, and brags indeed-y, of a muscular punch that's, incredibly speed-y. Brought FIght fans are runnin with Cash." -Muhammad Ali

Muhammad Ali took pride in his race and reached out to African Americans. Muhammad was a man of conviction and his influence in the world of sports shined through his speeches. His speech *"I am the Greatest"* proclaimed to all that he believed in himself, he knew that he could accomplish anything thru a superior mindset. Ali would not let anyone take him down.

People felt Ali's courage, which inspired new empowering beliefs. Muhammad Ali set the stage for others to follow, and he showed that African Americans can be extraordinarily successful in the world of sports.

When was the last time you heard anyone proclaim, *"I AM THE GREATEST!"* This is a powerful statement. Where did our Muhammad Ali's go?

What did Ali learn that is no longer being taught in schools? If you've seen the film, Waiting for Superman, you will see the difference between teaching for success, and teaching how to feel-good. Failing schools created the myth that feeling righteous about yourself is more beneficial than accomplishments to mask the trend of failing test scores, literacy and job preparation. A conscious effort was made to convince children feeling-good is just as, or more valuable than results. Administrators, bureaucrats, teachers, and parents alike attempted to bolster student's self-image with clichés and platitudes.

Renowned psychologist Albert Ellis and author of The Myth of Self-Esteem have publicly criticized the self-esteem movement as *"self-defeating and ultimately destructive."* According to Ellis, a healthier alternative to self-esteem is unconditional self-acceptance or as Napoleon Hill called it *"accurate thinking."* I know from my own experiences positive determination is used to generate results. Which is what actually creates a deep and eternal happiness and joy, is a complete success, real achievement. As Mary Kay Ash put it, *"You*

I Am the Greatest!

fake it till you make it!" meaning you don't have to feel complete until you have done something to feel virtuous about. Yet, you're about to learn what the schools, never teach. You are going to learn proven techniques allowing you to become a champion, tap your inner power, and get inspired, so you to will proudly declare to the world: "*I AM THE GREATEST!*"

My greatest attribute since overcoming my personal challenges was the ability to Inspire. Yet there's a difference between Inspire and Inspired. When you inspire others, its nothing more than a temporary feel-good moment, you've become a happy hour cocktail. To be truly Inspired is powerful, it is not only achieving success, its knowing the exact process to take action, and create anything you want in your life. Inspired is your freedom to cast off fears and create powerful changes in your life. Inspired is the fuel it is going to take to reignite the American Spirit, personal achievement and success. To me, success is achieving goals, continually casting a larger vision with a curiosity and thirst to become more. It is life's adventures, which allows us to grow passionately, culturally, spiritually, physiologically, brilliantly, and create wealth while making a positive impact on others. The road to success is written in pencil, because you'll always be erasing, and creating new roads, bridges, and scenic detours. The power of being Inspired, feeling your mojo flowing is the juice you feel from achieving, and creating, and dreaming bigger, that feeling never fades.

I want you to become inspired, overcome any negative aspect you have in your life while never settling for a temporary feel-good moment again. I want you only to achieve extraordinary success so you can exclaim boldly, "*I AM THE GREATEST!*" Applying the principles you're going to learn, I changed not only ways I felt about myself, but also accomplish tasks, achieving measurable results in my life. Laying dormant within all of us is the power massively to transform our lives into our biggest dreams. It's time to stand; it's time to dream again.

I could look at how I was able to turn my dreams into reality, and knowing I've only just begun, fills me with a sense of gratitude. More important I am far from unique. After seeing a financially struggling computer geek from Harvard become a Multi-Billionaire in just a few short years, simply by connecting friends, with other friends, it's easy to see what is possible.

We are living in the greatest of times for those who have a spirit of a dreamer. It is in these times where so many people are creating awe inspiring achievements as if by overnight, by achieving successes that would have been unthinkable in the past. I'm reminded of a dreamer we lost earlier this year who actually changed how the world connects on a daily basis, Steve Jobs. He was a kid in jeans who was penniless and had a passion for computers and built a fortune 500 company faster than anyone in history, today Apple is the most valuable company in America.

Look at Glenn Beck. What started as one family tragedy to another, a personal battle with drugs and alcohol, Glenn emerged as one of the nations leading talk show hosts. He pioneered the first online media network, which is still growing at record pace. Look at people in the entertainment industry like Steven Spielberg or Garth Brooks, or businessmen like Steve Jobs and Walt Disney. What do they have in common other than massive success? The answer, is Power, Inspired Power.

The word power has become a downright emotional word. And how people perceive the term has become opposites. Some people equate power with greed, control, with only negative sentiments attached. Some people lust after power. Others perceive it as a sin, a moral evil in society. What does power actually mean to you?

I don't integrate a historical character of conquering people, or imposing power over others. And I would urge you not to do the same mistake, historically we have several examples of the fleeing life span of power when it is used to exert pressure or control over people. Yet, we may not get the word used as much today, we all agree power is a constant in the world. You mold your perceptions, or someone will pick them for you. If you stand for nothing, you will fall for everything. However, Inspired Power is the ability to achieve the outcome you envision while inspiring and opening the doors for others to achieve their dreams. When you become, inspired you trigger a power which gives you the ability to change your life, to mold your perceptions, to establish the rules by which the game is played. Inspired power is shared, never imposed. It's ability to see the needs of people, and develop solutions of those you care for and love. It's the secret to living your dreams, and creating opportunities for others to live theirs. It becomes your compass to cast your vision, and stay on course, manage your brains thoughts, your behavior, so you avoid the storms and rough waters, and sail into a perfect sunrise exactly as seen in your vision.

Throughout time, the power to control our lives has been felt through an array of broad forms and functions. In the earliest times, it was a primitive as survival of the fittest, the strong had power over the weak. Although as societies evolved, power was passed down by birthright. The king, cast his crest, or family shield throughout his kingdom marking his realm of control, disobedience was snuffed out by the kings swift authority. Power was also obtained by the association or loyal obedience to the king. Capital didn't become the recognizable sign of power until the industrial age. We have read how those who had access to massive amounts of capital dominated the Industrial Process. Although many things have changed, many of these still play a role today. It's a lot easier to build your dream with capital, than it is being broke. Having strength, is better than being seen as weak. Today, the familiar saying holds true, Knowledge is Power.

Today information, technologies, systems, ideas, are evolving and changing daily. Students in school studying Marketing, or business graduate with knowledge gained through textbooks which became obsolete before they even went through the printing press. Everything from driverless cars, to the best marketed hamburger concept store chains. Consider Google; for example, and the power of information.

What is Google? Google began as a search engine, which simply put knowledge is power. is the ability to collect all information into a hub and categorize, filter, and communicated that information to the world. Google has gained worldwide power and dominance for the most part was achieved through their ability to collect all information and communicate it efficiently.

Through the collection of data and information, Google was able to create capital, while introducing the world to innovative new concepts, and products which became the ultimately Inspired Infused Power.

Knowledge is Power

I Am the Greatest!

Knowledge is Power, More Importantly Specialized Knowledge is Your Superpower.

AS ALVIN TOFFLER HAS WRITTEN:

"Knowledge itself ... turns out to be not only the source of the highest-quality power, but also the most important ingredient of force and wealth. Put differently, knowledge has gone from being an adjunct of money power and muscle power, to being their very essence. It is, in fact, the ultimate amplifier. This is the key to the power shift that lies ahead, and it explains why the battle for control of knowledge and the means of communication is heating up all over the world." -Alvin Toffler

Inspired Power is at the fingertips of us all, any excuse not to gain specialty education, is futile. In fact, not only is specialized information available online, but also the entire course catalog of America's most endeared institutes of higher learning. Today, for free, you can get full courses from MIT, Harvard, and Princeton just to name a few. Throwback to medieval times, is a reminder that if you were not king, the likely hood you could become one, was 0%. The same opportunity for personal achievement during the Industrial Revolution without capital was also pretty grim. Yet today, any kid in jeans can develop an idea, a company that can transform the world. Inspired Power is not exclusively for the achievement of capital. To get inspired is the ability to obtain specialized information, which can convert you and, in many ways, inspire the world.

LIKE MAHATMA GANDHI SAID:

"Be the change you want to see in the world."

I Am the Greatest!

Earlier when I discussed my reasons for writing this book, there's a question I had to answer. Why do some people get inspired, strive to become a champion, and achieve the results to where they can declare, "*I Am the Greatest!*" while others settle for comfort? Why aren't we all Inspired, empowered, happy, wealthy, healthy, and successful? You can be the smartest person in the world, you can think up theories, ideas, inventions, you can understand how to make all the changes in your body, yet it's not enough. There's a difference between a dreamer and a day dreamer, and it can all be summed up in one word, Action. Action is what creates results. Action equals reaction. Knowledge is your starting point, while your initial target, would be the desired outcome. To achieve your dream, you have to chart a course, develop a strategy, in order to use your knowledge from inception to conclusion.

Action is the system set in order to achieve your dream. The actual meaning of power is "*the ability to act.*" All of our creations in life are represented by how we choose to communicate to ourselves. What we relate to our brain as to how we perceive any circumstance or condition. Quality life is connected to how we move and use our muscles and bodies even our facial expressions. Motion becomes emotion.

Today, so many people get caught in the mental trap, reacting as a response, because they are envious of people's success. They allow themselves more often than not, to fall victim of wanting to feel like a victim, or it must be biased, any excuses in order to defend and communicate to their brain that success at the root, must be inherently evil. Yet, when you go beyond the surface the answer is obvious, yet difficult for so many, and the answer is the ability to take action. Think about it, other people had the same knowledge Steve Jobs had. People other than Glenn Beck could have seen the writing on the wall and embraced the creation of an online television network. But, Beck & Jobs was able to take action, and in doing so not only became inspired, but inspired the world as a whole.

We experience our lives through communicating to ourselves in two different ways.

First we communicate internally, which is how we communicate to our brain all the things we view, say, and experience within ourselves.

The second method we communicate is externally all the words, tonalities, facial expressions, body postures, and physical actions to communicate outwardly to others in the world.

This is easy to understand since we are taught early on the importance of body language. All the ways we communicate are actions, a cause set in motion. So when you discover how actions have consequences, it is saying all communications have a definite impact on ourselves and on others.

Inspired Communication is Power

Those Who Communicate Through the Power of Words Have Shaped History, Good & Bad.

Mastering effective communication allows you to create the story communicated to your brain creating events in your life in the most empowering positive way. Rather than, communicate to your brain a story of hopelessness during a particular event, which would ensure a negative outcome, you can change the story to allow focus on what is possible and solutions to take action. Behaviors and feelings are all originally rooted directly from a source of communication. What if I change the word communicate to influence, it takes on a whole new meaning doesn't it? Those who effect the thoughts, feelings, and actions of the majority of us are considered masters of influence. Right? See how communication is used, just swapping out the word communicate and replacing it with influence made you communicate to yourself an entirely different meaning.

I Am the Greatest!

The power of words, harnessing the Inspired Power of the spoken language, has been immortalized by, John F Kennedy, Thomas Jefferson, Martin Luther King, Jr., Ronald Reagan, Winston Churchill, and Mahatma Gandhi. These oratorical masters used their skill to shape and mold the world as we know it. In a much grimmer vein, think of Hitler. These men shared the power to communicate, to persuade, and ignite the action to create emotion, stir up a sense of passion within themselves and others. They were able to cast their vision. A vision was cast to expand man's reach beyond the skies, while slipping the surly bonds of the earth to touch the face of God.

While a vision was also cast through insecurities and hate, skillfully communicated through a gifted young orator whose name has become synonymous with hate. Hitler's desire to resurrect the Holy Roman Empire of the German Nation, communicated to others with such agreement that he induced the way the majority thought and acted. Today, the average person if asked what their initial sentiment of Hitler is, it's a safe bet. The answer would be decidedly negative, as it should be. However, our historical lens tends to become out of focus over time. We must never forget that Hitler, was not hated, in fact, he was revered, throughout Europe, and America. Those who communicated fears, or skepticism of Hitler was chastised in the media, and society. The warning signs were all there, yet Hitler's appeal through his gift of oratory communication masked the truth of his words.

Wouldn't this also be the case why a Steven Spielberg, a Garth Brooks, a Steve Jobs, a Glenn Beck, or a Ronald Reagan apart from others? Are they not masters of persuasion and influence through communication? Communication is not just a tool to sway and influence the masses, it is also the same tool we use to move ourselves.

Your ability to become an accomplished communicator in the outside world determines the success level you have with others - personally, emotionally, socially, and financially. More important, the level of success you experience within yourself - the happiness, joy, ecstasy, love, or anything else you dream of - is the direct result of your level of expertise to relate to yourself. The way you feel is not the result of what is happening in your life - it is your interpretation of what is happening.

I Am the Greatest!

Look at Glenn Beck, in his life he has had to experience some difficult and painful events, such as: He experienced an alcoholic mother who eventually committed suicide. Shortly after the loss of his mother Glenn dealt with the loss of his brother-in-law also taking his own life. Another one of his brother-in-laws died shortly after of heart failure. Coupled with his personal struggle with drugs and alcohol, it's a safe assumption that Glenn had an abundance of experiences which he could have anchored painful & disempowering meanings too. Those who are successful, inspired, did not allow events which took place on their life, affect their quality of life, rather it is determined by what they did about what happened.

For many people, the process of how you interpret events is set on autopilot. By this I mean, the process of how you interpret events or give meaning to experiences have become automatic. You are the one who decides how you are going to think and represent only upon how you perceive your life. Best part is, you can also turn off the autopilot and put the power of the controls back in your hands, now changing how you experience life.

This book is about taking the momentous leap, focused, consistent actions creating powerfully inspired results. Think about it. This is the essence of putting the mojo back in every aspect of your life. These skills are a core component to creating all change, creating lasting intimacy, creating a dream infused life! You want to change how you feel about yourself and your own world around you. Maybe you want to learn how to communicate with the ones you love better. Perhaps your goal is to enhance your personal relationships, so you can connect on an incredibly deep and emotional level. How to obtain a level of health, in a fraction of the time frame of any diet, with results, you never thought was possible. Maybe you want to earn more money, create capital so you'll have the vehicle to pursue your dreams, and open the door to help and give back.

This is it, here is your ability to create a dream infused life, to rise inspired, and inspire others through the energetic use of science and instruction in this book. Before you can obtain different outcomes, you must realize that as of right now, your already-producing outcomes. They just are probably not the kind of outcomes you want. The majority thinks of where they are mentally, and what's going on inside their head and believe that they're just things that happen outside our control.

I Am the Greatest!

Powerful Mind-Freak

Truth is you can control how your mind works, and your behaviors as you
never thought was even possible before.

Feeling depressed? You were the screenwriter who gave that story to your brain, and now your directing the show titled depression, as its being acted out. If the mojo is flowing and your feeling juiced, pumped you created that, as well. Depression in all honesty is not something that just happened to you. You don't catch depression. You create it, the same as all outcomes in your life, through definitive mental and physical actions. To be depressed, you have to continue seeing your life in explicit ways. You tell yourself things, in just the right tone of voice. You have to convince yourself, and use definitive posture and breathing patterns. In fact, right this minute I can help educate you how to be depressed. Make sure you collapse your shoulders and look down a lot. When you speak it needs to be in a sad-sounding tone of voice, while you are thinking of the worst-case scenarios for your life, this will help a lot. Throw your biochemistry into pandemonium through poor diet or excessive alcohol or drug use, assisting your body to produce low blood sugar and achieving an outcome of depression. Later in the book, we will discuss depression more, and some studies that will change your perception of depression.

I don't mean to sound as if I take depression for granted; in fact, it is quite the opposite; I know how real it is for so many people. It does not negate the fact that there is considerable effort in order to produce an outcome of depression. A series of specific actions and hard work is put into creating a state of depression. Creating a state of depression for some people is so easy it's as if they are on autopilot, they have been there so many times. The worst part is people have communicated to their brain these patterns, which have been linked to all kinds of external events. Some people get so much attention from others, sympathy, love, and so on - that they link depression to extra attention and love, which they communicate to their brain as life. Others have lived with it so long that it becomes a feeling that is normal and comfortable. Their identity becomes their state of mind.

In today's society, we accept, or justify negative behaviors, by saying the individual suffers from depression. Today, it is common practice to place blame, make excuses, or be a victim, because taking personal responsibility, telling yourself the truth, wouldn't feel-good or promote self-esteem. We can change our mental and physical actions which result immediately in changing our emotions and behaviors. You can become pumped or juiced by immediately embracing the point of view creating the emotion. You can picture in your mind all things that make you feel ecstatic, or juiced. You can change the stories you communicate to your brain, and how you perceive events. You can endorse breathing patterns and change your posture in order to create that state in your body, and Done! You will feel your mojo flow. Spielberg is a master at creating emotions, he knows specifically how to adjust the lighting, sound, and other variables on the screen to produce the effect. A director can film an intense drama or the next family friendly classic out of the same event.

The result you see up on the screen is the product of the directors sole discretion. You decide within your mind, how any event is directed, wicked or lousy, you're the director. You can direct your thoughts, and how your mind is focused, which underlines all your physical actions, with the same skill and precision.

People who dream and achieve their dreams develop a consistent road to success. The first step is to know your outcome, which means, precisely to determine what you want. Then its time to take action, only through taking action do you graduate from an ordinary day dreamer. You take actions you believe will result in fully realize your desired outcome. Even in the best laid plan, we run into roadblocks, there are hiccups along the way and these setbacks can railroad you. So another step, we must include is to develop a conscious recognition of the kinds of responses and results you're getting from the actions taken, while taking notice as soon as possible if they are advancing you towards your goal, or hindering your accomplishing them. You must be able to step back and see what you are getting from your actions, maybe it comes from a conversation or your daily habits. If your actions are not working out as you envisioned, you need to record what specific outcomes you have produced through your actions, in order for you to learn from every experience.

Finally, you need to develop the flexibility to change your behavior until you get what you want. Look at those who have achieved their goals consistently, you'll find they followed these steps. They cast a vision, with a set destination, because you can't ever arrive anywhere if you don't have a destination in the end.

They took action, cause everyone has a story about what they could have done, just never took action. They were able to read others, to know whether they were getting a favorable response or not. And they kept adjusting, changing their behavior until they found what worked.

Glenn Beck | Passion!

Glenn Beck, love him or hate him, in just over 10 years he went from Radio Show Host to Media Empire Owner.

Glenn Beck may be considered controversial, he finds himself under constant scrutiny, threats, boycotts, yet, the attempts to derail Glenn have failed. To know, how to stop Glenn Beck is to understand his past. A past which failed to destroy him, provided a stronger armor, any man who battles demons and perseveres can stand in the gap, for no man can breech nor tarnish, the spirit of a dreamer, and the heart of a servant.

Glenn Lee Beck is most notably known as a lighting rod for conservative political commentators, eclipsing even Rush Limbaugh. While also, rising to be one of the most influential people in media. Yet, this kind of success, is not what you would expect to hear about anyone who has the history of Glenn Beck.

At age 13 Glenn's mother, an alcoholic, drowned herself. His radio career also began the same year, after winning a local contest in his town. Again, a tragic family event forced Glenn to communicate to himself how to respond to a tragic event. One of his brothers-in-law also committed suicide followed by another brother-in-law who suffered a fatal heart attack. When Glenn learned of his daughter's condition living with cerebral palsy, he chose an empowering internal interpretation and meaning. He framed the news of his daughter's condition as a blessing from God bestowed upon Glenn. God, challenges us, his greatest blessings are through those experiences where we are able to expand as human beings and become ever more grateful. Early success, did not last long for Glenn, for how he was to fight with addictions as his late mother had done when he was a child.

Glenn was addicted to alcohol and drugs, resulting in a divorce in 1990. For most people, that's where the story would have ended. Or there would be a sappy VH1 Special Behind the Microphone pity fest, usually tragedies of what Glenn experienced, take down many individuals. But, Beck wasn't like most people. It seemed what started as the Glenn Beck Program, in Tampa, FL in 2000 quickly turned into over 400 stations internationally. Glenn went into television and was such a wild success on CNN that Fox News lured him away, and the viewers followed. However, this is where the real story of Glenn Beck begins, and when many in conservative talk radio and TV turned their back on Glenn Beck.

Glenn believed in his vision, he was not going to be swayed by no one, and he had an unwavering belief that he was just. Glenn was not only Inspired, he was commanding, he could articulate and relate not only the issues of today, but he had the ability to use historical reference; he was no longer a talking head for the conservative movement. This embolden him to launch a series of live event rallies, each one ignored or panned by the media, he was merely a joke. Yet, Glenn cast his vision, he stood in the gap, he wore his armor, and with passion, and without apologies he, communicated his message to the people, and he persuaded the masses.

His first Rally was quoted according to the Huffington Post Aug 29, 2010 "In front of multiple tens of thousands," others said, "a few thousand" although Glenn's first rally officially came in at over 500,000 and beyond. Glenn had faith which made him believe, in his ability to communicate his message, his vision to the people, and he achieved enormous success. His vision spread to the people of Israel at Glenn's second rally, also an immense success. Just a short time ago Glenn cast the vision to fill the new Dallas Cowboys Stadium, and create the first live event featuring, a speaker, music, and show. It was sold out for three days, attended by people from all 50 states and over 20 countries. On stage when Glenn spoke, tears became a regular scene in the crowd, because Glenn's vision, his passion, was no longer he's alone, it was passed and felt and meant to be shared by all those in attendance.

Glenn is of course in a line of work to, where he evokes strong feelings, by either political side. So, I hope you get the model we all can learn from Glenn, regardless of political affiliation.

What we all can learn is what all those in the media and political realm figured out, and turned Glenn into a threat. Glenn cast a vision, he created a strategy to achieve success, he left Fox news started an Online Television Network, mocked as a joke, and supposed to fail, it did not. Glenn, and his sponsors of the Fox Television show were under boycott, and when he left Fox Glenn, was supposed to be finished, it was only the beginning. When Glenn, stopped being just another paid commentator and cast a vision, and felt so strongly in his conviction that he not only took action he challenged a nation also to act and join him for the rally's he was supposed to be standing there alone, because no television star or news anchor, or radio personality has ever done this, yet hundreds of thousands showed up. Just one man, one common man, has so far in only a decade done what no entertainer, politician, or man have been able to do. This man who's mother committed suicide when Glenn was barely a teenager, couple more deaths in his family at an early age, Drug and alcohol abuse, doesn't have a degree from a prestigious school like most real journalist and experts. This common man, has specialized knowledge which he has perfected, and communicates with passion, and eloquence, and persuades, with a vision, a strategy, and is extremely successful.

Glenn was evoking such strong emotions causing hate filled articles, blog posts, comments, letters, screams and jeers. Worst of all Glenn lived with constant death threats on himself and his family. He lives a life which must include a constant 24 hour security.

I don't know about you, but aside from the standard offensive and unoriginal comments, letters, and emails, I have never faced threats against my safety. Well, ok once; however, I think it was justified, I can't blame a small business owner who built his dream of the best Chinese buffet in town, and when I came in still weighing well over 500 pounds and took it upon myself to grab a chair and seat myself at the buffet line. The owner was only protecting his investment, and All You Can Eat, could have put him out of business. I didn't understand the words, just the body language was sure leading me to believe that was his intentions, but I digress.

Here, is the overriding message I want you to take away from Glenn Beck's story. Tell me what's impossible? Because I saw a man with a tainted past become more powerful, influential, and passionate than any politician, celebrity, business tycoon, and he did it because he cast a vision, he created a strategy, he believed in the vision, and he was flexible to make adjustments, and he achieves and succeeds at all he does.

Garth Brooks | Effect

#1 Selling Recording Artist In History | Envisioned Himself to be Singing Country Music.

The legacy of Garth Brooks has been told as if he were an overnight success, where everything he would touch, turned to gold. However, Garth Brooks got turned down by every country music label several times. In fact, Garth's first trip to Nashville lasted only 24 hrs before he headed back to Oklahoma. At the constant encouragement of a talent scout, Garth returned to Nashville and started meeting Music industry execs. It wasn't until a recording executive caught one of Garth's live shows in a local bar, that his recording career began. Garth had to expand his belief system - he had changed his approach and combined his two loves when performing live, Rock & Country. Garth's ability to be flexible and change his style allowed him to stop trying to be another George Strait, and become Garth, the rowdy, infectious, Rock combined with Country Superstar. He had broken almost every record in his short 10 year run before he retired. His tours would sell out stadiums in cities within minutes and adding back to back dates Garth would sell out 5-6 shows packing stadiums in every city for days. His International tours were the most successful of any Country Artist, and he is considered the artist who made Country cool again. Did he follow the four steps? Of course, he did. Knowing what he wanted, he tried something, and if it didn't work, he kept changing and changing until he learned how to balance his life. In addition to being all time highest selling recording artist in history, he's a father, a husband, and a family man, as well.

Overall, this book allows you to oversee and manage your brain with efficient signals to inspire and empower you to take dramatic action. This leads you to a simple, inescapable fact. Success is not an accident. Powerful results are not a random act of God for some people, and just rotten luck for those who don't achieve the same success. There are constant, specific patterns of action, a route to achieve our dreams, they are within the reach of us all. We can all get inspired and utilize a potential to make the focus, drive, and fire within us all. We just have to learn how to turn on and use our minds and body in the most powerful and effective ways.

What do you think a Spielberg and a Brooks share in common? How about a John F. Kennedy and a Martin Luther King, Jr., what character traits did these two distinguished American leaders poses that allowed them to move so many people into an inspired and empowering state? What sets a Steve Jobs and a Ronald Reagan apart from the masses? They all have been able to make themselves take direct actions toward the attainment of their dreams. What is the secret that drives them continually to dream bigger, every single day, with more enduring vitality, and passion so that they accomplish everything they do? There's a lot of factors. However, I think there are seven inspired character virtues they have all emboldened within themselves, seven attributes that allow them the juice to do whatever it takes to achieve. These are the seven triggers & mechanisms which can assure you succeed.

Seven Inspired Character Virtues

Virtue Number One | It's all about Passion!

These individuals had a driving factor that took them past the point of a want, and ignited a deeper sense of commitment to where they were at the point of obsession, being unreasonable, it drove them to grow and become more! It's passion that drove Michael Jordan to train every day, even after setback, disappointment, and mediocrity, to the point his passion became almost an ability to fly effortlessly. It's an unreasonable passion that drives the resolute actions of a Steve Jobs in sharp contrast from all others. A pursuit of excellence which spurs a man such as, Richard Branson to assert that not even space will limit his accomplishments and set into motion commercial space flight. A burning desire to achieve what others have either failed to accomplish or had never dreamed up in the first place is what cause individuals to work late into the night and start work earlier. Its passion people want in their relationships.

Passion is the spark which ignites life, adds adventure it becomes the juice and substance. If you get inspired to pursue greatness it is passion which creates the strength to persevere, whether it's the desire of Muhammad Ali to declare "*I am the Greatest!*" or a master, a scientist, a parent, or an entrepreneur.

Virtue Number Two | Belief!

If you can't even believe in yourself, then it is foolish to try to convince others to believe. Religions of all faiths talk about the faith and belief correlation, and the effect it has on mankind. Individuals succeeding at such a high level believe at an entirely different level than those who don't. If you believe something is impossible, then it is. However, when you believe nothing is impossible, then there are no limits, and you refuse to accept any other result except for absolute success. If you believe in magic, you'll have a magical life. If you believe that the sky's the limit, then you've already capped how high you can go. What we believe is truth, what we believe is possible, Becomes what is true, becomes what's possible. Throughout this book, you will learn how to change your belief system, scientifically quickly so that you have beliefs which empower your attainment of our biggest dream. You hear the word passion thrown around all the time today, and many people have passion; they just never tap their full potential by limiting their beliefs about their own abilities, which stops them from ever taking action to achieve their dreams. People who succeed to know what they want, and believe it's theirs, they just have to go get it.

Passion and belief help to arouse our mojo gives us the juice to fire on all cylinders toward greatness. But just igniting our mojo, lighting a fire just to watch it burn out is no fun. If it were, we could trigger the passion in a hundred people, in one event, and they would all go on and reach every single idea they dreamed up. Besides that initial power, we need to establish a course, an intelligent journey to withstand all the storms, so when light pierces the storm clouds we arrive at our final destination; we need a strategy to our course.

Virtue Number Three | Strategy!

Strategy is a way of deploying all our resources. When Steve Jobs decided to create Apple Inc., he mapped out a course that would lead to the world he wanted to illuminate and make better. He knew what he needed to establish, whom he must know, and what he must do. He was inspired, had passion, and he would ask, what could be, Jobs, developed the strategies harnessing the power of all the listed virtues which allowed him to achieve his desired goals. Think of the Great Communicator, on a consistent basis, Ronald Reagan, developed specific communication strategies that he used to generate the results he needed. Ronald Reagan, would hand write quotes, short stories, anecdotes on note cards, and he carried them everywhere, in any situation he always had a story, a joke, a reference he could employ to create an instant rapport with his audience. Because just like every great entertainer, politician, parent, or employer knows its not enough to have resources to succeed. You must use those resources in the most effective useful way. A strategy is humility, to know that even with the greatest skill and determination you also need the right avenue. You can be a bull in a china shop, breaking everything until you've gotten what you wanted, or you can learn how to guide people to the outcome you desire.

Virtue Number Four | Defined Values!

Values are the person's belief systems about what is right or wrong in our lives. It's our compass as we make decisions about what make life worth living. A lot of people don't have a clear idea of what is essential to them. Many times people can be swayed to take a particular action, and then later they have regretted about making that decision because they haven't defined their values, which shape our decisions and actions. They certainly are not clear about what unconsciously they believe is right for them and others. Think of Barack Obama, Ronald Reagan, Martin Luther King Jr., John Wayne, or George Clooney.

They all have unique visions, but they share a foundational moral grounding, a sense of whom they are and why they do what they do. Defining your values, sets your parameters so you know which way will always be North, so you don't go off course in decisions you make.

All these virtues work together, they are all the chemicals infused to cause a reaction. Is passion effected by beliefs? You bet! The more you believe in something the more you're willing to risk all the cards on the table and double down. However if, you believe your going to experience the beauty of a sunrise and your strategy is driving west; you're going to be in for a surprise. Because believing in yourself and your dreams are not enough. When we set our course and develop a strategy would that be effected by our values? Yes; of course, your strategy involves doing things in contrast to your unconscious beliefs about what is right or wrong for your life, then your strategy has already failed to achieve the outcome. You hear people say all the time about someone, and they say They sabotaged themselves, or in their head, they lost before the game ever started. It's because there is an internal conflict between the individuals values and the strategic plan for achievement. Just like our first four virtues that we've discussed, they are inseparable from:

Virtue Number Five | Energy!

Energy can be the thundering sounds and dramatic arrangement of a Garth Brooks or Lady Gaga. It can be the entrepreneurial buoyancy of a Mark Zuckenburg or a Steve Jobs. It is almost impossible just to arrive in a magical land called excellence. People who obtain a transcendence took opportunities to improve them. They live as if obsessed with all the wonders and opportunities of each day, the curiosity of a child, yet the logic of an elder who knew no one has enough time. There are countless numbers of people in this world who possess a passion they affirm in. They have down pat, the course to set and strategy to implement which aligned with their values, but they just don't posses the physical vitality to take action. Great achievements are inseparable from the physical, intellectual, and spiritual energy which makes living each day magnificently.

Virtue Number Six | Connecting Power!

How many successful hermits do you know? Probably the same as I, none. Because almost all successful people have charisma, a charm the ability to connect to others in extraordinary ways, it's ability to bind, build an instant rapport with peoples of all backgrounds and beliefs. Sure there's the master hermit who invents something that changes the world. But, if the hermit spends all his life locked in seclusion, he may succeed on one level, but he fails on so many more.

Legendary successes - the Kennedy's, the Kings, the Reagan's, the Gandhi's all have an uncanny ability to create a connection which unites them to millions of others. Truly notable achievements are not on the world's stage. Our greatest success lies within our hearts and minds. Deep down, we all need to forge connections that last the test of time, loving connections with others. Without deep connections, love, any success, all achievements are but an empty victory. We touched upon our final virtue a little bit earlier.

Virtue Number Seven | Finesse of Communication!

This is the cornerstone of what this book is all about. How we use the power of words and communicate to others and how we communicate to ourselves determines our life's outcome. People who achieve remarkable things, those who succeed, are those who have learned how to take any trial or situation and interpret it's meaning in a way that they can react with empowering actions rather than negative behaviors. People who fail, accept challenges and failures and use them as a defining point for their life, unconsciously seeking out an external force to blame, being left with a feeling of being a victim. People who change the world who shape our thoughts and ideas are people who have a finesse of communication in order to persuade. Their words can form a vision, a new adventure, or a joy a mission. Finesse of communication is what make the extraordinary parents or artists, or a skilled politician, and our talented teachers. Throughout this book, all the topics covered will have an underlying theme in one way or another that has to do with communication. It's the origin of energy for bridging gaps, blazing new paths, and casting new awe inspiring visions.

Writing this book, my hope, and the goal were to provide tools and inspiration into the science of human development. Complete with time tested proven techniques and technologies to change personal, humanistic behavior. I wanted to provide the information in the most up-to-date techniques but written to be easily understood and most importantly seen as relevant to your life. I wanted to give you hope, a feeling so many have been thirsting for. Not only did I want you to feel hope, I wanted to spark a fire deep within you in order to start creating changes in your life so you can experience everything you dream of and deserve. I wanted to provide the information in a way that you can start creating lasting changes rapidly, faster than you ever imagined. I knew that many of the subjects I would be writing about could be books all on their own. To me it's invaluable to provide, as much as possible, a complete program that is not left lacking in any area of your life. I hope you find this book to be a source of power to ignite a passion, develop a new purpose, and to rise - Rise Inspired!

Why is it so many people are not living the life of their dreams? Because to simply dream without actually doing anything is nothing more than a common day dream, it takes commitment through action. It's time to get inspired.

Vince Lombardi the iconic Head football coach of the Green Bay Packers during the 1960's, where he led the team to three straight league championships and five in seven years, including winning the first two Super Bowls, said:

"Leaders are made; they are not born. They are made by hard effort, which is the price which all of us must pay to achieve any goal that is worthwhile."

I challenge you to become curious with this information, to read it all, share with others what truly is possible, and to enjoy it. According to several studies fewer than 10 percent of the people who buy a book read past the first chapter. I remember the first time I heard the statistics, I was thinking, No Way, then common sense took over, and I remember that less than 3 percent of the nation is financially independent, less than 10 percent has written goals, only 35 percent of American women, and even fewer guys feel they are in reasonable physical condition, and in many states one out of every two marriages finishes in divorce.

The world is ready to dream again, it's time to get inspired, lose the excuses, and design a life which will cause the mojo to flow!

What if there is a way to accelerate and execute the learning process? What if I could unveil how to master the exact lessons that people who inspired have already learned? Years of tinkering, learning and finally perfected, you are going to learn in minutes. The way to do this is through modeling, a way to reproduce precisely the inspiration and actions of others. What do they do that sets them apart from those who only hope of success? Some things are never taught in school, here are some life lessons on achieving.

Everyday a New Champion is Born

Chapter 11

The NLP Mindshift

"WHAT LIES BEHIND YOU AND WHAT LIES IN FRONT OF YOU, PALES IN COMPARISON TO WHAT LIES INSIDE OF YOU." -RALPH WALDO EMERSON

In 1962, a son was born, however, as a result of oxygen deprivation at the time of birth, the boy was diagnosed as a spastic quadriplegic with cerebral palsy. The new parents were advised to institutionalize their new born son because there was no chance of him recovering and little hope that their son would ever experience a normal life. Although he couldn't walk or talk, he was quite astute, and his eyes would follow them around the room. The public school system would not allow him in their schools. His parents took him sledding and swimming, even taught him the alphabet and basic words, like any other child, ignoring expert advice. Yet, no school would allow their son to be included, even after providing conclusive evidence of their son's intellect and ability to learn. With no resources, money, or support life gave the young parents all they could handle.

In every man, and women's life there comes that moment of unparalleled challenge, when every part of being is tested and consumed. A time when life doesn't just seem unfair, it seems it kicks us while were down, just struggling to get up. It's a time when our faith, our values, our patience, our compassion, and our ultimate ability to overcome, are all pushed to the breaking point, and then off the cliff's edge. Some choose to use these tests as opportunities to grow, become better people, yet so many more allow these struggles to define them, victimize them and ultimately destroy them. You've heard the stories, pertaining to both situations, the inspiring heroic tales of overcoming all the odds, and adversity, and so many more of the tragedy. Have you ever pondered what creates the difference in the way people respond to life's challenges? I have! Because to me with the challenges I have faced on my own life, I saw others go through tougher challenges and emerge as giant's and overcome all the odds, and all I could think was, how in the hell can I bitch and moan about my current situation, and these people represent greatness.

For the last 10 years of my life, I have been driven to discover the trigger points of human beings to behave the way they do. Ever since my first self-help seminar experience, one of my closest friends talked me into attending I got a glimpse into the realization of what truly sets some men and women apart form the rest of the pack. What is it that triggers an individual to become a leader, an achiever? With so much confusion and media saturation focused on all the negatives of society and adversity, how are there so many people worldwide living such happy lives, filled with joy, and love? While any store bought tabloid will show you examples of celebrities, top executives, public figures who seem to have it all live their lives of despair, anger, and depression?

Take this next story I'm going to share with you, and see the difference between the two lives involved. He was a man who I looked up to for years, he was a fabulously wealthy, enormously talented entertainer with a huge following. He was also a man who besides his weight problems, was loved by millions, made them laugh and to a Fat Kid like me, made fat cool. In 1990, he joined the cast of Saturday Night Live, surrounded by comedic greats Adam Sandler, Chris Rock, Rob Schneider, David Spade, they became the bad boys of SNL. He became a show favorite on SNL and was one of the famed television successes of the nineties. Then he becomes one of the nations hottest film stars. He has dozens of admiring friends, lived on the 60th floor in a prime, high rise Chicago Penthouse. He seems to have everything a person could ask for.

Which of these two people would you rather switch places with? I think we all can agree most would say they would choose the second life, over the struggles of the first. Here, is a little more about these people. The first is one of the most inspiring, strong, and motivating people I know. You may have heard them simply called, Team Hoyt, son Rick and his parents Dick and Judy. After all the struggles, setbacks, and only after investing $5,000 to have a custom built computer allowing Rick to communicate, was Rick at age 13 finally admitted into public school. You would think Rick going onto studying at Boston University and graduating with a degree in Special Education would be a truly inspiring story within itself. However, with his father Dick a retired Lt. Colonel in the Air National Guard, serving our great nation for 37 years, Team Hoyt, was poised to inspire millions more.

"In the spring of 1977, Rick told his father that he wanted to participate in a 5-mile benefit run for a Lacrosse player who had been paralyzed in an accident. Far from being a long-distance runner, Dick agreed to push Rick in his wheelchair and they finished all 5 miles, coming in next to last. That night, Rick told his father, "Dad, when I'm running, it feels like I'm not handicapped." (feasterfive.com)

This awareness began a passion of what would become over 1,000 races accomplished, including marathons, duathlons and triathlons (6 of them being Ironman competitions). Also, in addition to their list of accomplishments, Dick and Rick biked and ran across the U.S. in 1992, completing full 3,735 miles in 45 days. If you've never seen the countless video's on youtube I encourage you to watch greatness in motion.

The NLP MindShift

The second person is someone you probably know well, someone who I'm sure brought you a great deal of pleasure and joy. His name was Chris Farley. He was one of the most beloved physical comedians of our time, and one of the exciting entertainment success stories of the nineties. Farley was able to enrich countless lives, but not his own. When he was, found dead by his brother at the age of thirty-three of acute toxicity from cocaine and heroin, few who knew him could say they were surprised. The man who had everything had become a bloated, out-of-control drug abuser, old beyond his years. Externally he had everything. Internally, he'd been running on empty for years.

Examples are seen all the time and throughout history. Think of Helen Keller's awe inspiring story. Or when a mother had to bear the loss of her daughter hit and killed by a drunk driver, Candy Lightner founded Mothers Against Drunk Driving. She took the tragedy and loss of a daughter and founded an organization that has probably saved hundreds or even thousands of lives. Then we see the opposite extreme, such as iconic and legendary hollywood icons like Marilyn Monroe, James Dean, people who had immense success and ended up destroying themselves.

Have's | Have-Nots

So let me ask you, what's the difference between the haves and the have-nots?

What's the difference between the I-Can and the I-Can'ts? What's the difference between those who simply Just Do It and don't? How can some people overcome and triumph, while others, even with every advantage, turn their lives into an absolute train wreck? Why are there some people who can take any situation, and make it work for them while others make those situations work against them?

- WHAT IS THE DIFFERENCE BETWEEN RICK HOYT AND CHRIS FARLEY?

- WHO CAN WE BLAME FOR THE BIPOLAR DIFFERENCES IN THE QUALITY OF LIFE?

See, this is what I became obsessed with learning. Because when I turn on the TV, watch the news, hear a politician speak, they always tell us who we need to blame, for any and every situation in our life. I grew up just like all of you, and we saw people with vast fortunes of all types, great jobs, the perfect boyfriend or girlfriend, husband or wife, perfect cover ready bodies. I wanted to know what caused their lives to be complete 180° polar opposite of mine! The difference all comes down to the way in which we perceive our abilities and the actions we take. How do we perceive our abilities when we try everything we can and things still don't work? Successful people do not have more/less problems than people who fail. Truth is the only people who don't have problems are those buried six feet deep and dead and gone. It's certainly not what happens to us that separates failures from successes. It comes down to how we look at the problem and what we do about what happens that is the difference.

When Dick and Judy learned of the damage caused by the oxygen deprivation during birth to their son Rick, they had a choice in how they were going to interpret that information. Think about the situation they faced immediately after going through an intensive time in labor with their son. They could have taken the news and felt all hope was lost and given up on their son and wrote him off as dead, hopeless, unfair, even seen as punishment by god. Instead, the Hoyt's chose consistently to see only the possibilities and positives that this experience has allowed them to experience with their son, and found a way to share that courage, it became their purpose. They also learned overtime that because of this experience they had the opportunity not only to help their son, but provide hope, and possibilities for countless scores of people who struggle with disabilities every day. Not only did they choose to be great in the time of unparalleled adversity they had the honor and privilege to become inspired themselves, and in return inspire others. This is where true power and greatness lies within all of us, yet it is a fleeting opportunity which is either seized or denied in the matter of a single moment and decision.

As a result of the '*story*' they chose to tell themselves, they began to develop a set of beliefs and values that continue to control their lives from a position of empowerment and possibilities rather than loss or disaster. How was Helen Keller able to learn to communicate, speak and earn a college degree back in the late 1800's when she was deaf and blind? Simple. She mastered the story which she told herself, she wrote the script to which she based all possibilities and limitations placed upon her abilities, she chose to have no limits. When she faced challenges that she would recall as pain, as a limitation, as exhaustion, she just rewrote their meanings and continued to communicate to her senses in a way that kept her on a script of limitless possibilities rather than defeat.

"The world as we have created it is a process of our thinking. It cannot be changed without changing our thinking." -Albert Einstein

I always loved hearing about stories which would be inspiring, show the distinction that only a few truly astounding individuals could ever achieve. It was then I started thinking to myself, if I could learn the technique or the story these people would use to propel them from a negative to a positive then I could duplicate it. Does history have a way of repeating itself? Well then if this is true, and history has been well documented then just like a treasure map, success, greatness, real inspiration has also left us clues.

People who produce extraordinary results do specific things in order to develop and achieve those results. It dawned on me that it wasn't enough just to know that Team Hoyt or a Helen Keller created a story and wrote a script in a way that produced results. I wanted to go deeper, get inside their brain, their thought process so I could learn specifically how they did it. I knew that if I could duplicate those actions of others, then I could reproduce the same level of results that they had. If I sowed, then I would also reap. Imagine the power, the sheer inspiration you would now poses if there were someone who could be sympathetic even in the most dire of circumstances, and you could learn their tactics, and how they choose to look at things, how they used their body in those situations, we would become more tolerant. In a day and age when we hear of the announcement of a marriage, it is closely followed by the question, Which number is this for you? If a couple has shared their love for twenty-five years and they still felt deeply in love with each other, I could find out what actions they have taken, their belief system, which is the result we all want to experience a long lasting love. I could use those clues, actions and beliefs adopt them into the story I tell myself about love and relationships. Which by practice put into action I could produce similar results in my own relationships.

In my life, I had produced the result of being morbidly obese, and the story I told myself was the same lies and excuses you hear being told daily. To be me, being fat must be someone else's fault, it's genetic, it's my thyroid, just big bones, and all time greatest lie ever told to myself, 'I like being big'. You see it was these stories I told myself all the time that produced a result of lifelessly entrapped body of fat. Why would I ever admit responsibility for being so fat, I couldn't fit on a roller coaster, I couldn't walk the distance of the driveway without being short of breath, sleeping on a couch meant only half of me would get a decent nights sleep? Finally, common sense slapped me upside the head, and I realized that all I needed to do was model people who were thin, find out what they ate, how they ate, what they ate, what their beliefs were, and I could produce the same result.

This helped me in losing over 300 pounds, but then it propelled me in the opposite direction to where I was so proficient at the story, I told I became obsessed with becoming skinny. I was a personal trainer who became focused on achieving the body I saw on all the magazine covers, I became bulimic. Until finally, I was honest with myself again, and was clear on how I was communicating the stories I needed to tell myself in order to be healthy, mind, body and spirit. The story had to be fined tuned, yet the process worked!

Neuro-Linguistic Programming

Behind the Science of Neuro-Linguistic Programming (NLP)

Then one of my closest friends Erica, talked me into an event which changed my life forever, and created the clarity, along with the tools to produce the results I aspired to attain in life. Erica and her husband Alan are those dear friends who help improve your life, they never tell me what I want to hear, they make me understand what I want to be conscious of in my decisions. Erica, was working for a personal development seminar training company called Life Tigers, founded by Jase Souder. Erica convinced Jase to let me to attend their weekend long event called The Bridge because she knew I would never pay the $2,500 to go on my own. This was the weekend, where I became inspired, where I felt true power, and complete control over every aspect of my life. Later in the book I will also share with you how Erica, achieved her dream of running her,own business and making an impact in children's lives.

Jase, introduced me to a science known as Neuro-Linguistic Programming, or (NLP) for short. Consider the name, neuro of course is referring to the brain, and linguistic, refers to the language. Programming is of course the installation of any kind of plan or procedure. NLP is the study of how language, both verbal and nonverbal, affects our nervous system. Our ability to do anything in life is based upon our ability to direct our own nervous system. Every movement you make was instructed first by your brain communicating with that particular function of your body. People who are able to produce specific communications to and from their nervous system produce phenomenal results.

So what is NLP? you may not have heard the term NLP or even the name Neuro-Linguistic Programming yet I'm sure you've seen NLP in action, and you probably didn't even realize it. Some highly successful shows have showcased the practical and scientific uses of NLP in everyday life. One show in particular and one of my favorite shows is TNT's 'LEVERAGE', where actress, Gina Bellman, who plays the role of Sophie Devereaux a brilliant grifter who deploys the techniques taught through NLP to persuade, or guide her marks. By planting suggestions or ideas subconsciously into the minds of her mark Sophie is writing the script and creating the actions they will take to achieve the desired outcome. You have also seen NLP used in shows such as CBS's 'THE MENTALIST', CBS's 'CRIMINAL MINDS', and USA's 'WHITE COLLAR'. NLP studies how people actually communicate or Talk with themselves in ways that deliver optimized resourceful states of mind, which creates the largest number of behavioral choices. Like I've said, our script, is how we think about any particular situation or event, so what we know as true, or fact is purely because we have been programmed that way. Our choices, excuses, and ultimately outcomes in life are determined by the stories we chose to tell ourselves.

My first experience seeing NLP in action was at the Bridge, when Jase was in the middle of an exercise, and a decidedly depressed women in the audience were speaking about her struggles in life, and then became so physically upset, she blurted out her desire physically to harm herself. Jase, had her come up on stage, and through a series of questions, I saw as this brave young lady told Jase all of her problems, and fears. She spoke about her years of therapy, antidepressants, and her struggle with depression, which she had no idea where her depression came from or the cause of her emotional attachment of that feeling. In less than 45 minutes, Jase took her from present day all the way back to when she was merely an infant. She sat there and described in vivid detail her experience being an infant, to be in her crib crying. She recalled times when her parents came in to comfort her, all they did was try to hush her, turn off the lights and would leave her to be crying in the dark. She felt 'abandoned', she attached the feeling of abandonment to her infant need of love and affection. She grew up and lived her life trying always to, please, others, never asking for anything, never being needy, and giving all she had, even if it left her with nothing. Because rooted deep inside her, she communicated to herself that if she needs love, or asks for anything from those she loves, then they will abandon her. Now, what is the likelihood that she could actually remember any event dating all the way back to when she was only a couple months old? The answer is easy, it doesn't matter, because the 'truth' is whatever she has told herself is true.

Once Jase got to the initial experience which created this dysfunction, he then walked her through another set of questions asking her to think what might happen if she would make decisions based upon her needs, and what would make her happy. Every question was answered with a deeply seeded sense of abandonment, not being loved, and ultimately being alone. After more than a decade of therapy, a regiment of antidepressant drugs, Jase was able finally to get to the root of all her emotional dysfunctions, and then was able to suggest new experiences to replace the old. The final outcome was in less than forty-five minutes she discovered the source of all her emotional dysfunctions, the process for which she was communicating all these feelings to herself, and how to replace those experiences with new ones, and start to communicate a new story where she never was abandoned. I was hooked! I had to know it all! (Just a little FYI, many times the same result can be produced in five or ten minutes.)

NLP TEACHES US HOW TO DIRECT NOT ONLY OUR OWN STATES AND BEHAVIORS, BUT ALSO THE STATES AND BEHAVIORS OF OTHERS.

NLP provides us with a methodology to model outstanding performances achieved by geniuses and leaders in any field. Think about that, yes you can become inspiring, creating a dream infused life, achieving the success, personal power, body, and even the relationships you have been telling yourself are out of reach.

NLP provided exactly what I needed. It was the foundation for unlocking the mystery of how certain people were able consistently to produce extraordinary results in every aspect of their life. I bet right now your thinking to yourself that perhaps the bitterness felt for that an individual who is always able to wake up in the morning, quickly and easily and full of energy, is not merely to drive you nuts; instead it is simply a result that they produce. Now the question becomes, how was it produced? In order to create a result, we must first take action, so what specific mental or physical actions were taken to generate the neurophysiological process of waking up from sleep quickly and easily? Countless studies in the field of NLP show that we all share the same neurology, which means, you have no excuses, you can get the same exact result if you manage your nervous system in exactly the same way. This is the process of 'modeling' discovering specifically what people do to produce the desired result.

Once again, the only limitations we have on ourselves are merely a product of the stories or excuses we use, and tell ourselves. Because if it's possible for others in the world, then it's possible for you. See, it's not a question of whether or not you can produce the results that someone else can; it's the strategy we use to duplicate the process, how do they produce the results? Every aspect of your life can be enriched, can produce results that up to this´ point you thought were not possible. You know someone who communicates perfectly with their kid, they have a relationship that seems too good to be true unless the father's name was Ward and his son Beaver was learning the value of honesty over a milkshake at the local soda shop. Of course, some tasks are more complex than others and may take more time to model and then duplicate. However, once you instill the belief supporting you, continually adjusting and changing virtually everything, that any human being does, can be modeled. Your not reinventing the wheel here. Your finding the person who spent years developing the wheel, all the mistakes, trial and error which resulted in a perfected flawless wheel. Now you step in, model the actions that took years to perfect, and produce similar results in a matter of moments, months, or at least a fraction of the time it took the person whose results you desire to reproduce.

Neuro Linguistic Programming began with John Grinder and Richard Bandler in the early 70's. Grinder & Bandler were enthralled with human development excellence, which created the opportunity to explore and model behavioral patterns of chosen brilliance. Grinder and Bandler began by modeling three people, Fritz Perls, Virginia Satir and Milton Erickson. Grinder and Bandler had little to no direct knowledge of each of the geniuses speciality and little expertise in the field of psychotherapy. Grinder and Bandler spent two years studying and modeling the geniuses behavior. They displayed the first two NLP models to the world in the volumes Structure of Magic I and II. This put NLP on the forefront of enquiry and human behavioral skill. The two men conducted training courses in NLP. The courses they conducted - backed-up that NLP models were exchangeable to others, which allowed the students to use the NLP models successfully in their own work.

Grinder & Bandler's success is celebrated. Yet even with the tools available, many of the people who clearly learned the patterns for creating emotionally and behavioral change never had the personal capacity to utilize them effectively and produce results. Again, knowledge without action won't equal results.

As I read more and more books on success, NLP, and the process of modeling I started to notice a theme in some of the most successful self-help books being offered. One book I read many years ago, is a book many people have either read, or has heard of. It's a book by Robert Kiyosaki titled, RICH DAD, POOR DAD. His book is an International best seller, selling more than 26 million copies. The book highlights the different attitudes to money work and life of two men (*His rich dad and his poor dad*), and how they in turn influenced key decisions in Kiyosaki's life. Robert Kiyosaki's books all detail the modeling process of his rich dad, the behavior, and the actions taken throughout the process.

To me, modeling is the golden ticket, or the yellow brick road producing talent and inspired results. Modeling means that anyone in this world who is producing a result I am trying to get, allows me to produce the same result if Im willing to pay the cost of time and effort. It's the mindset of those who succeed, and throughout history, we are reaffirmed with the fact that those who history has seen fit to call Great Men showed an unwavering belief in themselves, their idea, and consistent actions taken until they achieved their desired result. If you want to be a better friend, create wealth, be a better parent, a better athlete, achieve more success in business, all you need to do are find models of sustained excellence.

We marvel at their talent, we use their inventions daily, we get inspired when they assert What if and then they satisfy their own problem, with innovations. They are the movers and shakers of the world, their the dreamers, and they are also pro modelers, they have mastered the art of learning everything they can by following other people's experience rather than their own. Malcolm Gladwell's New York Times Best selling book, Outliers - The Story of Success. Gladwell looks at everyone from rock stars to professional athletes, software billionaires to scientific geniuses, to show that the story of success is far more remarkable, and more compelling, than we could ever have imagined. He reveals that, by the time these legends first taste success, it is only after 10,000 hours of time. So when you hear about the next overnight success story, remember they may be off by about 10,000 hours.

The One Minute Manager Kenneth Blanchard and Spencer Johnson is a model for human communication and undemanding and effective management of any human relationship. Where did the material for their book come from? The authors were modeling some of the most successful managers in the country. These books are just a couple of an ever increasing list of books based off a series of models on how to direct your mind, your body, and your communication with others in a way that will generate tremendous results for everyone involved. I laid out a lot of the background to show you the advantage of modeling in your life.

However, it is my intention by the end of this book, for you not only to understand these patterns to Inspire internal strength to obtain a personal greatness in your life, but also to go even further by creating your own models. You invested in this book because you have made the decision you want more out of life, you double downed by realizing that you deserve more out of life. It is my passion to unlock all opportunities for you to do so, because just like me, I had the opportunity presented to me, it was still my decision if I chose to acknowledge it, and believe it, Im excited you already see the value and possibilities.

Building on the successes of others is a fundamental building block when it comes to learning. In technology, every advance in engineering or computing device follows naturally from earlier discoveries and breakthroughs. The ground breaking iPhone was actually modeled off of the iPad, which ironically was introduced to the world after the iPhone. Today we see the influence of Steve Jobs, his iPad has been integrated into most computer designs and mobile devices. In the business world, companies that don't learn from the past operate using state-of-the-art information, are doomed to fail.

But the field of human behavior is still stuck in the industrial age when it comes to how the brain works and how we behave. Today, we slap a label called depression on something or someone, and miraculously don't you know what happens, Bam! We're depressed. Labels, or the words we attach to something can be self-fulfilling prophecies. A small bruise, will never be called a bruise when examined by a doctor, no-no-no... so the bruise ceases to exist and is replaced by someone suffers a contusion. Is a bruise less painful or serious than a contusion, or are they the same thing? Yes, they are exactly the same, however, saying contusion, now that sounds hell of a lot better than an ordinary bruise, right!

The two words may represent the same thing; however, they can mean the difference of being called a wuss to your face, or just when your not around. I'm going to teach you a technology that's readily available, it's a technology that can be used to create the quality of life you truly desire and deserve. If you can't say with confidence that you deserve the best for yourself, then don't ever expect someone else to give you their best.

The New Code of NLP

In 1994, John Grinder introduced the world to a new code of NLP, which is based on three distinctions. I envision a medicine wheel, broken into three parts, mind, body, spirit alone the medicine wheel, or circle is broken, it takes all three pieces working together to complete the circle and work as one. Without your brain telling your leg to move, your leg won't function, and this is easily seen by a quadriplegic, who's neuro paths have been cut off to parts of his body, and the communication doesn't exist and they lose the function of their legs.

Breaking the Code | Your Belief System

The first part of the medicine wheel represents a person's belief system. What a person believes, what is possible or impossible, what he sees as his limits. His beliefs are a gauge of what he is capable of actually doing, either he believes he can, or he believes he can't. Henry Ford once said, "*Whether you think you can, or you think you can't--you're right.*" Henry Ford hit the target with his statement. Look at it this way, anytime someone embarks on a new weight loss diet, the outcome is almost predetermined. They go all out, and they lose weight, they feel better, self esteem is on high, and then at some point, the pounds come back, many times multiplied, and they're looking for the next substantial weight loss craze. Take a step back and consider what kind of belief system they have when it comes to losing weight, diets and the lasting effect? It will fail, I WILL FAIL, I AM A FAILURE, without saying those words, isn't the belief consistently sending messages of doubt and failure to your nervous system? You're sending your nervous system consistent messages that limit or eliminate your ability to obtain that result. If, on the other hand, you are sending your nervous system messages consistently which embolden the belief that YES YOU CAN achieve any body that you desire, then they signal your brain to produce the result you envision, and this opens up the possibility for it. You can model a person's belief system, which is creating the same mindset which achieved the result you will reproduce.

Breaking the Code | Your Mental Syntax

The second part of the medicine wheel is a person's Mental Syntax. Mental syntax is a person's filing cabinet, its how they manage their thoughts. Syntax is like an account number. You have a set of numbers show on your credit card, yet all the numbers must be entered in exactly as they appear on the card or else it does not work. The same is true in reaching the part of your brain and nervous system that could most affectively help you get the outcome you desire. The same is true in communication. Many times people don't communicate well to each other because different people use different codes, different mental syntaxes.

The easiest way to differentiate the differences is a conversation being attempted through text messages. The communication that is achieved, through text messaging is rudimentary at best. One person is typing the words from the conversation being held within his mind, and vice verse on the other end of the text message. So for the person who reads the text is knowingly translating the meaning of the words and patching together his own version of the conversation. Communication fails because, in a typical conversation between two people conversing face to face, they can hear the pitch adjustments given to specific words in order to increase importance to a particular point.

When we make a joke, change facial expressions even body language are all used by our brains so we can communicate effectively. However, just like with artificial intelligence, unlock codes, and you've now connected over half of the medicine wheel toward modeling people's best qualities.

Breaking the Code | Your Physiology

The third part of the medicine wheel is physiology. The mind and body are interwoven and totally linked. The way you use your physiology is much like a battalion of Marines marching in full formation, the way they breathe, marching with their heads held high, chest out, shoulders back, marching with precision and perfect posture, projecting an overwhelming sense of confidence, pride, and valor. The nature and quality of your movements, actually determines what state you are in. The state you're in then will determine the range and quality of the behaviors you're able to produce.

In reality, we're modeling all the time. In fact, when you think about it, we are acting daily, and every hour of our lives, always playing to a different audience. We are always selling, sure it is not the same as the traditional sense of selling a product, yet your always selling yourself, selling your ideas, selling your point of view, are you not? Just think of a first date, we all can agree a first date is not only a sales job, but an interview, where your hoping you bring your A-Game or else your going home to play by yourself. No matter your role in life you have always been modeling, acting and selling, so it makes sense put into practice the knowledge of how to model success, in order to achieve success.

Consider the success of modeling when it comes to business structure and systems developed to achieve their desired outcome. You know them as franchise opportunities, anything from a 7-11 to most fast food restaurants, hotels, fitness clubs, direct sales, and the list goes on. Remember modeling just like franchises can be clearly explained by the common saying, work smarter, not harder. Who do you think is going to achieve substantial financial success, more free time, and less time at the office? Will it be the small business owner working 80+ hours a week managing every aspect of his single store operation? Or will it be the entrepreneur that develops a system and hires employees to model the system, while he expands his business, by merely finding locations and implementing the same system modeling off the original? Of course, the person who creates a system to achieve the desired outcome has the greater opportunity to grow, while laboring less.

Consider the richest man in the world Carlos Slim Helú. How did he get that way? Simple: He modeled the Rockefellers, the Morgans, and others of similar financial standing, while keeping his fathers frugal business sense. He read everything he could read among his favorites of history is Ghengis Khan, studying the beliefs of prominent historical leaders and business tycoons and modeling their strategies. Why was Rick Hoyt able not just merely to survive, but to prosper from a condition he was born with that would stop most people. His parents never allowed to him feel defeat, they would allow him to experience as much as possible life had to offer, regardless of the logistics. Rick had a model of possibility, and that positive model was stronger than the negative experiences he underwent. The difference between those who succeed and those who fail isn't what they have - it's what they choose to see and do with their resources and their experience of life.

Through this same modeling technique, I began to see instant results both for myself and for others. I continued to seek out other patterns of thought and measures that produced significant results in short periods of time. These patterns are your fuel, it is what allows you to experience life and more importantly get results firing on all cylinders firing and life in full throttle. It is these strategies you will not only learn about in this book, you will know precisely how to implement, and employ directly into every facet of your life. My goal, my outcome for you are not just to provide the opportunity for you to master these patterns, additionally enhance your own strategies. I have learned never to assume anything too much, for if you think it, there will always be a place where it just doesn't work. NLP is a powerful tool, and it's just that - a tool you can use to develop your own approaches, your own strategies, your own insights. No one strategy works all the time. Modeling is not a new concept. Every great inventor has modeled the discoveries of others to come up with something new.

Trouble with modeling in today's fast paced, information overload society is we model with no focus or precision, sometimes even forgetting the original result we are trying to duplicate. Life's so random? Well, many times the way we deploy modeling is by picking up random bits and pieces from this person or that and then we entirely miss something much more important and valuable from someone else. We model something good here and something bad there. You set out to model someone I respect but find you don't quite know how to do what he/she does.

"Luck is the combination of passion & opportunity colliding, it's talent and drive which decides your staying power." -Tollie Schmidt

Think of this as a guidebook into your most powerful asset, your mind. Learn how to guide your mind consciously and unconsciously with greater precision. This is your chance to become conscious of something you've always been doing in your life.

Bluntly put, we have positively NO EXCUSES with all the resources and strategies all around us, with access at our finger tips online, and in our daily interactions. My challenge to you is to start thinking like a modeler, continuously being aware of the patterns and types of actions that produce astounding jaw dropping results. When someone is able to do something extraordinary, the immediate thought should not be of jealousy, since being jealous will never lead to a positive outcome. Instead, you should be asking, *"How does he create that result?"* I truly hope you will continue to look for excellence, for the magic in everything you see, and learn how it's produced so that you can create the same kinds of results whenever you desire.

Let's look at how we respond to all the different circumstances in life because you can never move forward with one foot still stuck in the past.

Chapter III

Powerful Mojo

"THE EMPIRES OF THE FUTURE ARE THE EMPIRES OF THE MIND" -
WINSTON CHURCHILL

What do you get when you play a country song backwards? You get your house back. You get your dog back. You get your best friend Jack back. You get your truck back. You get your hair back. Ya get your first and second wives back. Your front porch swing. Your pretty little thing. Your bling bling bling and a diamond ring. You get your farm and the barn and the boat and the Harley, and your first night in jail with Charlie. This would be one hell of an experience, you would be on top of the world, Right? And of course we all have more or less had the experience when it feels as if we lost everything, there was no possible way things could get worse, then they did? You've probably remembered times you fumbled up things you usually do easily, when the lid popped off your coffee and spilled down the front of your shirt. Running late to work, and it seems as if every single light were red, and everything you tried turned out wrong.

What's the difference? Did you enter the twilight zone? You're the same person. Nothing about you has suddenly changed; you didn't suddenly get hit in the head with a baseball. So why is it at times it seems the world is against you, and other times your on fire? How can someone such as Tiger Woods goes from killing it tournament after tournament to all the sudden nothing works, it's as if he forgot how to play the game of golf?

The difference is the mojo. Just like when Austin Powers lost his mojo and all of a sudden everything stopped working for him, until he got it back. Your mojo is the term I use to describe your neurophysiological state. Your mojo enables all your inner powers: confidence, love, inner strength, joy, ecstasy, belief. When you lose the mojo, you lose your power and it gets replaced by confusion, depression, fear, anxiety, sadness, frustration.

Have you ever gone into a restaurant and had a server snarl, "*Whaddya want?*" you answer "*a new server, sunshine!*" Do you think she always communicates in a way that makes you wonder who in the world took a spit in their Cheerios that morning? Ok, sure it's possible that the server has had such a terrible life, and their sunny disposition is just how they are. But, I more than likely they just had a terrible day, too many tables at one time, maybe stiffed by a few customers. They're not a bad person; just lost their mojo. If you could give them their mojo back, you can change their entire behavior.

Your Mojo...

Your Mojo's Effect | Empowering to Disempowering

Understanding the mojo is the key to understanding change and achieving a new level of personal excellence. Our behavior is the result of the mojo flowing through our body, or loosing our mojo. I know this is going to be hard to believe, but I know in my life there are times where I just couldn't get the mojo flowing. Someone looked at me wrong, and I would fly off the handle and do or say things I was later embarrassed or even ashamed by. Maybe you have, too. One of my previous employers back in high school that would allow a customer just to tear into him, screaming and blaming everything from our mistake to the weather on him. Then after his little temper tantrum he would calm down quickly, and my employer could have a rational discussion with him.

MY EMPLOYER WOULD SAY TO ME AFTERWARDS:

"Look, sometimes you just need to let them vent, say nothing, and let them get it all out before you say a word, because you never know what might have happened prior to walking through the door."

I remember this because to this day, I still find times that I use his advice, and it works. The customer's rant had nothing to do with us; instead he just got off the phone after learning his mother passed away suddenly. You never know what events are transpiring in life, triggering them to lose all their mojo and their behavior shifts for the worst immediately. What you always have control over is your actions, feelings, and behavior.

Remember the server, the ranting customer, are not their behaviors. The key is to take control of our mojo; thus, our behaviors. What if, in a single moment, you could create the energy and flow where you're pumped, the mojo is flowing, your mind and focus become a laser of precision. You can!

When you finish this book, and recommend it to all your friends and family (*Insert Blatant Advertising Plug Here*) you're going to see how to get your mojo flowing with an intensity level, to where you get so empowered that, in a moment, you can get yourself out of a dis-empowering funk.

Controlling Your Internal Communications

Remember: Power = Action

My goal is to share with you how to get your mojo flowing, which leads to decisive, congruent, and committed action. In this chapter were going to learn all about the mojo, and exactly how it works and flows. Also, were going to learn why we CAN control the mojo and how to make it flow and work for us.

Your mojo is made up of millions of neurological processes happening within us. Most of the time, how your mojo flows happen without any conscious direction on our part. We see something and our mojo is on autopilot and responds. That response could be a positive effect or negative, but there are not much we actually do to control it. The difference between those who fail to achieve their goals in life and those who succeeds is the difference between those who cannot release their mojo and function in a funk, and those who tap into their mojo let it flow and use their inner power to propel their actions to achieve all they want.

Almost everything people want is some possible form of mojo. List the things you want in life. Do you want to love? Well, there's love mojo, a feeling or emotion we signal to ourselves and feel within ourselves based on certain triggers from the environment. Confidence? Respect? They're all things that we create. We produce all these unique and different forms of mojo within ourselves. Maybe you want money. You don't care about the physical pieces of the green paper with photos of dead presidents staring back at you. You want what money represents to you: the love, confidence, freedom, or whatever forms of mojo you think it's going to create for you.

The key to love, the key to joy, the key to the ultimate power that man has sought for years: the ability to direct his life = is the ability to know how to direct and manage your mojo.

To direct your mojo's flow so you can achieve the results you're ready to achieve in life, is begun by learning how effectively to run your brain. Before we can even start this process, we need to know a little bit about how it works. We need to know how the brain directs our mojo, and state, the emotions we feel at any particular time and moment. Since time began, man has been obsessed in ways he could alter his mojo, create an instant sensation, feeling or emotion, creating a new experience. Fasting, drugs, ritual, music, sex, food, hypnoses, even chanting has been tried. Immediately, you can zero in on anyone of these examples and point to their uses, and their limitations. Here, is where the downright groovy mind freak fun comes into play. You're now going to be opened up to direct ways that are not only just as powerful and often twice as fast with a laser like precision.

Since all behavior is linked directly to our mojo, we produce different communications and behaviors when our mojo is flowing than when we are stuck in a funk. Then, the next question is, What creates the emotional state were in? Any emotional state is caused by two main components. The first is how we feel about a situation; the second is how we are responding to it. What and how you perceive things, as well as what and how you say things to yourself about the situation in front of you, creates the emotional state you're in and all kinds of behaviors you produce. The easy examples, how do you treat your lover when he or she gets home a lot later than they promised? Well your behavior and response are all going to be determined by the mojo your feeling, your emotional state. To a large degree your reaction is determined by what you have been communicating to your brain, or the story you've been telling yourself. If you've been sitting there for hours picturing the one you loved, hurt in a car accident, bloody, dead, or in the

Powerful Mojo

hospital, you may breathe a sigh of relief, drying your tears on their shirt while hugging them as tight as you can when the person walks in the door. Your emotional state was one of concern, your mojo was determined by you picturing situations that scared you, made you worry.

However, if instead you pictured your loved one in a hospital where the nurse was wearing knee-high stockings, and she's a naughty nurse, while hearing the sounds of a slab bass guitar in the background to the beat *bam chicka wow wow*, your response when your loved one walks through the door will be a stark contrast to our previous example. Your emotional state will be one of anger, feeling used, and a whole new set of behaviors will result.

What causes you to picture situations that make them feel concerned while, another person communicates to anger, or distrust to themselves? What triggers their emotional state to be one of concern or anger? Many factors are involved. Maybe we modeled the reactions of our parents in similar situations, which wrote the script we use for the story were going to use on ourselves. Look at it this way, if you saw your mom worried and concerned when your dad would come home late, would you are more inclined as an adult to see the situation in the same way?

Yet, if your dad were cheating on your mom, and she expressed her anger with you, fearing he was cheating. You might model her pattern of anger, resentment, and mistrust. These might be feelings you recall. Our beliefs, attitudes, values, and experiences with that person all effect the kinds of stories based on how we tell ourselves about their behaviors and how we processed the event.

Another huge factor in how we perceive or process the world around us is how we use our own physiology. Our physiology encompasses everything from muscle tension, what we eat, how we breathe, our posture, and our overall level of biochemical functions, and directly affects our mojo's emotional state. How we choose to process an event to communicate to our brain and physiology works together automatically in a cybernetic loop. Anything that has an imprint on one will automatically affect the other. So changing your mojo's emotional state involves changing how you process the event and your physiology. If when your lover is running late, and your body's mojo is in a healthy emotional state, then you probably will process the situation and tell yourself that their just stuck in traffic, or on their way home. In a physiological state, of immense muscular tension, you can feel exhausted, you feel pain, or even low blood sugar, your tendency to create a negative emotional state will only magnify.

How often have you been sick as a dog, yet your mojo was flowing and pumping and you just felt totally alive? The point is; your physiology changes the way you represent and experience the world around you. When you process things as difficult or upsetting, doesn't your body react, and a tense feeling takes over, or you feel a knot in your stomach? So our mojo is effected by not only how we are processing events in our mind but simultaneously our body's physiology. Our mojo's emotional state will determine our behavior. To control and direct our behaviors, we must control, and direct, our mojo's emotional states. To control our states, we must control, and deliberately direct, how we choose to process events to communicate to our brain and physiology's. Weight loss, Depression, happiness, love, achievements, the list can go on forever, when we consider what is possible by being in control of our mojo's emotional state 100% of the time.

The Map is Not the Territory (NLP)

There's a crucial concept that's used in NLP: The map is not the territory

Studies show individuals recall events they experienced in their life as never being a precise, factual account of the event. It's just one interpretation that has been filtered through specific personal beliefs, attitudes, values, and something called metaprograms. Metaprograms are how your mind processes an event, stores the information from feeling or emotions you placed on the event and direct your behavior.

If we can't recall any event with a precise non bias entirely factual account, then why not process the event and communicate to our brain in a way that empowers us and others instead of creating limitations? There's no reason not to, and using memory management and consistently create the most empowering states of mojo. In any event, there are many things we can focus on. You have a craving and feel hungry, and your mojo goes into a funk, you communicate to your brain how hard losing, weight is, you are depriving yourself of things you love, you're miserable, it's not worth it, and you can take yourself into a feeling of depression. Does, this scenario sound familiar to you? That same craving could have been used to empower yourself in a way that you would strengthen your resolve not only to lose weight but create the body of your dreams. What if instead every time you consistently feel a craving you communicate to your brain that a craving only lasts 5 minutes so its no big deal. You change your physiology by moving around, get up off the chair and just move, start laughing for no reason, drink a full glass of water. Just by changing your physiology your creating a positive mojo and your emotional state becomes one of pride for changing behavior and it makes you happy.

Successful people can tap into their most resourceful state of mojo on a consistent basis. Don't you think that's the difference between those who succeed and those who don't? Think back to Rick Hoyt. It wasn't what happened at the time of birth that mattered. It was the way he chose to process the event and communicate it to his brain about what happened. Despite not being able to use 90% of his body, speak, or communicate without the use of a computer, he found a way to focus on what he could do, and allowed his mojo to empower himself.

Remember, nothing is naturally bad or good. Value is placed after we have processed, and then communicated to our brain how to think and feel about any event, person, object, place, and the list goes on. We can represent things in a way that we create a positive flow of mojo, or we can do the opposite and take our mojo into a funk. Think of a time, when you were in a powerful, emotional state.

If I asked for you to put down the book right now, and walk across a bed of broken glass barefoot, I doubt you would get up and do it. It's something you believe you can't do, or you associate pain with the idea, you'll cut your feet. And you probably did not associate any resourceful feelings and states for the challenge. So, when I speak of it, you would probably not go into a mindset that would support you in taking action.

If instead you were picturing people cheering and encouraging everyone, while they were dancing and celebrating, if what you were experiencing was a scene of excitement, a spontaneous party, your mojo would flow into a state of extraordinary confidence and probability. If, during this party, you were now visualizing yourself walking across the glass, almost floating across the glass, and during this means you didn't see any sharp edges, the perceived risk was gone. Now, you start saying YES, lets do this, and instilled with confidence you launch your body into action and walk, your neurological triggers would create a state where we will without hesitation take action and walk.

Remember Jase's event The Bridge I talked about earlier? At the Bridge there we can walk across a bed of broken bottles, and glass barefoot. The reason is to change the mindsets and to communicate a different message of empowerment, and trust to the brain. Changing how our mind is processing the walk across broken glass allows us to act and achieve the result. Despite fear or other limiting factors. People who take off their shoes and socks and then walk across a bunch of broken glass isn't different from the way they were when they came in the door thinking of walking across broken glass was impossible. But, we learned how to change our physiology, and learned to change how we processed and communicated the idea to our brain so we could trigger only the resources to act.

The Glass Walk | Jase Souder's Bridge Event

Walking across glass is an opportunity to do something you thought was impossible and taking action. Your mojo is always flowing, in life, results are always being produced. If you don't take, conscious control deciding the results you desire, then outside influences will put you into a negative state. You can end up in a negative state simply from a conversation or watching television. A dream is like a river. You can be at the uncontrollable whim of nature. Or you can be specific, and deliberate with your actions.

Choosing your actions, allows you to steer in a chosen direction. You decide. You set the course. You will achieve your goals. If you don't sow mentally, physically, and logically you will end up with a crop of weeds automatically.

Without consciously directing our minds into a powerful state, then our mojo will not flow and the environment we allowed to take hold will provide a state where we are in a funk. The results can be rough. It's essential, daily that we protect what is communicated to our brain. We need to be aware of how we are representing events and the meaning we are communicating to ourselves. Every day you've got to take out the trash, and weed the garden.

Karl's Death Premonition

Sometimes being in a funk and allowing yourself into an undesirable state can be dangerous sometimes deadly. Have you ever heard the story of Karl Wallenda of the Flying Wallendas? For years, Karl performed aerial routines of death defying stunts with accuracy and success. Karl was so confident in his ability that failure, or danger to his personal safety never was even a question, or concern. Failure wasn't even an option, and mentally the concept of failure was never a part of his mental code.

One day Karl, uncharacteristically began commenting to his wife that he envisioned himself to be falling. After all those years, Karl consistently started to communicate to himself falling. Karl fell to his death within only three months since the first time he saw himself fall. Was Karl's death a premonition? We can only speculate; however, a better answer could be explained that Karl gave his nervous system a continuous representation, a trigger, throwing him into a state that supported the behavior of falling, which the outcome is one he created. He directed his brain to follow a new path, which eventually, it did. This is why it is essential to focus on all the things we want in life, let our positive mojo flow, and not allow ourselves to focus on what we don't want.

If all you see in your life is nothing but problems, roadblocks, a bleak future, and a laundry list of awful things, it's because you're in a state that supports those behaviors and results. Would you consider yourself the jealous type? No, you are not.

Earlier, maybe you created jealous states creating negative behaviors directly connected to them. Luckily, you are not your behavior. Don't buy into the generalization that you can be classified as a particular behavior, based on one event, or you're past. Because if you do, you create a belief that will control and direct all your future actions. Keep in mind, your behavior is directly linked to the state you are in, and your state is a by-product of how you represent things internally and your physiology, both can be changed instantly. Earlier if you have been jealous, it merely means you chose to communicate the situation and event in a particular way to create a state of jealousy. So now you can create a state by representing things in a way that will not produce anger or jealousy. It is our choice of how to communicate and represent things to ourselves. Keep telling yourself that your lover is cheating, pretty soon you'll put yourself in a state of hatred and anger. Although, there is no evidence of any cheating, you experience it in your body as if it were true, because of this, your loved one comes home and you're already on offense, suspicious, angry. How do you treat the person you love, when you are in this kind of state? Be honest, more than likely you are acting like a grade A jerk. Worst part, is maybe you abuse, or attack them verbally, or just feel crummy inside which festers and creates some other retaliatory behavior later on.

Remember, your lover might not have done anything. But, the kind of behavior your producing out of such a state, will make he/she want to be with someone else! If you're jealous, you create that state. You can change your pictures of negativity to images of your loved one working hard to get home. This new picture process will put you in a state when your loved one does make it home, your behavior will make them feel wanted, increasing the desire to be with you. Maybe your lover is doing what you pictured, but wasting many negative emotions is destructive. You need to find out for sure, and communicate those concerns. Most the time it's unlikely it is true, yet you created all kinds of pain for both you, and for what?

"The ancestor of every action is a thought." -Ralph Waldo Emerson

Chris Williams Story

Tragedy, Faith, Strength & Forgiveness (LetitGo)

As we learned earlier, The map is not the territory, concept proves that every individual recalls any event in their life is never a precise, factual account of the event. So it shows how our metaprograms are shaped and created by our interpretation of any event. Even in the most emotionally heart wrenching moments in our life, we CAN create an empowering state of mind and take a tragedy to redemption. Chris Williams made a decision as he stared out his shattered windshield at the overturned car, fully and painfully aware that his wife, their unborn son, 11-year-old son, and 9-year-old daughter were dead. Chris could direct his thoughts, communicated his interpretation of the event to his mind so that he could be in the most resourceful, empowering state possible.

As Chris writes in his book, Let It Go. Chris chose to forgive the driver who caused the accident, killing his loved ones. On Feb. 9, 2007, the Williams family was on their way home from a night out when 17-year-old Cameron White, driving from the other direction, slammed into the side of their car. It happened too fast for Williams who was driving, to get out of the way. White was driving under the influence of alcohol, and he fled the scene of the accident. Here, where a powerful state of mojo truly flows for Chris, before he even knew the teen's name or the circumstances, he knew he had to let it (*the act*) go.

REMEMBER THE VIRTUE OF BELIEF & FAITH WE DISCUSSED IN THE PREVIOUS CHAPTER?

We discussed how influential and powerful our belief and faith is. Chris had faith, believing good would be discovered and God had a larger purpose. He refused to interpret even his own horrific experience in such a way it would cause negative emotions. "*As a disciple of Christ, I had no other choice,*" Williams that was then serving as bishop of the LDS Crystal Heights Ward, Salt Lake Highland Stake, told the LDS Church News two days after the accident. At the time, Williams did not realize the imprint his decision would have on the community. In the years since Chris surviving that fateful accident, his story is one of healing and forgiveness. Williams has become a beacon of strength, and hope, he reached out to his community to help people he didn't even know, how to heal, and overcome personal tragedies.

During a press conference and interviews he gave shortly after the crash, Williams often spoke about his decision to forgive and let go of what could have been a miserable burden of entwined grief, righteous anger, or even resentment, choosing instead to separate his feelings about the deaths of his family members from the teenager in the other driver's seat.

In turn, many news articles written about the tragedy included Williams' appeal for forgiveness and loved, including an invitation to "extend a single act of kindness, a token of mercy, or an expression of forgiveness … by Valentine's Day and then, if you feel so to do, write that experience down and share it with my two surviving boys by sending it to the address that the radio and TV outlets will provide."

The key to achieving your dreams, and to creating inner peace, happiness, and joy, is to interpret things to yourself by communicating ways which will put you in the most resourceful state so that you are empowered and your mojo flows and your actions are positive and ultimately create the result you demand. Failure to see the good or the possibilities, usually means a failure even to attempt your dreams. If Chris interpreted only the event in a way that spurred anger, hate, a sense of unfairness for his circumstance, he would have lost ALL faith, he would believe in nothing, and more important all his good he could spread, would have never happened. Even in life's most tragic, horrific, events we have a choice on how we interpret the event, what emotions we will feel, resulting in our direct actions and behavior, choose to find the good, because from goodness comes greatness.

If we interpret to ourselves things will not work, they won't. If we communicate to ourselves that things will work, we create the flow of mojo we need to provide the state that will enable us in achieving only positive results. The difference between a Steve Jobs, Glenn Beck, Chris Williams, and other people are they

Powerful Mojo

see the world as where opportunities are available to develop and obtain any result they dream up. We all can have an off day, where we feel the mojo flow, but we can't get exactly the results we are trying to get. However, when we are in state, the mojo is flowing, we create the greatest possible opportunity for using all our resources in an accurate and effective way.

Those who have created their dreams, transformed their lives, and produce monumental results are masters of creating the mojo by tapping into the most empowering parts of their mind. This is what separate the men from the boys, the women from the girls, it's how you get up each morning, put on your big boy britches and make things happen. The most important theme of this chapter is the powerful mojo you create through your state, and you control it.

LUCKY MOJO

It's Not Luck... It's your mojo baby...

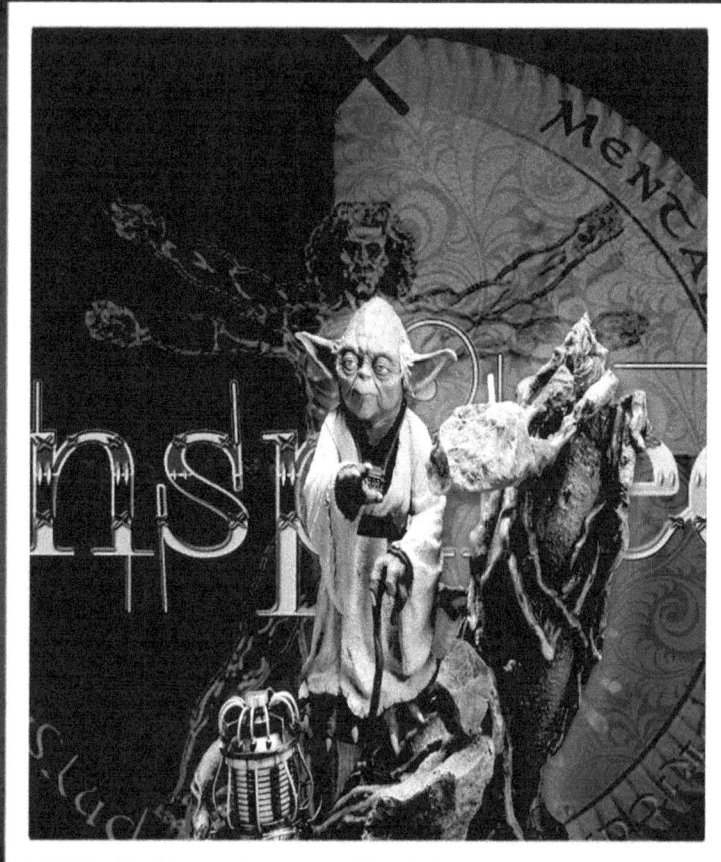

Chapter IV

The Art of Fulfillment

"WE WANDER FOR DISTRACTION, BUT WE TRAVEL FOR FULFILLMENT." -
HILAIRE BELLOC

As I stated at the beginning of this book, we will experience an inspired life. To obtain an inspired life, you need the skills. Acquiring diverse skills is the science of achievement. Step-by-step here is how you do it, you can achieve anything, everybody has, anybody who wants to can make it happen if they will follow certain laws. You sow you reap as I've already said. But, you can succeed and may not be fulfilled. Success without fulfillment is failure. I've dealt with people from around the world, some of the greatest achievers throughout the world, but I've met few who are truly fulfilled. See to have an inspired life, you need to have the ability to support the discipline of achievement, but you also have to master the art of fulfillment. And it's an art, not a science. There are principles that if you use them, you can create joy right now although you haven't achieved your goals. And you know what, if you have more joy right now you have more energy to go after them.

See most of us have been trained, at least in the Western world, were supposed to go do things so we can achieve, so we can eventually feel good. In the East, you're supposed to feel good and enjoy yourself right now because this is all it is, one is focused on the future, the other is focused on the present. We need both. Listen, if you live here in the West and you just sit around, and you bliss out at the world, you're going to be fulfilled. But for how long? You know, if you just sit there and be fulfilled, people come and take your furniture. You got to do something with your life; requires that we do things that allow us to contribute to the world. Life also requires that if we will be fulfilled, we also need to find a way to enjoy the things we do. And if you can do that, now you're at the top of the ladder. Because, if you don't do that, you'll bump into the experience I bumped into. I achieved and made it all happen. I felt so excited about my life, I was juiced, I was giving, giving, giving, however, there came a point, where I was so focused on giving, giving, giving, that I wasn't taking any time for myself. I started to lose my mojo.

I remember one time, being on stage, speaking in front of all these people, receiving a standing ovation, being stoked that I could contribute to all these people. But at the end, I felt empty. I mean it was a truly scary moment for me. I realized, that there were some things in my life, that I had not focused on, and they were hurting. I contended that they were okay, truth is they weren't, much of it had to do with the relationship I had with myself, I had never taken enough time for myself. I began doing that, every day, every single day I was doing my hour of inspiration, but now I was so swept up in doing, therefore, I wasn't taking care of me. So here's what this is about, you will start a process if you're willing to. It's a process about taking time for yourself, it's about taking the most scarce resource that you've gotten, which is time, and

The Art of Fulfillment

giving it to yourself. And were not going to think about problems, but better yet go through a remarkably straightforward system that will line you up for a deep fulfillment of success.

Because problems will not go away, so how are we going to have an inspired life? Well the answer to that question is to realize that problems and happiness have no link. I learned this, because I felt like all of a sudden I had all these problems, in the midst of problems, big changes, and anytime you make some changes; you're going to have some problems. People will agree with your change, or they won't like it, or they will judge it and say things such as, why did you do that? I don't like it. Change, always, always creates problems. As you run into problems, you create solutions. (*Which, by the way, are more changes.*) There is a constant process here, simply stated, as you create more changes, you create more problems. So problems are here to stay. They won't be problems for you, they'll be challenges, and we love a challenge don't we? Remember as we learned earlier, how are we going to perceive a situation and communicate it to our brain? We will communicate the situation to our brain in the most resourceful state that will provide us the best opportunity to solve, and achieve our result. Nobody wants a problem, but we love a challenge.

Why do we watch sports? Because people take on a challenge, they want to see what they can do. When you start a new business, you thrive off the opportunity to take on a new challenge. What is it that makes you attracted to someone, you might start thinking in your head, oh my gosh, can I connect with that person, can I even get through to this person? How can I get this idea across to them? See, It's a challenge, challenge is necessary for growth, and growth is life. So it's a cool system.

Life is Beautiful | Developing an Unprecedented Psychology

An Inspired Life | Where You Are Juiced Your mojo Flows Daily

Then having an inspired life simply means you will have a life where the primary emotion of your life are the ones that you want. See it doesn't mean that life works out every way that you want, sometimes it rains on your parade. Sometimes the events of your life, you cannot control. But, you can control what it means to you. And when we can control what it means to us, this is the greatest power of your life, you will not only be inspiring, you will be powerful. The ultimate advantage, here's a perfect example.

Did you see that movie that won the Academy award, Life is Beautiful? Maybe if, you have not seen the film, I'm sure you've seen on YouTube or Facebook the clip of the man jumping up and down after winning the oscar, which was the lead actor in Life is Beautiful. It's a story of a man who has an extraordinary and inspired life. Not because he has more money than anybody, not because he's in a situation where everything is easy. But because, he's alive! He has this joy about him, and, by the way, if you've actually ever met the actor who plays this character, you would know that he lives this way, day-today. You know he was offering this thing, and it became clear that this thing was, himself. He was such a joyous man when he won the Academy award. We have never seen so much emotion, he was like a little boy, and we all loved it. Because nobody else would have the guts to be that way. Or they've forgotten what it feels like just to feel, to be alive, what makes him inspired? He has an unprecedented psychology. He has an inspired mindset.

He sees the world from a state where he is inspired and joyous. And in the movie, the man has that, doesn't he? And who does that affect? Everyone. Everyone within the realm of his influence is affected by his inspiration. His wife feels like the most cherished person on earth, and, therefore, so does he. Because when you give that kind of love that kind of joy, people give it back. It's infectious.

His son seems so happy, and in the middle of the Nazis taking over their country, you know the story already. You know they get picked up. And they're such a connection among the family, that the wife who is not getting sent away, gets on the train with them. And they're in the middle of this camp, this man with his unprecedented psychology, figures a way, at looking at the situation, for his son. Presenting the situation so his son sees it as a game.

Isn't life a game anyway? Because he has an ultimate psychology, his family survives the horror of the Holocaust. See, if you want your family to survive, if you want them to succeed, if you want them to have joy, if you want your kids to have a lasting love, if you want to be able to give gifts in your life, not to just take care of yourself, then you need an inspired psychology, within yourself.

Daily Mojo to be Grateful

It's Not Where You Live Physically | It's Where You Live Internally

There are two worlds, as we have discussed earlier, the inside world and the outside world we cannot control the outside world altogether. But, we have absolute control over the inside world. But you know what, most of us are too busy; to take any time and see what's going on in. We just accept the status quo, this is just who I am; this is my life. Or I'll get to it later. I want to invite you, to take the time to say, I will make time for myself and start with an hour of daily mojo. Every day, I will have at least 30 minutes to thrive. Or 15 minutes to be fulfilled at the very minimum. So I want you to take those 15 minutes, and I want you to focus on everything you're grateful for. If we want our life to have a greater purpose, we must make the time to be grateful. This personal time must have some specific things we do, and one of those things, is gratitude. If you want to know what is the quality of your life, it is, how much time do we spend in gratitude. How much time are you grateful and appreciative to the point that emotion swells up in you? I'm feeling it now, I'm so grateful for God; I'm so grateful to have the privilege to serve you right now. So if, you can get to this state, everything changes.

I will give you an example, if you think about being fearful, and you're fearful, you're not grateful. If you want to get rid of fear, everybody has said, I'm not fearful, I'm just stressed. Or if you live in places like LA or New York, they're called achievers, they can't even be stressed there. They have angst, which is a higher-level, a more sophisticated level, of stress. But you know what, if you focus on stress, ultimately it will bring you to fear. And everybody has fears, fears that I'm not enough, fears that it won't work out, fears they won't be loved. Everybody has that fear at some level unconsciously, were only human. So you can put that fear aside, when you are being grateful. I don't mean just intellectually, yes I'm grateful for this, I'm grateful for that, but I mean stopping, thinking, seeing, and feeling. So I will walk you through a system that includes gratitude. Every day of our life, we must have a vision. Every day of our life we must have something that excites us. I hear people say, they are bored, there is nothing to do. They will constantly complain about the mundane life they have, detail their boring job, go to another boring dinner, in and out of boring meetings. I'm bored, nothing excites me, NO you're boring.

How you Feel, IS Your Life | Discovering Your Negative Feelings

If Nothing In Your Life Excites You | You Haven't Come Up With a Vision

We all need something that will make us use more of our potential. Our courage, passion, our joy, face our fears, start building our emotional muscles. But, you don't build emotional muscles when you do the same thing day after day after day. What you get is a life that is unfulfilling. So we've got to have a vision, every day to become inspired. I will take you through an easy process that will get you to expand your vision. Once you start expanding as a human being, your start feeling life and you cast a compelling future, you become juiced in life making you get up early and staying up late. There's a reason, you don't have a reason.

Anytime you achieve a goal, as you get close to it, you better set up the next one. If you don't have that next goal already set in a cue, ready to act on, it's like postpartum you eagerly await that baby, and now you've got it. And sometimes in the middle of the night, you're thinking what have I done. Have you ever had that experience? But you know what, you also have experience on the other side, something wonderful. It's kind of like, the man who went to the moon for the first time, the first astronauts, they achieved this monumental goal, they walked on the moon. Then, they came back to the earth, are met with parades in their honor, instantly recognized as national heroes, they shook the president's hand, but now what? What do you do now that you walked on the moon? Maybe you have to find how to get fulfillment out of a smile instead of a space-flight. Maybe you need to cast a new vision, a vision of what your life is about now.

You've got to have a daily vision that will excite you. Otherwise, life becomes mundane. There's nothing worse than an okay life. I told you, starting today, you will not have just an okay life when we are done here. I promise you, if you get in the habit you will not settle for an okay life; instead people will ask, what happened to you. There is nothing more exciting, then the ability to create. There's not much excitement in maintenance. I mean you have to maintain your body, and you have to maintain things, but creating is something that God created us for. He gave us the gift to make choices, create new things, build businesses, ideas, families, and friends. Creating your own garden, by planting seeds of ideas, and consistently weeding out the junk that prevents us from achieving a perfect harvest. Inspired to create is free to all, it's available to every one of us but, if you're not a creating a vision each day than the day will not have much juice in it. So every day there's got to be a little time for vision, a time to be inspired, Right!

Don't you want your mojo back? It's time for gratitude, time for vision, and every single day, you got to move; motion equals emotion. I'll tell you why most people are unhappy, it's because they don't move.

Look at our lives today. Most people live in a box, and then what do they do? They get up, get a box cereal for breakfast, they get their box car, and they drive, to their box office, they go up a box elevator, they talk on a box, eat a box lunch, they drive their box home; they turn on a box to be entertained. Maybe, just maybe, they decide they need some variety in their life, and pop the top to a cold refreshing, cylinder trying to change their state. Listen, life must become a constant flow of movement. When you move your alive, emotion comes from motion. The more you move the more you feel, the emotion in your voice, even as I'm writing this, I'm wiggling in my chair, changing it up, anything to get my emotional juices flowing it's all about the mojo. That's how you feel, and, by the way, the less you move, the less you feel, the less alive you are. If you are totally rigid and totally inflexible, no movement this is known, as death. So if, emotionally you're stuck, move. Every day you got a move, now that can be as easy as walking, for exercise, but it's something that's got to happen. And, by the way, if you want a passionate relationship with anybody what do you need? You need time to spend with that person. Maybe even have a conversation with that person, it's a crazy idea, I know, but their worth it, your worth it.

Most of us have conversations in our head. I want to show you how to take control of those conversations, much as if a director will direct a show. It is a way of directing your thoughts, shaping your mind, conditioning your mind, it's kind of like going to the gym and getting in the best shape of your life. But it's the best mental, emotional, spiritual, physical, shape you've ever been in, and you don't need me to do it. I don't have to follow you around the rest of your life this is something where you will do it for yourself. I'll be here till the end of the book. If you want to visit with me again great, if you want to come to a seminar, I would love to meet you. But, you don't need me, I'm not here to create dependency, I'm here to remind you what you know is true. If you create on new habits on a continuous basis, you will create the results you want and deserve. So how does it work? Let's do this first, it's time for you to make some discoveries. The quality of your life is the quality of the consistent emotions you experience. Again, the quality of your life is the quality of the consistent emotions you experience. How you feel, IS your life. What are the feelings you have on a consistent basis.

So I will ask for you to take a moment, and if you have our journal there, or any piece of paper you will not make it rules driven, don't just do this in your head. I want you to write down all the emotions you experience in an average week. On one side write down all the good emotions you experience in a week and on the other side right down all the bad ones. Now when I say the bad ones, I mean there are no bad emotions, but the ones that are painful and you don't want. All I want you to do is write them down. And when you write them down do not edit them. If you experience any of these emotions at least some time during the week then write them down. The emotions you consistently feel, not the ones that you feel occasionally because what this is going to tell us is whether or not we are truly living right now. This doesn't tell me your income; I don't care. But, I care what you're passionate about, I care about what hurts you, I care about what you love and care about what moves you, and you do too. And you don't even have to tell me the, "*What's*" lets just figure out the feelings first. So, please, take a moment and write them down because now we will stop talking and start doing.

The first step here is to figure out where you are.

Write down now on one side all the emotions you consistently feel in a week, in a positive way. Flip the page over and write down all the emotions you consistently feel in a week that is negative. So stop reading, and, please get yourself to do this right now. If you're still reading, you're not writing. I swear this book will explode in 10 seconds if you do not start writing. Really? You need me to beg. The point is, thinking is not enough, things become real when you write them down. Writing down your goals and dreams give them some weight, it's imperative so please do this, I promise it's worth the time. You are worth the time.

So now you truly have some emotions you want, but how do you create them? You have some emotions you don't want, how do you get rid of them? Here's the best part, you can change how you feel about any situation or event, in an instant! We know this is true by your past experiences. There were times when you were downright upset, from your experiences, and then something caught your attention, all of a sudden you're laughing, right. People can be in a horrible place and immediately changed their state, the location, or event has nothing to do with your emotional state, except which you give it. You can be veritably, at a funeral, and suddenly something cracks you up, I mean it's pretty rare, but it has happened. People can be in an even worse situation, but somehow they find all their determination and change their state into one of resourcefulness. How to do that specifically is what I want to show you. I will show you how to do this, right now, real quickly.

Here is a quick overview about what you should do to shift your state to one of empowering resourcefulness. Three things you need to feel anything, these are the reasons why you feel anything. If you feel sad or upset or depressed or frustrated there are these three reasons, and if you change one of any of these three, you're going to change how you feel. And if you change all three, you will change how you feel altogether. If you're feeling happy, if you're feeling excited, if you're feeling euphoric, and you are on a roll and you want to know why it is that you felt that way. Maybe exciting things are happening in your life, but there is a reason why you felt a strong emotional anchor to that past event.Sometimes you have extraordinary things happening in your life, but you still don't feel passionate. So how do you do that?

Three reasons, three things, have to be in place for you to feel great. I call these three reasons, the trilogy, because, there are three patterns that if you do these three patterns in your body, in a certain way, then

The Art of Fulfillment

you'll get a certain result. It's like a recipe, you do one recipe, you get one result, you do another one, you get a different result, you get one kind of cake, or another, so let's give you an example.

A Dreamer's Revolution Seminar

I Have a Seminar I Do, Called, A Dreamer's Revolution

A dreamer's revolution is the initial seminar most people attend, a weekend to Inspire your life through casting a new vision. We don't just change things or make them a little better, it's a chance to go-all-in, to step up and say, "*I will transform my life!*" I don't care if it's my body, my emotions, my fear, my job, it's time to rise and act, it's time to get up, and go DO.

People are in an environment for three days of total immersion, even Frank Sinatra, would leave saying, "*Coo-coo, that weekend was the gas,*" because people come out transformed in the process. From the onset, I will ask for you to tell me, what it is, no-ifs-ands-or-buts, you want in your life. Here are a few of the recurring answers I have been told. I want to make a million dollars, or I want to make one billion dollars, I want to help my kids get through college, I want more confidence, I want to lose 57 pounds. Why do you want these things? If you lose 57 pounds, make a million dollars, what are you going to get through those accomplishments?

Sooner or later they say, "oh! Well... *if I change the world, I would have contributed to others in a deep and profound way,*" and I reply, "*yes, but what will it get YOU?*" Eventually, they'll say, "*well... I'll feel good, because my life will have significance,"* or they'll say, *"you know if I lost 57 pounds, I'd feel sexier, or I'd feel more energetic."* Or they'll say, *"if I had this money, I'd feel free, complete freedom,"* or power, security.

Whatever it is you want, you want it, because, you think it's going to give you a feeling. Your sense of wanting, is your cause, and if you can obtain, what you want, then your effect, will be a new feeling. You can look at anything you want in life, and review it from a cause and effect, approach. Truth be told, you can have that feeling right now, by changing these three patterns.

The first pattern that determines how you feel is not the event, but rather what you do with your body, in this moment. Right now, you're feeling, and whatever you feel right now in this moment, as you're reading this, is related. First, your feelings are being created by how you're using your body. If you're not using your body, and you are slumped over, feeling tired and beat up, it's safe bet to say, you would feel different right now if you were walking. Okay, now I'll give you a more specific example. Behind curtain number one, I have a person who suffers from depression. For $100,000 to be donated to your favorite charity, can you describe for me what they might look like? Can you describe him/her physically? I bet you could do it. What is his/her posture like? You know the answer, so just say it, or at least think it, but just say it out-loud! Seriously what does their physical body look like? How do you think their posture is right now? Do you think their posture is more than likely, slumped, what about their eyes, you think they're probably looking down? Where is his/her head, would you agree it is safe to say it is also down? What's his/her breathing like, is their breathing deep or shallow? His/her breathing is shallow. What about their facial expression? Is their face up in tight, or, more slack? You already know their face is slack. So how come you know all these things without me telling you? The answer is, because, you have practiced this stuff before, haven't you? Any feeling of sadness or depression is the acknowledgement that you have experienced this state.

U.C. Berkley's Depression
Research Study

Now, if you do this with your body, I don't care who you are, if you do these things, with your body, you're going to feel lousy, and you're going to feel depressed. Now, if you change the way you use your body, such as your shoulders back, you breathe, you use your voice in a different way, you start to move or gesture in a different tempo, then it becomes hard to feel depressed. There was a depression research study done a U.C. Berkeley. They did something that sounded insane, because traditionally, if someone is depressed they go to a traditional psychologist.

Today, the current philosophy is depression is merely a Prozac deficiency.

Society's Answer? Better Living Through Chemistry. If It is Prescribed by a Doctor, It Must Be Good For Us!

Today, if things are not working out for you, and day-today events are overwhelming, our culture feels that the solution must be in a pill form. Our society would rather us drug you, then resolve what's going on within you, it's called better living through chemistry. Sadly, living through chemistry successfully became the cultural norm, allowing chemical dependency to become another tool in raising our kids. Because today, we've got this attention deficit disorder, also known as ADD, or now it's been upgraded to ADHD, attention deficit *hyperactivity* disorder. Could this maybe be explained by the fact that kids are overstimulated, don't get enough focus, they don't receive enough of our attention? Kids, don't know how to use their energy in a world where things are going so slow, and what they're learning in school, and how they are on the Internet, on TV, or anything else, then it must be that we need to drug them.

Drug kids into submission, so they become as slow as their adult counterparts, which allow the adults to feel more comfortable.

It's an intriguing way we look at life today. The truth of the matter is these kids are using their bodies in a way that is unacceptable, but they're not being directed. Today, we go for the quick fix, we want the instant solution, even if it will not provide a long-term solution, which will support making us healthier. You can get a solution, but it may not be sustainable in a healthy way. The bottom line is, using that approach we usually end up drugging people. U.C. Berkeley, tried something different, and their approach involved no drugs. They did something that you're going to think sounds utterly ridiculous. They came up with a simple approach, they took people who were clinically depressed, this means you've achieved high levels of depression, yes, they are now certifiable. You are clinically depressed. You have achieved depression level, meaning, you practice this pattern of depression on a consistent basis.

I know this may seem a little obnoxious right now, I'm not trying to make people who suffer from depression sound terrible. Because, a long time ago, I also felt sadness in my life. I do not allow a state sadness to control my behavior. I recognize when I am feeling sad, and appreciate the message it is communicating to me. A message of sadness is an action signal, telling me to change. You will learn how to break the pattern of negative emotions, just as I have learned. I could not have the life I do today, helping others, if I were not in control of my emotions.

Again, emotions dictate our behavior. So, please understand where I'm truly coming from, it's an understanding and practiced principle I know works, and have used.

U.C. Berkeley's study was conducted over four weeks. Participants were asked to stand and face a full length 3-way mirror when they arrived at the research clinic. Standing facing the mirror participants received simple, clear instructions. They were instructed to do one silly thing, simply to smile as big as they could. The participants had to smile for no legitimate reason while holding the expression for 20 minutes. Now when you're doing this, your smile is so big, that it actually creates crows feet on the side of your eyes. Crow's feet are this little set of thin lines, which appear when you're smiling so big. Now interesting, they had to keep their shoulders back, while they were doing this, and breathe full, deep breathes. Dumb idea, right? But what happened? Not a single person was able to remain depressed; including a woman that claimed she was depressed even while she slept. I will even admit, being able to be in a state of depression while asleep, is one heck of an accomplishment! You know what's intriguing, at the end of these 20 days many of these individuals did not need medication anymore, and that's all they changed. This physical change is only one part, of what we call a trilogy.

Just the physical part of the trilogy, that's how powerful it is. See, if you get up, and if you move, moving your body in a totally different way, you shall feel different. Emotion is created by motion. We have 80 muscles in our face, how many are you using consciously, are you doing anything different with your body, so you can feel different? What do you do? Do you do the same things, so you feel the same things? Look at your list, if you have written it down, and the list represents, a few patterns that you do with your body regularly, and you don't even think about it. Whenever you do it differently, you feel it. Some movements will make you feel good, when you do them, while others might make you feel crummy.

Think about a movement to breathe. You got to move to sing. You got to move to speak. If I start speaking quicker, my pitch goes up, my organs in the body start moving in a different way. But, if I start speaking like a host on NPR, slow mundane and boring, how's that going to make me feel? What if when I spoke there was no energy, I had my head down, speaking slowed, with no change in my dialect, nobody would listen to me. There's got to be some combination of energy, And that energy does not come from sitting in a chair, or having a TelePrompTer in front of me.

Instead, let me tell you what I am doing to create energy as I'm writing this. I'm picturing your face, and I'm trying to think what I can say, and give to you, that I know will make a difference based on the last 10 years of experiences. I'm telling you, I know, the number one thing to create a new state, is too deliberately, and powerfully, change the way you move.

Change the way you use your body, and you will change the way you feel altogether. Instantly. It is unimportant how crummy you felt, right now while your reading this, take a moment and just change your body's movement. Move your hands up for a second, just make this minor movement, you'll get a minor change in feeling. But, if you make a radical change, and you say, yes! I'm doing this now! I'm sick of this! I promise you; you're going to feel different. I know this sounds a bit odd, but it works.

Do you know what the best studies of life teaches us? The answer is, what works, even if it's simple, it's fine to have things simple, why do we have to make it so hard, just to feel good.

The Female "Coregasm"

Here, is another example of how movement, can drastically change how your feeling. According to a study by Indiana University and, the Center for Sexual Health Promotion discovered the truth behind a taboo myth concerning women and exercise. For years, fitness and women's magazines have touted the apocryphal "*coregasm*," but now researchers say that hundreds of women are getting the unintended benefits of those tummy crunches. Forty-five percent of the women who responded to the researchers, cited exercise-induced orgasm during abdominal exercises, weight lifting, yoga, bicycling, running and something as basic as walking. Emotion comes from motion. Here, is the second part of the inspired trilogy.

Awareness | Breaking Your Pattern of Negative Thoughts

The Second Part Is The Pattern of Focus and Belief and How They Relate to One Another

Whatever you focus on, or your dealing with, whether it's true or not is irrelevant. As we have discussed in detail earlier, and how past experiences can have a negative or positive effect on future behavior. Have you ever had an experience where somebody did something, or you thought somebody did something, or even better, you merely thought you heard about this something, and they did, something, to take advantage of you. As you focused on that you got angry, you said or hurt, the one you love, only to discover later, that you were dead wrong, or they never did something, it wasn't true. And you felt bad about your behavior, or you felt embarrassed, and you wondered how could you have felt all those things.

Whatever we focus on, we feel, whether it's true or not.

Focus equals feeling, just like the way you move, effects our feeling.

- See, right now if I said to you, what are you juiced about in your life, what excites you?

- If you truly wanted to be excited about your life, right now, what could you be excited about?

- What are you proud of?

- Could you name something that makes you proud, if you wanted to be proud?

- Who in your life do you truly love?

- Who loves you?

Think about these questions for a moment. Who do you truly love? Who loves you? By the way, right now as your thinking about these questions, how's it feels, when you focus on someone you love, when you attach the feelings to that person? Maybe as your focusing on your lover, you recall the warmth, and security of a hug, how they make you feel as if no one else in the world exist just by a tender kiss. See, whatever you focus on, you're going to feel. Focus equals reality for the individual, although it's not reality, in actuality. I'll say that again, focus equals reality for the individual, although it's not in actuality. It's a complicated way of saying, anything you focus on, you're going to feel, whether true or not, because your brain doesn't know the difference between something you vividly imagine and focus on, and something you actually experience.

Direct focus can be immensely powerful if you use this to your advantage. It's simplicity, for you, proves how fast you can change how you feel, is determined on how fast you can change your focus. So how fast can you change how your feeling? Simple, as fast as you change the way you move. See, right now if you focus on something that is terribly upsetting, or something to worry about, or something you're fearful about, you're going to feel those feelings. But, if you focus on something that you're grateful for, you're going to feel a totally different set of feelings. See you are in control, you can change your feelings in an instant. The problem is we don't believe we can change that fast, and the second problem is, we have patterns of doing this, don't we. Regularly, we tend to focus on what is overwhelming, or focus on what we're upset about in our spouse, or focus on why we failed earlier. If you keep focusing on things you didn't succeed at formerly, you're going to feel as though you failed, which is to make you feel like a failure, and you're not. Acting to make things better, can't be built on a past that didn't work. But, instead of focusing on what did not work, you can focus on what you want and you can focus on the solution whenever you have problems. Because everybody's got problems, but 95% of your time needs to be spent on a solution, 5% on the problem.

See most people spend all their time describing the problem, they go into more and more and more detail, and we wonder why people feel overwhelmed. Focus is the secret key to changing how you feel, and you can do it in an instant. One way to change your focus is to change the third thing in our inspired trilogy, our language patterns. See all day long were thinking. Which means all day long you're asking and answering questions with yourself.

EVERYDAY QUESTIONS YOU UNCONSCIOUSLY COMMUNICATE TO YOURSELF.

- "Should I do this?"

- "What does this mean?"

- "Why is this?"

- "Where's that?"

- "Why is this going on?"

So, what initiates thinking, is the question we want answered? We know what the problem is, we have questions that we ask that don't serve us. Some of us have questions like: "*Why is this always happen to me...*" Well it doesn't always happen to you, but, if you ask for a lousy question like that, regularly, your brain will tell you because you're an idiot. "*How come I can never lose weight?*" Well, you CAN lose weight. Asking a lousy question (*ask and you shall what? You, receive.*) How come I can never lose weight, because your brain answers back, because you are a pig. You need to come up with a better question! Questions direct our thinking and focus, questions are a form of language.

If you want to change your life, I hope you discover the questions, you ask on a constant basis, also take note of the phrases you tend to say a lot? Because phrases hypnotize us, we have certain words by themselves can change the way you feel. Someone says to you, "*hey listen, I've been thinking you're mistaking about that,*" you might have one interpretation, such as you're wrong; however; you feel something decidedly different just by the language. If someone says you are lying, you have a whole different feeling. One word can change the way you feel when someone else speaks it to you. The words you select, powerfully affect. I don't mean, just being positive and doing the Stuart Smalley thing, where you got positive self talk. "*Can you say, I'm good enough, I'm strong enough, and by golly people like me.*" No...! I mean noticing the habits of the words, and the emotions they create.

Third part of language is the phrases that we say, and we say them with such emotional intensity that we start to believe them.

We call those incantations.

Incantations are like if you remember studying mythology, the sorcerer would tell a prince over and over again, a phrase and over and over again with such intensity that he would be hypnotized, and he thinks he's a frog.

So of course, he was a frog, that's what he experienced. We experience whatever we focus on. We feel whatever we picture. We feel whatever we say to ourselves, we feel whatever we do with our bodies these are the three patterns. Changing these three patterns, or any of the three, you're going to change how you feel. If you change all three, you will radically the change how you feel. If you change the pattern of how you use your body, and you change the pattern of what you focus on daily you will become inspired, with a growing intensity to act.

I want to show you a technique that could change your life. Very simple, if you change the pattern of what you say to yourself, with the emotional intensity, of the way you say it, then you're going to change the pattern of how you feel. This means you could pick any feeling you want.

- When I'm not feeling good, what am I focusing on?

- What do I actually focus on? What does it mean to me?

BECAUSE YOU CAN FOCUS ON ANY ANYTHING, AND ONE PERSON LOOKS AT IT, AND SAYS:

"Because that happened, that's why I can never be close to another man or woman in my life, that's why I could never trust again."

SOMEONE ELSE HAS THE SAME EXPERIENCE, AND CAN SAY:

The Art of Fulfillment

"You know because that happened, I've learned so much about myself, and because that happened, I appreciate the person I'm with now, so much!"

You can have a foreground without a background. Right... That's the secret of life! Some people believe their life is over, because something happened because they gave, it that meaning.

SOMEBODY ELSE SAYS:

"Gods challenging me, it's time to go to the next level."

We have absolute choice, about how we feel, and whatever feelings we put in our lives regularly, determines the quality of our lives. So you can have frustration, anger, upset, overwhelmed, and insecurity. You know, if you want to be fearful, you can live in a state of guilt, worry, or whatever. Or you can live in a place called, passion, mojo, Joy, thankfulness, gratefulness, connection, love, wonder, and if you create those emotions, regularly, do you think you will have a different life? You bet you are!

Okay, so how do we take these three understandings, and make it to where we don't have to think about it? Instead, we actually regularly condition ourselves to have the perfect emotions we want. Getting rid of emotions we don't want. Well, first up is awareness. See, the next time you start to feel frustrated and angry, stop and notice:

• What you're doing with your cheeks?

• Notice what you do with your mouth?

• What's happening with your breathing?

- What is happening to your eyebrows?

- Are you tightening your fingers in your hands?

Because, we all have extremely specific things we do, which moves us into our version of anger or frustration. We are tired, we feel overwhelmed, does that make sense?

Just notice what's happening to your body. Here, is an example of the kind of conversation you might have with yourself.

"Okay I'm not breathing, okay that's a clue, so I need to make a little change there. Wow, my mouth is so tight, I can't even talk; I can't even get a jellybean through there! OK! That might be a clue why I'm a little uptight."

SECONDLY:

- What am, I focusing on? *"I'm focusing on how this isn't working!"*

NOW TO HELP YOU UNDERSTAND THE BELIEF PART, ASK YOURSELF THIS QUESTION:

To feel this way, what would I have to believe? To be frustrated and upset, what do I have to believe? I have to believe, things should better than they are, and they're not, and this is NOT working.

The Art of Fulfillment

Well, maybe it isn't working, but it's not going to help you to focus on what isn't working. Let's focus on what we can do. Or you say:

"I feel like it's hopeless, because to feel hopeless, I've got to believe there's nothing I can do."

* Is that actually true?

* Is there nothing you can do?

* Or are you just caught up in a dis-empowering state?

* Are you just caught up in a pattern?

See, if you would ask yourself instead: What would I have to believe, to feel this way? This question, will help, in breaking down that part of the trilogy, and will leave you to be saying, *"well that isn't really true."* All right... that will help you there.

THE THIRD PART OF AWARENESS IS BREAKING YOUR PATTERN OF NEGATIVE THOUGHTS AND QUESTIONS.

HAVE A CONVERSATION WITH YOURSELF, HERE IS AN EXAMPLE:

* "Okay, well, what am I saying to myself?"

* "Why did they do this?"

- "How come they always do these things?"

- "Why don't they ever listen?"

NOW; HOWEVER, YOU CATCH YOURSELF AND START A NEW CONVERSATION; FOR EXAMPLE:

"I'm asking many lousy questions, they may listen sometimes, though I say they don't."

I've seen these types of conversations after complete awareness, with total intensity! Then, the conversation turns into demands, you demand more from yourself, and you will not accept anything less.

AN INTENSE AWARENESS CONVERSATION SOUNDS MUCH DIFFERENT; HERE IS AN EXAMPLE:

- "Of course, I'm going to feel bad!"

- "Let me change what I'm asking!"

- "How can I turn this around?"

- "What do I need to focus on, to make this work?"

- "What's the truth here?"

- "Maybe I can't control it all, but I can control, what it means to me."

- "What does this actually mean?"

By being aware, you can break your pattern and get yourself out of a negative pattern of emotion, immediately.

YOU CAN SAY:

- "How do I want to feel?"

- "I want to feel as I did when I had my strong, attractive body, I loved working out."

They want the feeling of being strong, confident, attractive, and sexy back. They asked a well-defined question of them self.

So now what kinds of questions would direct our minds in the path of answers and success?

- What do we need to focus on right now?

- What would we have to believe?

BEING AWARE OF THE RESULT HE WANTS, NOW THE CONVERSATION WOULD SOUND LIKE THIS:

- "I'd have to believe, that you know what, I can turn anything around!"

- "I may not like it, but I can make it happen, it's just another challenge God's given me to sculpt my muscles, sculpt my soul, so throw it at me!"

* "God is the greatest trainer on earth!"

Because, a skilled trainer pushes you. Just when you think you've got nothing left, what do they do? They yell out, *"give me six more, you go six more."* Even if, you don't think you have another, but your trainer knows, they say, *"Yes you do!"* Sure enough, you've gotten at least three more in you, and you develop, real muscle. Now, you're stronger, physically and mentally, because what used to be hard, becomes easier, each time you go though it. That's what this is all about.

Now, here's what you can do that will make this part of your life. We are going after that piece of life that was missing. Do you remember what is missing? What is after all this verbiage that I've given you? Time. I gave you needed time with yourself. But, we will structure that time so that we create a daily inspired trilogy, putting us in a state of mind where the mojo flows.

Remember, perfect moments, where everything was perfect, and your mojo was flowing. It's like, "yes, I know what to do, oh yes, it's a challenge, big deal brings it here, let's handle it, no big deal, come on don't worry." Have you been in those states, where nothing shakes you? You can hope that you pop into one of the states, if you're lucky. Or you can create it every morning, or you can pop into one of those states so you can start with a foundation, which is so powerful, it affects not only yourself, but all those around you. You can make life beautiful. Life can be beautiful for you every day, if you do the things, he did, with your body every day. If you focus on life, the way he focused on it if you use language, as he used. He became the man in the movie. See, that's a role model. If you sow the same seeds as he sowed, you'll reap the same rewards. But you must schedule. Like I said:

"If you talk about it, it's a dream, if you envision, it's possible, but if you schedule it, it's real."

So here's what I'm asking for, it's an invitation, and a challenge. I want you to give yourself that missing time, and I want you to give yourself, ideally an hour to inspire it's your daily mojo, at least five days a week.

Now, what does that mean? It means, for one hour I will walk you through three things to do for one hour. These three things will undoubtedly connect you to yourself and will give you a new level of focus, Joy, and happiness. You will gain the strength to deal with not only the challenges, but also the joys of life more. If you don't do it, you will always be driven by the technologies of life, by demands, and by people, by our kids. What is beautiful is that you want to give to everybody else. But, if you keep giving, giving, giving of yourself, to everyone else and you never stop and fill back up, then there's nothing left to give. And, I know, you know, that's true.

So, here's what it looks like, and, by the way, if you can't do and hour, then give yourself at least 30 minutes, 30 minutes to influence. If it's not in your power, then give yourself at least 30 minutes, it's just 30 minutes of your life, if you can't allow yourself 30 minutes then, at least 15 to infuse your mind, body, and soul.

I will explain step-by-step how to do this, so there's never going to be a day, you should not do this. Because, there are always 15 minutes. But, I know you can lock in that hour, and go. But, real quick, before I tell you how it works, if you can do just the 15 minutes, it will grow to 30 minutes it will grow to the hour. Because, you get inspired reinforcing your life's passion. What does a breathing cadence look like, here it is. It's quite simple, it's only three parts, and here's how it goes.

The first step, is you want to make sure that the moment you wake up in the morning, there is no hesitancy to get up, so you start to train your body, which is just training your mind. Remember, body and mind are linked. Whatever you do with your body, it's going to affect your mind. You want to train your body to jump out of bed immediately, with energy, without hesitation, and start moving. Remember, emotion comes from motion. We've got to move. Now, ideally, you would exercise in the morning, there are lots of reasons to do that. Because, of all times, if you exercise in the morning, you turn on your metabolism and you have it for the whole day. But, if you don't exercise, you don't turn on your metabolism, and you just keep gaining fat. Your body loses its strength, and you lose muscle every single year. Especially as you age, but if you can train yourself to do that in the morning, first thing, even if you have to get up earlier, go to bed earlier, or just take one hour less sleep. Or 30 minutes less or even just 15 minutes less sleep. If you can do that in the morning you turn on your metabolism, but you also turn on your emotions.

The Art of Fulfillment

Breath Walking | Altering Your Brain Function

Movement and Breath Are the First Phase.

So what you're going to do, is put your shoes beside your bed, and if you've gotten somebody to do this with it's even easier and better. I mean if you've got your lover, and the first thing you do is gotten up in the morning and started walking with them, then that's great. But, if you get up and just physically move, go for a walk, anywhere. You get outside, you get out of the house; you move immediately.

Now, walking doesn't sound extraordinarily dynamic, and you may want to run, but you walk first, start warming up your body, warming up your metabolism. As you're walking, there is a pattern of breathing that when you breathe in a particular way, it stimulates your body to cleanse yourself.

So you start to move and walk, while your walking, you will breathe to the following cadence. You Inhale four deep breaths through your nose, and then you exhale four deep breathes through your mouth.

1. (Inhale - Inhale - Inhale - Inhale)

2. (Exhale - Exhale - Exhale - Exhale)

As you're doing this, you're actually going to be tapping fingers, your redoing the same pattern again and again.

This pattern of breathing will alter your state, and you will feel your mojo flow. After doing this breathing cadence for five minutes, you will begin to feel radically different.

BUT NOW, YOU'RE GOING TO INHALE THROUGH YOUR NOSE AND EXHALE OUT YOUR MOUTH, REMEMBER THE CADENCE:

1. (Inhale - Inhale - Inhale - Inhale) *through your nose

2. (Exhale - Exhale - Exhale - Exhale) *out your mouth

M.I.T. Research Study | Breathing Alters Brain Function

There have been studies done on this at MIT, and it literally alters brain function. But, you don't have to believe the studies, to feel what it does to your system. So, all you're going to do for the first five minutes, is enjoy yourself. Get up, and start to walk. You walk for about five minutes with this breathing cadence.

The Art of Fulfillment

Step two. You get grateful, and you begin to visualize. So in step two, you're now going to cultivate the emotion of gratitude. Remember, I said fear disappears when you're grateful, the minute you're grateful you're rich, when you have everything in your life to be grateful for. When you don't have that emotion, you have nothing, you're poor. So, this has to be a daily emotion, because this is the antidote to all your problems, stress and all the frustration. But, you got to cultivate it, because if you go into a state of depression, regularly, pretty soon your body goes there automatically. Your body is conditioned, it's trained. You're going to drop anchor. Anchoring, is when you use your entire body's physiology to perfectly replicate the state of the person or thing you want to achieve. You'll start breathing and visualizing, and focusing on what you want exactly, then when you start feeling all the things in life you're grateful for; you will anchor your state into a state of gratefulness.

So, you're outdoors, you're moving, so your pattern and your physiology will make you feel good. You got movement; you got emotion. Now, as you're moving, you're thinking about everything you're grateful for. I think about all the things that I'm grateful for, and I have in my life. My health, family, the people I get to work with. When I think about my family members, I start to send love to them and a spiral of thought going out. I think about my close friends and my close business associates and all the people that I get to serve through my work in the world. And I just expand it. You think of moments are grateful for.

I remember a moment I shared with a friend of mine. Sitting on the floor of his new bedroom. He was unpacking his belongings, all which, were neatly placed within a single suitcase. Smiling, singing, and bopping up and down, like a kid in a candy store, barely just 18, he had been on his own for 2 years. Never having his own room, or an actual bed to sleep on. But, with a smile that spanned from ear to ear, I watched as he gently placed his clothes on hangers, while organizing his first closet. This was one of life's special and random moments. Captured as a teaching opportunity on the importance of humility and the value we overlook in the smallest of gifts, in our life. Before he could notice, I quickly left his room, because it was a perfect expression of the word, joy and it just made me cry; it was a beautiful moment. And the gratitude I feel for life's significant moments, make me realize how truly blessed I am.

So what are we doing, we're moving, were outdoors and were breathing and that's changing our physiology. We are being grateful, and that's focus, which changes our state. Okay, so now what you focus on is everything that you truly want in your life. But, you already focus on it from the state that it's been

The Art of Fulfillment

achieved. I honestly start giving thanks for it, as if it's already done. "*I'm so grateful about that business deal; it came together exactly as planned.*" So I start to see it as if it were already done, all the pieces came together. Remember, your brain cannot tell the difference between something you vividly imagine or something you actually experienced. So, I see it, I feel it, I think about it, I focus on the emotion as though it's already achieved. The more you can program your body and your mind and your emotions as though it's already achieved, your brain can do things that your body is totally unaware of. And if you focus on what you want continuously you will automatically start to move to it. Whatever you focus on you move towards.

The problem is most people focus on what they're afraid of. For example, if someone is out of control while driving in their car, immediately they will look at the wall, that they don't want to hit, but as they look at it, they start to steer straight to the wall. The same thing happens in life, where you focus that's where you go. So don't focus on what you fear, focus on what you want and make it real. The more certain you are about what you want, you can have or achieve it, much easier. It is for your brain to figure out a way. When you say, this is important, your brain starts noticing anything that will get you to what's important. If you believe it's already happened, you know enough about life that with that kind of certainty your brain will find a way.

NOW, YOU START FOCUSING ON TODAY:

- What you want to create today.

- You think about meetings you will have.

- You think about what is the result you want.

MOST PEOPLE THINK ABOUT WHAT IT IS I HAVE TO DO, INSTEAD THINK ABOUT WHAT YOU WANT TO DO:

- Who do you want to turn on, excite, make happy, and laugh?

- What do you want to achieve?

- What do you want to accomplish?

Because, remember everything that happens in the outside world, started from the inside. I mean everything in your life up to now, your family, your career, your hobbies, they first started from within, from thinking about, and then they became your reality. Most people think about what they don't want and focus so much on it, they actually manifest it, and create it. So the point is to focus, on today. What it is, today, you want to achieve, the result, what feelings and what is the perfect day?

So, now what you need to do is exercise, ideally 20 minutes no less than 15, and 30 is even better. And if you can do 45 minutes, that's awesome and that's how you get to the hour. So, at the end of our daily mojo, you will feel so magnanimous, you will be vibrating your mojo will flow.

NOW, YOU MIGHT SAY:

"Tollie, I'm not going running five times a week."

You don't have to. Just go on a walk, and you can do this process, this hour to inspire and truly focus. You can spend 10 minutes in gratitude, ten minutes on visualizing, and 10 minutes on what you want to happen throughout your day, and be done in 30 minutes. Lately, we hear a lot about freedom, trust me this is YOUR freedom.

The Art of Fulfillment

I can tell you that if you can give yourself an hour, where 15-20 of those minutes are based on these three things you will see enormous changes in your physiology making you feel unstoppable. Monumental changes in your focus making you feel grateful, so you can visualize what you want, but more important feel as if you already have it. Create monumental changes, where you push your body to be stronger. You will make some incantations, and you will say powerful phrases over and over, at least 5 to 10 minutes a day. You will have conditioned your mind, your body, your emotions, and your spirit will soar. And now, you will deal with problems in a radically different way and all your problems, they won't be problems, they will be challenging. More important, you will be excited to connect with people, you will be excited about your projects; you will affect people around you in a different way, because you will have an extraordinary psychology. Don't you want an extraordinary body? It takes a ritual, doesn't it. A ritual of diet, and a ritual of exercise. You want extraordinary emotions and spirit; it takes rituals.

Something you might want to add to your daily mojo is prayer. If you believe in the power of prayer, this is it, this is a form of it. Maybe the greatest prayer is not asking for things, but maybe it's saying, Thank you, Saying Thank You Lord emphatically! Getting in a place of gratitude, daily, for more than 15 minutes to fulfillment and ideally the hour to inspire, will change your life more than anything else.

If you don't read any other book, and all you did was this, I promise you that if you do this for six months, your life will never be the same. Because all the research shows that if you even exercise for six months you will exercise for the rest of your life, because it becomes physically addictive to you. If you get away from exercise, you will be attracted, to do it. All you need to do right now is give it a week, or 10 days. Do this with me for 10 days, and I promise you; will get some momentum. If you want guaranteed success, do it for 30 days.

I know this book is longer than most, but it is caused by I honestly wanted to engage you, I don't know whether I'll ever see you again, but my goal, was to do everything I can, to get you, to give yourself what you deserve. And to tie in the three things that you've got to take control of and remind you of the fundamentals, that your life is nothing but your emotions. If you get the right emotions, you will go work out. If, you're determined, you will workout.

The Art of Fulfillment

Building Momentum | Today and Every Day

This Book, Is For You To Create What You Want, For the Long Term

If you will do this, even if you do only four days a week, you will create a habit, that you will commit not to break, and your pride will soar. Because, you just need to discipline yourself. A tiny bit, by the way, this doesn't feel like discipline, it feels like joy, when you do it. But, if you just discipline yourself a little bit, you get a positive habit, you consciously created; it spills over into all areas of your life. And, if you stay with me on this journey, over the next few chapters, were going to address those areas, with the best tools that I know of. So, thank you for reading this far, and here is what I want you to do tomorrow.

I want you to begin your day by doing this hour of daily mojo, or this 30 minutes to influence or these 15 minutes to infuse your mind, body, and spirit, just do it. By the way, this sounds complex, and I've overloaded you with a long chapter, but don't worry, I will walk you thru it fresh as we do it. Make sure you get started. The hardest part to do, is go to the gym, so just do it! As they say in the Nike ads that are a great reminder of how those athletes achieved so much success. You will get what you truly want. So my friends, I plea with you, give yourself this gift, each day. I mean, this is, really one of the most momentous decisions of your life. I hope my bunt, and outrageous approach pushed you in the right direction, and didn't push you away.

I Hope somehow, I found my way into your heart or into your intellect or whatever part of you, we must reach, to push the button that launches your life to the next level, the level it deserves to be.

So this is the beginning of a brand-new journey, and I'm tremendously grateful that you have allowed me to be your partner, in this first part of the process. I think we can make immense progress so let's start taking real action, lets not just talk a good game between us. Let's do it. Just get your butt out there, because once you get out there, you'll get out there again and again. You will get that momentum that takes over, and the best of you will start showing up every day. When the best of you, shows up every day you will start to appreciate it and so will everybody else. So today, look around you, keep your eyes open for magic moments.

Special moments are all around, be sure that today, you live with passion. Today and every day. Now, Lets kick this pig, it's to dream BIG!

The Art of Fulfillment

A LITTLE NONSENSE NOW AND THEN IS RELISHED BY THE WISEST MEN.

- Willy Wonka

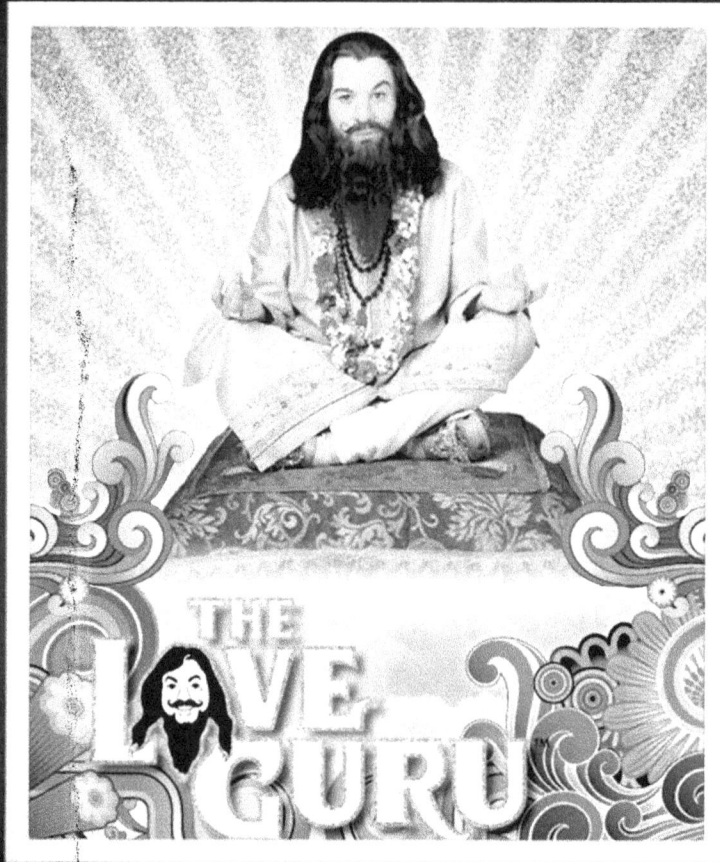

Chapter V

The Love Mojo

"GIVE ME A POUND... LOCK IT DOWN... BREAK THE PICKLE... TICKLE TICKLE!..." -GURU PITKA (MIKE MYERS)

Welcome to the Love Mojo, where we shall talk intimacy, it's like my mentor the Love Guru once told me:

"INTIMACY IS LIKE PUTTING YOUR WIENER ON A TABLE AND HAVING SOMEONE SAY, THAT LOOKS LIKE A# @&! $...ONLY SMALLER."

Well... Ok, not exactly, but this chapter is nothing you have heard before. I can guarantee that by the end of this chapter, you will have a new lust for life. But first, I wanted to say congratulations for continuing to become inspired; I'm really impressed. Today, I want to talk to you about what I think may be one of the most important, if not the most important areas of your life. This area of your life, can give you the greatest amount of joy and ecstasy, when it's handled correctly. And probably, most of the peaks of your life have some aspect of this in your life. And then, if it's handled ineffectively, This is the place of pain. This is the place where people really feel themselves devastated. This is the place where life seems to lose its meaning. So the area we will talk about, is that vehicle of life, that thing we focus on called relationships. If you handle it well, My Gosh... I mean, when your in love, when you feel that connection, when you feel that bond, when you feel that oneness with somebody, you know what that's like. I mean, what can actually compete with it. Now making money might be nice, and achieving something is peachy, but if you do it alone, it's worthless.

If you don't have someone to share that joy with, what's it like? Nonetheless, being upset, upset with yourself, is one thing. But, when you get someone else, to be upset at, you can positively do a number can't you. You can really get yourself upset, you can certainly get yourself wired, you can make yourself feel massively inferior or massively superior, angry, upset, frustrated, hurt, and devastation, right? You can do, nearly anything, to yourself, that you want, with this vehicle called relationships. I call it a vehicle, because, we forget that relationships are a way of relating, it's a process, it is not a fixed thing in time. Relationships are always changing themselves; it's always moving. One of the challenges we have as human beings are that we all want to get things done. You know, we need the whole thing done, we want to get all that financial stuff handled, so we never have to work again. If you never work again, you would be totally unfulfilled.

Everyone I know who never has to work again, usually works harder. They are just doing what they love now. They're focus, is on doing things because they want to, not because they have to. But, most of us think, we need to achieve this level where we can just stop, but when we stop we just die. There are two laws of life, and they are so fundamental, and they are true of everything; they are surely true of relationships. Everything of life must grow, cause if it doesn't grow, then it dies. That's true of a relationship, that's true of your body, and that's true of your mind. That's true of a plant, and that's true of anything in the universe, you grow, or you die. When you're green, you grow, and when your ripe you rot. When you start thinking its over, it is over! See, you can't look for a fixed time, when all of a sudden, your finances, your body, and your relationships are done. It's never done, your body is in constant challenge, to continually improving and strengthening and developing powerful and passionate, so you can live life at the highest level. So you can become inspiring, and that's what we are talking about. Being inspired is how you feel that indescribable quality of life, and the same thing is true of a relationship.

Most of us are juggling so many things in our lives that when it comes to a relationship, we just want it to take care of it's self. But, if they were just handled, then you wouldn't have to grow, you wouldn't have to expand; you wouldn't have what you deserve in your life. You wouldn't have that little bit of resistance when you need it, and you wouldn't have that comfort when you needed the reinforcement. And most importantly you wouldn't have love. You wouldn't have the deepest love of all, the level that you're able to share, whether it is with your creator, or with your children, or with your lover, or your best friend. And that's what relationships are all about.

The Key to Avoiding A Conflict

The Second Law of the Universe Is You Must Contribute

Because, if you don't find a way to contribute in meaningful ways, you're eliminated that is the law of life, that's the law of the universe. Anything that doesn't contribute is eventually eliminated by evolution, if not by something else. So, In our lives, for you and me to feel fulfilled we have gotten to grow and we have got to contribute. You know we have gotten to grow, and we need to contribute in a way that we believe has some sort of meaning. If we don't do this, then it doesn't matter if anyone loves us or not. We won't be happy with ourselves. So a relationship is a place we go to sculpt our souls, to sculpt our spirits, to sculpt our emotions, and to enjoy life to the fullest. And when relationships are handled properly it's the most incredible feeling of joy and pleasure, filled with variety, and excitement. When relationships are handled poorly, Oh boy... it is pain, absolute misery. I know you have loved and lost, you have experienced the pain of a relationship and the ecstasy, I know I sure have. So how do we develop those deep and loving relationships that we all thirst for as human beings?

THE SECRET TO DEEP AND LOVING RELATIONSHIPS IS DONE BY LOOKING INTO THREE SPECIFIC THINGS THAT NEED REEVALUATION.

First lets talk about how you create an unprecedented relationship, an unprecedented relationship, not a pleasant one, not an agreeable one, but one that's outstanding. Now, I don't care if your starting from scratch, or if you have one that you're already in and you want to create it, recreate it, or rejuvenate it into an unprecedented relationship. The principles are pretty much the same.

The second part, we want to talk about, is how do you handle the exceptional challenges that show up in any relationship. There are always going to be there, because, when you have people who have different values, different ways of looking at life, different rules, you will have conflict. It is a matter of time, no matter how much you love someone one, it will show up at times. Some conflicts are small; some conflicts are enormous. Conflicts have more to do with the personalities or the rules, or the values, than the people involved.

Then thirdly, how do you nurture and expand this relationship geometrically? How do you make sure there is a constant growth factor present, which is necessary. You're not just creating a relationship, but you keep expanding it, so that the fulfillment is a spiral that moves up, as opposed to deterioration showing up.

Entropy shows up in most things, doesn't it? Most things just naturally break down, if you're not moving forward, your moving backwards, its gravity, it's just the way life works.

So, now if were going to do this, you might start by saying where are you now. Because, we have talked each day, about this constant of having the ability to close the gap. I mean, how do you create an unprecedented life? You close the gap, between where you are now, and where you want to go. The secret to closing the gap, is first being honest with yourself, that there is one.

Almost any area of your life there is a gap, if you are a healthy person, it is that a healthy person is always looking to become even healthier. They may love where they are, but they are always looking for more. More love, more connection, more intimacy, more spirit, and more playtime. Some of us, will listen more, feel more, and give more. We all want more, if we are healthy, growing, and expanding, then the urge for more is in our nature; it's a foundation to achieving a quality life.

The Gap In Your Relationship

This Will Be the First Question We Will Focus In On

Maybe, we should start by saying where are you now? We can all agree that actually there's only two positions that people are in right now. So, right now, you're either in a relationship, or you're not. Time to get dirty, let's talk about an intimate relationship for instance.

If you're not in a relationship, then we genuinely only have two perspectives. The first reason is, you want a relationship but, you don't have one. So, then the question becomes, if that is true, why? Honestly, I can tell you. The answer is, if you truly desire a relationship and you don't have one; it's just because you have mixed emotions about what a relationship will mean. You want a relationship because you don't have any love and connection or intimacy, which comes from a relationship.

HOWEVER, YOU DON'T WANT A RELATIONSHIP, BECAUSE OF ALL THE EXCUSES YOU CONTINUALLY TELL YOURSELF, SUCH AS:

- "Oh my goodness, I don't have the time, or energy."

- "I've had Fights and frustrations."

- "I don't want to feel like a failure."

- "I don't want things not work out."

- "I don't want someone to disappoint me again."

So, the truth is, if your, not in a relationship, unquestionably there is only one reason, it is not a (*must*) for you to be in a relationship.

Like I said before, there's got to be a must (*to not be hurt*). If you're going to be in a relationship, let me tell you the good news upfront. You will get hurt! But, nonetheless, you are probably going to hurt other people as well, without even meaning to. That's just part of, the nature of life. You can't have joy, without having some pains, sometimes. Everything in life, has a reciprocal, you can't just have one dimension of life. This would be like saying, I want the rainbow, but not the storm. I mean it's part of life, and it is, what you learn to do. You see, those who have an unprecedented life, are people who learn to enjoy the storm, as much as the rainbow. They have learned to find value in the storm, the beauty in the storm.

Think about it this way, when all that rain comes down, and people are complaining about the rain, well the plants are gobbling it all up and loving it. Sometimes, you need to adapt, you need to be a plant, you need to be a seagull; you have gotten to change perspectives.

SO, IF YOUR, NOT IN A RELATIONSHIP ITS EITHER:

- (A) - you want a relationship, which we just described

OR

- (B) - you don't want a relationship.

Is There a Purpose To Love?

You're Clear About Not Wanting a Relationship

In which case, it's obvious what the problem is. You have associated so much pain to relationships that even your natural desire for a connection is being shunted. The sad part about this, is ultimately these negative associations create even more pain, than if you were in a relationship. Because, all human beings have a deep emotional, spiritual, and psychological need to connect at the deepest level. We need this intimacy. It's not something we want, its something we must have. So, we need to deal with and tackle, those negative associations. Ok, well not we, but, you. You, will have to deal with it actually, I would just like to help. You know you will have to deal with this sooner or later. And more than likely, you wouldn't continue reading this now, unless, you are truly ready now to create the relationship of your dreams.

Now, the second position you could be in, is you are already in a relationship. If you are already in a relationship, then there are three perspectives we need to look at:

(A) - you want more from your relationship, which, by the way, would be natural. I mean it's human nature, no matter how strong the relationship is, we always seek more.

SO, THE NEXT PERSPECTIVE IS:

(B) - you want out of your relationship. Wanting out of your relationship is the other extreme, but, you're not quite sure how to navigate it, or you just cant end it. If you can't end it, then why? Why are you not out of it?

If you want more, that's natural, if you want out of it, well it's because your associating a lot of pain to it. If you're not out of it, it's because your associating pain to leaving. See, relationships are all about emotional association. It is not about the real, thing. We don't actually respond to life anymore, we respond to what we associate to life. Somebody, at one point or another, said something and we decided what that means; for example:

- "That means... they don't care."

- "That means... they don't love me."

Right... See how we go off on a tangent. This is caused by most of us are not responding to what's happening in the moment, but we are responding to our past.

When someone does something that resembles pain from our past, boy-o-boy we run quickly! Not only do we run, but we often tend to shoot off all the old feelings at our partner. We pretend, this is what's happening now. One of the secrets to a great relationship is learning (*This is not That*). But, the person you're with right now, in this moment, deserves to have a clean slate, and you deserve, to have a clean slate with them. But, what really messes up a relationship, is walking around with all these wounds. It's like if I walked up to you and patted you on the back right now, more than likely it wouldn't hurt at all. But, if the day before you lay out at the beach all day with no sunscreen. And now, you have a wicked sunburn, and I come by and barely touch your back, you will jump out of your skin. You will say, "*You know what? This relationship is horrible!*" You see, it is not the relationship that is horrible, it is the conditions, your bringing to the relationship.

The conditions, you are bringing into the relationship, are your past. So, if you are in a relationship which you want out of, or you have been pushing your partner away, here are couple things to look at first. Are you making this person into someone else? Are you responding to them as if they are your mother, or your father, or a brother, or that horrible person you would do anything to get out of a relationship with, but you stayed there too long? Or are you reacting, out of fear, and magnifying the situation? Or are you adding meaning to the situation, which is as we discussed, not quite accurate? If you command, the meanings of your life, and you don't make things into more than they are, then relationships become more inspiring. Frequently, what is happening in the relationship, is we are making things bigger than they undoubtedly are. We are making a mountain out of a mole hill. Almost all stress comes from making things more serious than they actually are.

Ok, so you want to revamp your life. You need to ask yourself some new questions whenever you're about to get upset. With any person, in any relationship, the questions you need to ask are these. "*What else could this mean?*" The question, what else could this mean, will change your life if you ask it. Because, what happens is when you're upset, you're upset not because of what someone did, not because of what someone said, but because of the '*meaning*' you attached to it. "*They said 'this,*' therefore, it meant '*that*'." So you must ask yourself, what else could this mean? You have got to make yourself come up with, as many positive meanings, as you came up with negative.

The Love Mojo

Let's say, for example, someone promised to do something and then they don't show up. Then, you go maniacal...

- "I can't believe this!"

- "They don't care!"

- "Look at this, they left me stranded!"

- "Once again..."

- "You know, every time I start to count on them they're not here!"

SO, NOW YOU HAVE COME UP WITH THREE OR FOUR MEANINGS. YOU HAVE ATTACHED MEANINGS SUCH AS:

- "They don't care."

- "You've been stranded."

- "Because they are irresponsible."

When you start stacking negative meanings, you're going to go, into a state that makes being in a relationship with you, well, an adventure, and not the fun kind. A relationship with you will be quite difficult. In this state, how do you think, you will treat this person you're in a relationship with? You will probably treat them in a way that will make them not want to be in a relationship with you, if not leaving the relationship permanently. In the moment, they won't want to relate to you, you lost the juice, does this make sense?

So, instead what you have got to be able to do, is come at that relationship with new and open set of possibilities. Whenever people screw up, they will beat themselves up, a lot more than you ever could anyway. So, why beat them up? Why push them away? You are supposed to be their lover, their friend, their manager, their associate, their partner, their mentor, their father, their mother, their son, their daughter, whatever relationship you have. Why not cultivate them? This doesn't mean you have to accept unacceptable behavior, but the way you do this, is you don't assume, ever, that the person deliberately has done something to harm you. When people do things, it's rarely, if ever, about you. Usually you're not that significant, they're trying to meet their own needs, they're trying to deal with their own fears, their own frustrations, you just happened to get in the way. And that's true for you and I, as well as anybody.

So you have gotten to remember it's not about you most the time. Usually, when someone is upset, you are reacting to something in their past, or it's that they are feeling frustrated internally, and they act out. If they are frustrated with you, it's only because they have the illusion that you are preventing them from experiencing something they need, some certainty, or some significance, or some love, or something they think they need. So get real and know its not about you. Ask yourself, what else could this mean? Well, maybe they are not here, and you've got to come up with empowering meanings, instead of negatives. *"Well maybe it means their really a jerk!"*

WELL, NO THAT'S, NOT THE WAY TO DO IT, YOU COULD SAY:

- "Well, what else could this mean?"

- "Well maybe they have been in a car accident."

- "Well maybe there's something else that is happening."

- "Maybe their actually doing something for me."

- "Maybe I didn't make it clear, that I needed to have them here at this particular minute."

- "Maybe I overloaded them with too many requests."

If you come up with enough other meanings that are empowering, you will finally get yourself into balance. When you communicate, two things will happen. Number one, you will be elegant when you communicate, and you won't assume the worst, which is what truly hurts people. When you assume the worst, even if you're right, you injure people in relationships and when you injure someone in a relationship you injure yourself. Because, you injure the relationship and that's something you share together. So many people in intimate relationships, will take the opportunity of the first argument, to blow up and attack. Now, the problem is, your attacking your teammate, your attacking your shipmate. We are all on this lifeboat, called earth together, and half the people try to blow up half their own boat, and it doesn't work. A relationship is about unity, it's about, how do we help each other, to move each other, to the next level, not how do we punish each other.

The biggest challenge you'll find in relationships is people would rather be right than be in love. Ask yourself, what this could mean? At some point, you may need to ask yourself:

- "Do I want to be right, or do I want to be in love?"

- "Do I want to learn?"

- "Do I care about this person?"

- "Let me focus on different questions."

So, I have gone off the main road a little, but ill tell you why. Because, if you want committed relationships, then you have got to become a jedi master of meaning, and you have got to find empowering meanings. Even if you're wrong and you assume the best from people they will appreciate that, and pretty soon that expectation becomes something they want to meet. Rarely, do people respond from negative reinforcement. But, consistently people respond to pleasurable reinforcement.

The third perspective is, you may be in a relationship, and you may just be immobilized. Maybe you have just given up, or maybe you're in a depression. You don't want out, you don't want more, you just kind of accept the fact, that this relationship is, well it just is... That is probably the worst place to be, because you know what, pain and pleasure will at least move you. Now, if you are in a rut, then you're in trouble. I hope someone zaps you with a cattle prod in your rut, because it will get you moving, it will get your attention because if you want a life you must have some movement.

SO, IF WE WERE TALKING ABOUT AN INTIMATE RELATIONSHIP, THEN THE FIRST THING I WANT YOU THINKING ABOUT IS:

- What am I doing in that relationship?

- Are you in a relationship or not?

- What's your perspective?

For example, if you wanted your spouse to call you every night at 6 pm, when they are on the road, and one night they don't call. When they finally do call, you tear into them, what have you taught them? You taught them, that calling you equaled pain. "*No, I taught them that not calling me, equals pain.*" Wrong answer, see they wanted to call you, they called you on their own and now is the time to give them positive reinforcement.

Negative reinforcement is not your goal. So, how I got off on this scenic road trip is, if you're in a relationship and you want out of it first apply these principles. Don't respond from the past, don't assume the worst, find empowering meaning and then, if you still see that this is not meeting your needs (*and I will describe how to decipher that in a bit*) obviously then you need to take action.

ALL RIGHT, SO YOU NEED TO ANSWER THE QUESTION:

- Do you want a relationship?

- Do you not want a relationship?

- Do you want more from the person you're in a relationship with?

- Do you want out of your relationship?

- Are you immobilized?

Because, you need to know where to start. The next question, I have for you is, where do you honestly, really, want your relationship to be? What would your ideal relationship look like? I will guide you thru a process, in this chapter to have you actually describe your ideal relationship in detail. But, I want you to begin, to think about, even fantasize for a moment.

I mean if you could have it, anyway you wanted, what would your intimate relationship be like?

- What would the two of you talk about?

- What would you laugh about?

- What would you share?

- What would you learn together?

- What would do to grow?

- What would you contribute to each other?

- How would you make love?

- What would be the magic times that you would share?

- How would you surprise each other?

You know most of us are so busy with all the demands of our lives that we don't take time for the things that are most important. Most peoples lives are not working for them, because they are more focused on the to do's part of their list, instead of the relationships that truly matter. See at the end of the day I have a straightforward question I ask. "*If you die today, what would it matter?*" It is a question that is unique to incite a unique thought process. If you consider your death, which to be honest, you can be hit by a bus tomorrow.

SO, SINCE WE LIKE TO BELIEVE WE WILL LIVE FOREVER; REALITY TELLS US THIS IS NOT THE CASE.

- If you died today, do the ones you love, truly understand how much you loved, and cherished them in your life?

- Have there been words left untold to those you love?

- Have you allowed pride or stubbornness to undermine you in a past relationship, you held so preciously?

- If you die today, would you Find yourself thinking about the merger, or your next business deal?

You would probably be wishing you had one last chance to hold your loved one tight. You would want to say with all your heart, I LOVE YOU, YOU ARE MY DREAM COME TRUE! Now, the day is a victory, because you shared a strong connection with someone you love. Life is love. And the quality of your life is directly related to the kinds of relationships that you create, and you expand, and nurture through. But it's easy to get off track and get caught up in the doing isn't it

SO LETS TAKE A MOMENT NOW AND LETS ANSWER AN EXTREMELY VITAL QUESTION.

- What's the purpose of a relationship?

- Is there a universal purpose, to any relationship?

- Is there a universal reason?

So often in life, we want things, but we forget what we want them for. I mean, have you ever said, "*I want a relationship*." Then, you get one, and you thought to yourself now, "*I don't want a relationship!*" Because, you thought what you wanted was a relationship, but what you honestly wanted, was something else. Maybe, you were seeking intimacy, maybe you sought to love, maybe it was sensuality, or maybe a connection of spirits.

Maybe it was someone who would tease you, maybe it was someone who would provide variety, or maybe it was to provide that challenge in life. But, what happens for most of us, is we just don't know, what we are after. So we get disappointed, we don't achieve, we don't even know what we want.

You need first to be clear, what's the real purpose of a relationship, of all relationships? Some people would say, "*well, to communicate," some people would say, "well, to learn, to share, to know.*" You know, to understand, you know, to experience things. All those answers are accurate. But, the real purpose of a relationship, the purpose that feeds outward to all these things we just described, is one simple thing.

THE PURPOSE OF A RELATIONSHIP IS TO MAGNIFY THE HUMAN EXPERIENCE.

What Do I Mean by Magnify the Human Experience?

Well, lets think about the feelings involved. How does it feel, when you experience something on your own? If you can have a phenomenal experience on your own, then why would you want to share that feeling? Because, in the act of sharing, we not only get to experience the event again, but there is a magnification in the overall experience, isn't there? When the other person gets excited, we get more excited. When they feel sad, we get even more sad. When that emotion is shared, there's synergy, there's a power, where one plus one doesn't just equal two. There's a third power, there's something visceral, there's something infernal, which occurs when this connection happens between two people, and they share their emotions. They share their feelings, not just their ideas. See, it magnify' our experience of life, that's why we search for it.

How would you like going to the ballpark for a game, and have only four people there with you in the stands, or would you prefer a hundred thousand people around you? Sure, you might say, "*Four, I'll get better seats!*" But, what I'm talking about is the feeling that comes from all the people in the stands. When the ball is hit out of the park, and only three people react, "*Yayyyy, way to go, nice one...*" Not quite the same experience as when you're in the middle of the super bowl, or in the middle of the final game of the world series, and everybody jumps to their feet screaming and shaking. Every part of your body is vibrating when your team scores, and you are going, freak'n nuts! In fact, the entire city goes nuts! So, why don't we all just go off and say, "*hey see you all later,*" and off we go to celebrate alone? *"YEAHHHH, Yeah You... I love the sound of my own voice..."* all by ourselves later on?

Celebrating alone there's not enough power in that. The power of the experience is through the sharing. Sharing is power in a relationship. The quality of your relationship is in direct correlation to yourself that you can share with someone else, that's how you relate, it's thru sharing. The amount of emotions and feelings, you can experience with that other person is powerful for your spirit. Start by listening, and hearing them, you've got to feel them, you've got to experience them, it can't just be a lame data dump into them. Taking and not giving, might feel good for a while, but it won't last. A community comes from a relationship, just look at the internet, if the web were just a place, you could go and get information that would be nice, but it becomes a community when it's a place you go to give. Look at the most talked about sites, Facebook, YouTube, dating communities, these are where people are located in masses, on a regular daily basis. When both the give and take are occurring simultaneously, and when you can pitch and catch, you've got something powerful. Because now there's a growth in the relationship, there's an expansion, a magnification, and now there's life.

The Love Mojo

Sharing is what relationships are all about. So if, you're in a relationship and you're unable to share, then you're not really in a relationship. If you're unable to care about someone else's sharing, then you are not in a relationship, or you are in a low level relationship. Obviously, there is a difference of levels and quality but not an extraordinary one, not the kind of relationship, that a person who invests in reading a book titled inspired wants to be in. Now when we talk about becoming inspired, we are not talking about getting inspired to have an advantage over someone in a relationship. If you have something, over somebody, then you're no longer in a sharing mode, you're in a controlling mode, and that isn't a related state. That is not a relationship. When your relating together, your moving in a direction, like that ship, were in a related moving the ship forward, right.

Were experiencing that joy, were experiencing that happiness, and were experiencing that pain, and were experiencing that learning, were experiencing all the human elements. All those elements of the human experience.

So, we have got to share in a relationship. It's as you always hear about how the internet will isolate the world, keep us separate. Most people who use the internet are using it to connect. Or people say, *"Well, people will never go to out to the movies or concerts."* It's totally absurd, because even if we connect online, we want the visceral experience of being together. There's a certain amount of relatedness that comes from physical proximity with people. If you want the most out of your life, an extraordinary life, then you get inspired thru extraordinary emotions, extraordinary psychology, and you do this through your capacity to share. With quality people and deep level of relatedness on an ongoing basis that expands your ability, to enjoy your life. Some of that relatedness will cause you to find a way to grow, as you've never grown before, because someone can find a way to move your spirit and challenge you and you can do the same for them. Some of it will cause you pain, which makes you look at your life, which will make you grow. Some of it, will give you the sense of contribution you've always been looking for, some of it will stimulate you and give you variety; some will add certainty to your life. All the human needs can be met in this way. Now, you can meet these needs by yourself but never at the same level of intensity. You have the potential to, but you won't.

If relationships are so vital, then why don't we always magnify our emotions? Well, we do, but the question is which emotions do we magnify. If you have dominate and negative emotions, one mistake you can make

The Love Mojo

is getting in a relationship with a partner who's primary psychology and emotions cause them to experience regularly, fear, rage, worry, frustration, jealousy, and envy. Let me tell you what's going to happen if you are in a relationship like this. Two people with negative emotions will magnify their negative emotions. Now, if your predominant emotions are positive, if your emotions are love and excitement, passion, compassion, and honor, if you experience peace, centeredness, and you're with somebody else, you will augment each other; you'll magnify those good feelings. Most people are not so extreme in the emotions they experience. Most people are not just one, or the other in their emotions. So, for most people their relationship is the place of their greatest pleasures and their deepest pains.

Give More | Give Often

The Real Secret To An Extraordinary Relationship Is To Give.

You've got to understand a relationship is a place you go to give, not a place you go to get. See, as long as you go into a relationship wondering what you can get out of it, then what you actually have is a transaction not a relationship. You are trying to figure out what you gave in the relationship, what percentage was given, "I gave 50% so they need to give 50%." When you start measuring how much you give in a relationship, the relationship is over, and now you have a transaction. Because a relationship is about unlimited sharing, a relationship is about unlimited giving, and when you share at that level, you magnify all that's good. But, when it becomes about who's done what, when a relationship is driven by rules, and not by love, a relationship begins to die. Everybody needs certain rules to feel comfortable to meet their values. But, the more rules you have, the more pain you have in a relationship.

Most upsets are because people have so many ways to be upset. There is a trend in our society, so many people look to be offended, by anything or anyone. There's a cultural shift to where the status symbol is best displayed through a victim, some seek out the opportunity to be offended, so they can become a status victim. But, what are they truly trying to accomplish? They are trying to gain acceptance from others through compassion, and love, they just want to be noticed. In a relationship; however, there are so many things that can make everything go off the track. We know, the purpose of a relationship is to magnify, so we need to decide, only to magnify the good. But, we will still screw up don't we? Maybe, if we make a conscious decision, that our relationships are truly about magnifying the good in the one we love, now the relationship is a place we go to give. Approaching our relationships this way means that we will also receive ten fold; it's a law of life.

So the question is, why don't we only magnify the good in our partner.

And the answer is that we get hooked, we are triggered by things that happened in our past, as we have already described. Triggering our past emotions has to do with us and the nature of human beings. As I mentioned earlier in the book, everybody has the same needs, despite where in this world you may come from. I've had the privilege to work with people from different countries, cultures, backgrounds, religions, and I have pretty much seen it all, not to mention my own relationships where I've made mistakes, and have felt the pain but grew from each experience and am thankful to all the extraordinary people who touched my heart. And I have worked with almost every type of person you can imagine. During that time, I could see that everyone has the same needs.

EVERYONE HAS DIFFERENT GOALS, DIFFERENT VALUES, AND DIFFERENT VIEWS, BUT THEY ALL HAVE THE SAME NEEDS:

- We all need certainty.

- We all need the feeling of comfort.

- We all want to avoid pain.

- We all want to gain pleasure.

- We all have a need for a variety in our lives.

- We need some uncertainty.

- We all need some surprises.

- We all want a challenge.

Fear? Your Not Special It's Human Nature

We Need These Things To Make Our Lives Exciting and Juicy

We all have a need to feel significant, feel important, feel unique, feel special, and to feel we are needed. The only question is how do you make sure we are meeting all these needs in our relationships. Do you demand it, or do you give it, or do you just notice its there and appreciate it within yourself?

Everybody has a need to connect, and to feel love. As we have already said, we all have a need to grow and contribute. These six needs must be met by all human beings, but what's interesting, is everyone pursues these needs in their own unique way. Some people try to meet all their needs through their job. They don't have any real, intimate relationships, because all their focus is becoming significant through achievement. To these people, connection is kind of a secondary thing.

Sadly these people usually end up unbelievably unhappy later in life, if not already. Some people will end relationships with friends and family, placing all their energy into one relationship with their lover. But, then if that relationship gets in trouble they have no life.

So for now, please know that relationships are about meeting others needs. If you can help your partner in life, feel certain that by being in a relationship with you, they will feel comfort, joy, and feel love. Help them experience more variety, by being in a relationship with you, surprises, learning, growing, some challenges and stimulation. Help your partner, to feel totally special and unique, and they need to feel you mean it. Ensure you truly value your partner by seeing the unique qualities they have we all have unique challenges, but value their unique qualities.

It is vital that you appreciate them, and you acknowledge them in a way so that they feel it. If you can genuinely connect regularly, if you can relate and share but also if you can get them to share you will have your needs met, as well. If both of you can grow and contribute to each other through your association and how you relate, then you will be in a relationship that is legendary. But, if you are trying to get out of a relationship currently it's because many of these things are missing. You don't feel relevant to that person, you don't feel significant, you don't feel special, you don't feel unique, and you feel as though you don't matter.

That's the first thing that starts to break down, when you don't feel a connection, they won't share something you want them to share. Maybe there is some dishonesty, which shuts down any kind of connection. You simply feel bored, no variety, doing the same things and so you're not growing, there's no contribution in your relationship anymore. Now, you feel uncertain, and you are afraid that, at any moment, they might leave you. These are the stigma that creates stress in a relationship.

But, here's what undoubtedly creates the stress in a relationship. All human beings share the same fears.

The Love Mojo

The primary fears of all human beings are the following.

- NUMBER ONE: IS THAT WE ARE NOT ENOUGH

- NUMBER TWO: ARE THAT WE WON'T BE LOVED

And let me explain to you why we have these fears. I kind of started in on this earlier in the book, I'm not sure if you recall, let me give you a little reminder. Every human being that has ever been to therapy knows, that something happened at some stage of their life making them feel insignificant and unloved. And they live with that fear forever. You don't need to go to a therapist, let me just tell you, we have lots of those experiences. And the reason is that human beings have something rather unique, in their makeup. It has to do with the way in which we were raised. In the animal kingdom, most animals are not dependent upon, another animal whether it's a mother, a father, brother, or sister. They're not totally dependent upon another animal for a long period of time. If you are a bird you're butt's kicked out of the nest in a few days, or a few weeks. If you are a snake, or a turtle you're dropped off and you're left to fend for yourself in the first moment, there is nobody around, you've got to step up. But, if you are a human being, your one of the few creatures on earth, like primates that's one of the other creatures like this that has a long period of time in which your survival revolves around a total dependency upon another human being, putting your own needs above their own.

As human beings, we weren't born with some special venom, or special scissored teeth, or even claws. Our evolutionary advantage is our ability to relate to each other to share. We share ideas, thoughts, feelings, emotions, and produce an unprecedented advantage in life, and that's why we as a species, have flourished. But, leave us alone and how do we deal? If a baby is left alone, it dies, a human baby. Why they get something called a failure to thrive syndrome, if the baby is not stroked, if it's not physically loved, if it's not given as the doctors say, tactile stimulation, also known as love, then the baby has failure to thrive syndrome, they can't explain it.

The baby dies. Love is a need that is deep inside us all, a survival instinct, and without love, we die. That's how powerful love is.

But here's what is unique about human beings that make your mother and hopefully your father but not always fathers, always mothers have to love you if they are biochemically healthy. The reason is all women when they are pregnant have something called oxytocin that flows in their body.

What this hormone does, is it makes this mom, have to love it's child even if the child is butt ugly. Immediately, this child who looks like a total mess is the most attractive thing on earth. Now, you know this is true, because we all have had those moments when a proud mommy pulls out the photos of their new baby, and with one glance you are like, *"Crud! Dang not right before I eat!"* Yet, the mom's looking and cooing over her little bundle of joy, telling you how precious and adorable it is. Now what's amusing is he has all this fat around him, it's the last time someone will say your cute when you have fat around you. He burps, and it's glorious, he pukes, and it's just so adorable, it's like a scene from the Eddie Murphy movie The Nutty Professor, when they are all sitting around the supper table, and Eddie Murphy's character passes gas, and the mother just pats him on the back and says, *"Ohhh my baby gots him a little gas, isn't that cute."* Now, granted that baby is now 35 plus years old, but you get the point. And when you're a baby it doesn't matter what you do, you are loved. And guess what, it's a nifty thing. Because, all you have to do is make a little noise, and everyone jumps to meet your needs. I mean anything you need it would just appear. When is the last time you felt that way about your life?

Human beings survival was depended on by another person. In various cultures, in the world, some fathers do leave, because they don't have oxytocin. Most fathers become connected to their child simply through a sense of what their child represents to them. The father feels as if life is more significant than themselves, and that there is this child who has been brought into this world because of them, which form an emotional connection and bond. But that's an emotional, a spiritual perception it's not necessarily biochemical.

So, that's why women, if they're healthy do not leave, it is biochemical, resulting from the oxytocin in them.

The Love Mojo

Now, here's what's interesting, as I said earlier, there's a point where this oxytocin leaves. When that stuff wears off, you are no longer momma's little pride and joy, let's put it that way. Suddenly, the same stuff you used to do, which was seen, as cute and adorable are no longer seen that way, and if you act out with inappropriate behavior you may get swatted, or a tongue lashing, or maybe just flat out ignored. Suddenly, there are all these rules that need to happen before you receive love, which is your substance for survival.

Mama's Little Pride & Joy | Why Oxytocin Makes Your Mother Love

Think about it, now Momma's little pride and joy, must do something significant now, to receive the love they crave. Before, you didn't have to do anything, now you have to act a certain way. Good or bad, if you don't get attention, doing good things as a child you'll do bad things. And, by the way, adults are just big kids, so you have the same patterns on some level. Unlike, other animals, whose dependency only lasts a few weeks, these days for human beings, it can continue 5, 10, 15, 25, 35, even upwards of 50 years!

So we live in a world where we have become connection freaks, because we know that if someone doesn't care for us, we aren't significant, or if we can't generate enough love then we will not survive, So while you may remember going to your therapist and recalling a story similar to this one time where your father or mother said something, or another child said something, or someone dumped you, and they didn't give you love you deserved, and that's why today you have this inferiority thing, then that must be the reason you have a fear of not being loved. Yes, because of a past experience, the therapist will help you verify that the event is why you can't be intimate and that is all a hefty load of crud.

Remember in earlier chapters, I spoke about the lady at the bridge event that had the same sort of feelings. She recalled being left in the dark when she was only an infant, well every time she would see a therapist they would make her relive that event over and over and over, all the emotions, feelings, and fears. So she's always going to have those feelings, she's not allowed ever to look at the event in an empowering way, no instead she reinforces those negative feelings which she carries into her daily experiences.

And the truth of the matter, all those feelings she had, we all have had, it's called being human, just some of us indulge in it.

Some of us live there, others discipline it and whenever those feelings come up, they recognize it and say to themselves:

- "Hey, hey, no here's the truth, I can love myself."

- "Here's the truth I love my creator my creator loves me."

- "Here's the truth, this problem is not a problem I just need to reconnect with this person."

Breaking The Conflict Cycle

Conflict = Pain

Now, the minute someone looks as though they aren't loving you, or they're not treating you significantly enough, the fear of losing love, creates a fear that you're going to die emotionally. And what most people do when this fear shows up in their relationship, is they try to get out first to avoid pain. People either try to hurt the other person first, figuring hurting them first, puts them in a position, to avoid pain. They take their fear, and they push it out, or they hurt themselves by going inside and getting depressed. Because, they feel that there's nothing they can do, and their world shall end. Or they distract themselves with alcohol, drugs, television or over working or something else that will make them feel righteous in the moment. This way they hope it will help them not to worry about feeling insignificant. Some people get that love the need, by just giving love to other people, even when the other person physically abuses them. They are so afraid of losing that feeling of significance or love.

THEY CREATE WAYS IN THEIR MIND TO JUSTIFY THE ABUSE.

- "At least if I'm being beat, I'm getting attention."

- "Maybe there's still a chance for love."

JUST AS DAMAGING, WE HAVE THE ACHIEVERS APPROACH:

- "If I make enough money..."

- "If I accomplish enough..."

- "If I achieve enough then people will notice I'm important and I'll feel the love..."

However, one thing, which cannot be denied, is these behaviors are the basis of the psyche, of human beings.

Most people have no training whatsoever on what's driving them as a human being. They don't know why they do what they do, they just have these things that they do, without any understanding of why. They are in response, just trying to get the job done. You put two of these people together, and you wonder why we have a situation where there is so much pain out there in the world. Also, taking into account that there are two types of people, males, and females who biochemically are different. And, therefore, think differently, somewhere I heard it compared as Men are from Mars and Women are from Venus, I think I read that on something.

Some males are more feminine in their energy, while other males are more masculine in their energy. Same thing with women. It was always a joke, when I lived in Russia one of my favorite people as the sweetest woman named Irina, she was the director of the languages at Moscow State University, and she was the sweetest loving woman, yet you would hardly ever see her smile. And I would tease her, *"Yes, in Russia where the men are men and women are too."* Because during the winter they are so bundled up like an eskimo with big, bulky coats that make them look like a line backer, and no smiles, they looked just like the men. And if you even look at a seat in the metro that they plan on sitting in, without warning you will be met with a sizable massive shopping bag smacked across your head. I always wished those magnificent lady's would take their Midol before venturing out with other humans.

But, anywhooo I digress, the male energies just had a different focus. Masculine energy is about achieving, breaking thru, experiencing freedom. However, feminine energy is about connection, and love. We have both energies in our body, and the question is which one do you develop most? And because of their drastic differences, the two energies themselves, create conflicts.

Now your saying to yourself, *"Tollie you helped me understand where conflicts come from but, what's the solution?"* Well that is an excellent question, first we need an awareness and appreciation of what any particular feeling, is all about. When issues start to happen in a relationship you've got first to take a look and say to yourself, *"Ok, right now I am starting to react, but I know it is fear which is triggering these feelings."* People say continually how they are stressed over this, and over that, well stress is a code word for fear.

The Love Mojo

The fear is that if you don't achieve this, or if they don't do that, they don't respond that way. Or, if they don't like this if they don't respect this, and this doesn't happen, then you're not enough. You won't be loved, which means, you will die. This is the basis on what is happening unconsciously within in your mind, all because of past events. So the way you make your relationships work, is you first create a strong relationship with yourself. It is imperative that you first learn to love yourself.

Because, if you are going into a relationship with the absence of love and are merely seeking love, then you'll be two people starving.

Both of you will be trying to take the other person's food just hoping some scraps fall on the floor. And you know that's pretty much the definition of hell, the only thing worse is the song to it's a small world, stuck in your head. All that your looking for is inside you.

So the way, you create relatedness is you start with you, and the way you start with you, is you've got to say, to yourself the following:

- "What do I love about myself?"

- "What is worth loving within myself?"

And you've got to create an action plan, as I've said earlier that can allow you to start creating that feeling. And the way to do that is to ask a straightforward question of yourself. *"If I want someone to feel totally loved by me, what would I do."*

What would you do? Everyone one knows actions speak louder than words, right. So now you start thinking of some of the possible answers. Maybe you would say to yourself, *"I love you."* But, this time you want your words to connect on a deeper level with yourself, so you will say, *"I love you,"* in a sincere, slow, confident voice. Also, as you say *"I love you,"* you will look into your own eyes using the mirror and say *"I love you!"* When is the last time you have looked in the mirror, and told yourself, *"I love you?"* I mean honestly looked and said it, and meant it! You're now sitting there thinking, *"I'm not going to be staring in no mirror like an idiot telling myself, I love you, you're crazy!"*

Well, when's the last time you genuinely did that? And before you think its crazy, remember the effects of the mirror and the depression patients within the U.C. Berkeley study? If depression can be erased, then I'm pretty sure you can also create a better state for your love mojo.

For that matter, when's the last time you looked into someone else's eyes who you are around always and stopped and with intent focus said, *"I love you."* Into their eyes and, not just with the mere words. We all know we can't give to other people what we haven't given to ourselves, because there's nothing to give. You can't go into a relationship empty and expect to fill someone else up. And you can't go into a relationship empty and expect that person to feel good about being in a relationship with you, they will feel as though you are a taker, not a giver.

So fill yourself up, what else would you do if you wanted someone else to know that you loved them? Well, you might do things for them:

YOU MIGHT TAKE SOME MEMORABLE TIME FOR THEM.

* What are you going to do for yourself?

* What momentous time could you take for yourself?

* What else would you do if you really, really, adored somebody.

The Love Mojo

What else would you do? You might tell other people how great they are, and now maybe you are saying, *"Well, can I tell other people how great I am?"*

And the answer is, well, yes you can if you can do it elegantly, you totally can. As long as you can put a little smile on your face when you say, *"Hey I'm good, can I tell you what I did?"*

And you know what, if you do it, and you're not full of yourself, and you're just acknowledging the truth inspires other people. But, if you do it and you pretend like your not doing it, and you go, *"Well yeah, let me tell you what else I've accomplished."*

Well, that's not connecting with yourself, and so you can't connect with anybody and you're just seen as a blowhard. Well there are other words to use, but they are a little more graphic and I'll keep this rated PG. But, you know what I mean; you've got to connect with yourself.

So before, we do anything else. I have talked about so many things here, maybe you want to take some notes, and jot down a couple of these principles and maybe you say:

* "Ok, one of the things he has written about, is that when I get upset, I need to ask myself, what's really happening here?"

* "Am I responding to the past or the present?"

* "What else could this mean?"

* "I'm just going to ask myself these questions over the next three days, maybe next couple weeks, I will do that all day long, in any upset I have."

THAT MIGHT BE A MARVELOUS THING TO DO.

I know we have already covered a lot. But right now, I want you to see how we could reinterpret any event, so that we are not simply reacting and making things worse.

Remember the questions, and answers we should always use when we step back and focus on other possible meanings. Such as:

- "Why am I in this relationship? To magnify my emotions."

- "Now, are these the emotions I want to magnify, in this moment, NO!" "Very good, in order to feel this way, I have to give it meaning, what's the meaning I'm giving this?"

- "What else could it mean?"

Remember, it's not about you, if they are doing this stuff and coming at me, it's because they need significance, they're screaming for significance, and they just need some love. It's not about me, they're not trying to hurt me, they're trying to meet their own needs. So we've talked about a lot already haven't we? If I'm really in a position, where I'm really, really, upset with somebody you know is it something I'm upset with myself about? Asking quality questions, will get you quality answers. Which will get you a quality life?

Let's do one thing right now, because in a few moments were going to talk about the most important principle in creating a relationship. But before we even do that, I want you to stop reading for a moment, and when you do, I want you to write down a game plan, of what you will do, so you really, love yourself. And I don't want you to use the story, *"I can't love myself, I will never love myself."*

Forget all the stories, The only thing keeping you from getting what you deserve and what you want are the stories you tell yourself about why you don't deserve it, or why you can't do it. So put the story aside, give yourself this gift. If you shall really, cherish yourself.

If you were honestly going to let yourself know that you truly love yourself, what would your action plan be? And, by the way, how serious is it to believe that you love yourself? If you don't love yourself can you honestly love anybody, truly 100%?

Do you genuinely think you could give, if you can't truly love yourself? And let me tell you the good news, you do have that love for yourself, or else you wouldn't be alive. You would have taken your life and be gone. So don't say you don't love yourself that might have been something you've just said to yourself repeatedly. Let's just be more demonstrative.

So I want you to create an action plan, what actions are you going to take? You say:

"I will take two minutes in the morning, for the next seven days, and I will do this stupid thing Tollie said; no one will know. I will look in the mirror, and I will say, a little incantation again over and over, I will look at myself and say, I love you, I love you, and you're going to say your name, and you will look right in your eyes and say; I love you. Now let me tell you what I love about you, I love your commitment, to people. I love your caring heart."

AND SAY YOUR NAME, SO IT BECOMES REAL TO YOU, SOMETHING LIKE:

The Love Mojo

- *"Tollie, I love your caring heart, I love your commitment to people."*

- *"Tollie I love your playfulness, I love that you're off the wall, I love that you're willing to do what it takes, to help people. I love that your so committed to being strong physically, and healthy, and I love your love for God."*

I love, I love, I love, and look into your own eyes. Because then it is not just sitting there saying, I love you, I love you, I love you. It's giving real reasons. It's like when you give someone a compliment, in a relationship, a little tip, don't just say your great, or golly gee whiz you're swells, your super duper in a far out groovy kinda way.

BUT, IF YOU CAN SAY:

- "You know what's really great about you..."

- "You know what I love about you..."

- "I have to tell I noticed this, and this..."

Hearts & Minds of Your Toughest Critics | The Tom McBride Story

I've got to tell you about a relationship I was involved in that started off on a bit of a rocky start. This was back in high school, and I was a bit of a challenge for my teachers, to put it lightly. It was the beginning of a new school year, and at one of my schools, The Center for International Studies, we had a new teacher named, Mr. Tom McBride teaching International Geo-Politics. I was used to the teacher from our previous year, whom I thoroughly loved, he was crazy, unpredictable, and allowed us to do anything thing we wanted as long as it would pertain to the discussion.

Well, Mr. McBride was used to a structured class, and I started off being a real, wise crack in class, which to my surprise he did not find charming or endearing what so ever. Instead, he took offense to it, which then he challenged me on my attitude. Which I fired right back at him, since I never did back down from a challenge, even when it would have been the smarter choice. So after that, I found myself, my parents, the administration at the school in a conference, because Mr. McBride wanted me thrown out of school.

Yes, I know what you are thinking, and I agree, he undoubtedly over reacted, but, he got my attention. I loved that school, it was the only school, that I enjoyed the process of learning. So, I made all the concessions I needed to make, which essentially came down it was his way or the highway.

I was unquestionably fuming, and felt that he might have won that battle, but come class time, it's on like donkey kong!

First week, was challenging, he'd ask me a question, I'd ignore him, or blow him off. Then one day he asked me a question, and when I tried to blow him off, he shocked me with his response:

"Tollie, it's ok it was kind of a trick question, I know your stupid, and the reason you always act out is to cover up your pure ignorance on any subject, and that's why you can sit there and continue to be the failure you are."

Well that didn't just get my attention that pissed me off! And for some reason I was always gifted with speech, and found it remarkably easy; however, when I would get mad, and was challenged in the right way, I seemed to kick myself into high gear, and it was game time, and I brought my A game. I debated him for solid 25 mins, no pauses, no stop back and forth, completely cordial, and intelligent thought provoking, debate. Then after that 25 minutes, Mr. McBride stopped and just started laughing. I paused to see what would be said next, and he looked at me and said:

"Tollie, I was told from your previous teacher that you are a grade A pain in the ass. I was told that you were not a good student as far as the rest of the traditional students, you don't do your homework, you march to the beat of your own drummer. But, if someone could only get you to realize what you were capable of, there was a brilliant young man inside."

He said, *"Thank you for a thought provoking debate."* I was shocked, by his kind words. After class, he told me that if I would agree to remove the giant stick from my *ss (*Mr. McBride always used abundantly colorful words with us, although he never was a sailor.*) I promise you that I will make sure you pass, and learn while you are challenged as you have never been challenged before. If you do this, I will also stand up for you anytime, when your intelligence is ever called into question. I appreciate your fire, passion, and tenacity, you just need to realize inside a classroom it can be distracting and intimidating other students.

Long story short, Mr. McBride always had my back, all the way until I left high school, and was the man who convinced my school to let me live in Russia for a year and study on my own. His letter of recommendation is the only high schoolteacher recommendation I still have to this day, not that I had many of them.

Tom McBride was the first person to convince me, I had a talent, and I was intelligent. And as much as I wanted to be a class clown and do my own thing, I strived to make that man proud of me, because he was the first teacher to shut me down, took me on one on one, and believed in me.

He remains as a dear friend, and someone I can tell anything to, without judgement, and always pushed me to believe in myself, and go and take on the world. And it was all because he took the time to engage me, and make me feel significant. And no matter who you are, we all want to feel appreciated, and special.

The Love Mojo

Positive reinforcement will always trump negative attacks.

WE ALL WANT TO BE LOVED; WE ALL WANT TO FEEL THE SIGNIFICANCE IN OUR LIFE.

Now, we don't want any bull or fluff; we don't want people to lie to us. We don't want fake things, but a sincere compliment gets us hooked. So, how about starting with yourself. Because you know whether you can give to yourself, then you can give to other people. So that's one thing, that's one assignment. In fact, if you do nothing else in this book, I'm going to ask you to do that for the next seven days. That you take two minutes, and you sincerely compliment yourself each morning. And look directly in the mirror, and I know your thinking to yourself, *"Yeah but what if my spouse, or somebody else is around, and they see me do this stuff?"* Inspire them.

Make it playful, have fun with it. But, what I'd like you to do right now is stop reading, and I want you to write what else besides that will you do that will get you to feel that love. Because if you have that love already, then you will not have that fear of losing it. And when you don't have the fear of losing your primary fear, and when that primary fear is gone, because you know you can't ever be not enough because you're enough for yourself.

You can't ever lose the love, because your giving it to yourself. Or you've connected to God, and you know that's ever lasting love. Whatever works, then you don't have to react in relationship whenever someone says something that makes you feel like Well maybe they don't feel I'm significant. Or they act like, they may not be there for you, or they may not love you, and you don't have to overreact. And when you are no longer over reacting the quality of your relationships transform.

Does this make sense to you? Then stop reading now, and write a list of at least ten things you will do, to teach yourself, to learn, to appreciate, to acknowledge the extraordinary human being you are and how much you love yourself. Please take the time and do that right now. Stop reading.

Ok welcome back, I hope you took the time thoroughly to do this. But, if you didn't please stop reading and go back and do, you can't love anyone or give love if you can't love yourself first. And we all know that intellectually, when you begin to do things for yourself that demonstrate beyond the shadow of a doubt, that you love yourself, all of a sudden your, not in a place of scarcity. And see when your in scarcity it's extremely hard to attract somebody who is full. Because you know like attracts like.

A Dream Come True

Law of life, water seeks its own level, like attracts like.

When you feel full of love, you can't believe all of a sudden there's this abundance, it's like in life when you're barely surviving financially, no one will help you. And suddenly when your rich everyone wants to give you stuff for free, it's bizarre.

So you must become within in your soul, in your feeling, in your emotions that which you want. And if you do that it's easy, it flows, and yes the love mojo will flow. Now, what were the things you wrote down? And what were the patterns? Did you notice any of them, were some of the patterns things that you would do for yourself, as a demonstration, that you loved yourself? Were they auditory things, things you said to yourself? Are these things that you would do, to cause you to be around other people who would love you? These seem to be primary patterns people seem to have.

Struggling With Anorexia | Emma Needed to Love Her Self First!

Let me give you an example. I worked with a young girl who was struggling with Anorexia, so as you can imagine the idea that she could love herself would be a monumental feat. I asked her to remember a time when she could love herself. And she, sat there and looked at the ground and told me about when she was younger she always kept a diary, and she always wrote in her diary every day. At the end of her diary entry, she would write I love you Emma, your one sexy lady, xoxo, and she giggled as she would say, *"I know stupid right."* And I just replied, I don't know when did you stop doing that? She replied about a year and a half-ago.

So I then asked her again, when did she start have the Anorexic tendencies, and she looked up and said, well I guess couple months after I quite writing in my diary, then she followed up her answer quickly, and asked me, but there's no way writing stupid things in a book could effect my mood or my body. No, it wasn't stupid, I told her about a man I knew named Roy who was a consultant for the FBI and several private companies and such. I told her how Roy could examine handwriting, and he could see so many personality traits; character flaws, and so much just through someone's handwriting. I told her; it's not just crazy talk, because it was a proven science that was admissible into a court of law as evidence. I told her; Roy examined one of my Granny's old letters. Without knowing her, he could describe health issues she had, personality traits and intimate details only close family members would know. What Roy taught me was to practice writing my name a certain way, 10-20 times a day, every day for a week, and see how my mood changed. So I did and as he predicted I felt an intense confidence.

So, the point is, by writing down all the reasons you love yourself, everyday writing down the specific things you love about yourself anchors it to your body, so real that it shapes the emotion, and behavior. Remember from previous chapters, what you communicate to your brain, is what your brain will seek out.

So by only communicating to your brain positive and loving things about yourself, your brain will take hold of that script and this will become your new programming, so once you feel loved, your emotions and behaviors will follow.

Now after, you do all this, and once you feel complete love with yourself, also once you are living your life in a truly inspired state where your mojo is flowing, everything is clicking, then there is one more step I want you to take.

Write yourself a love letter. Write your letter, as if God were coming through your hand. Write ever feeling, touch, smell, experience with no filters, or concern about the appropriateness. You know you can sit there and brag about your kids, and you mean it. You can say how remarkable, talented, beautiful they are and go on and on and on about them. Just don't pull out the baby pictures, before breakfast, please. Just kidding, but I want you to write about yourself the way your parents could write about you, or God would write about you. Then give it to a family member after you have it sealed in an envelope and it is not to be opened. Then have your family member mail that letter to you, in six months, and I can assure you it's a pure emotional moment, and it reinforces as a great reminder about whom you truly are.

So many people spend enormous amounts of time each morning in front of the mirror, doing their hair, makeup, shaving, and other fun stuff to get ready for the day. But, why not take that wasted time in front of the mirror to send yourself love each morning? It may sound silly to look in the mirror while your doing your hair and say, Dang, you look hot! But it's just those words, and the intensity you put behind them, which start to anchor the actual feeling to your brain. And it creates a playful state with yourself. Sometimes, you just have to hug yourself. As stupid and silly as hugging yourself may sound, a hug is vital, and it anchors a warm and loving feeling to yourself. I mean you have to think about it, what would you do for someone else, you'd give them a hug; you would pat them on the back.

One of the things I do some times, is when I do something on or off stage that I just know is awesome, I will reach back and give myself a pat on the back. I will smile, kind of mocking it and myself, but my mojo is flowing and I am in the moment, saying to myself, *"Yeaa that was pimp!"* and I don't care if no one else noticed, as long as I did. Besides, in my world, I make Dork, cool!

Because part of the challenge in life is, that most of us are not busy looking around to acknowledge other people so if you don't acknowledge yourself sincerely, for doing things that are unique or exceptional, or just being loving, you will not feel that feeling you deserve. And the more you give these feelings of love to yourself, the more whole you'll be, the more centered you'll be, the better person you'll be in a relationship, you'll have something to give, instead of going there to get. And you know what, you'll be more selective.

Choose Wisely

So now let's talk, we have talked about so many different ideas on relationships.

Let me wrap up with two principles that we surely need to focus on. What is the most decisive factor in creating an unprecedented relationship? Well the most decisive factor in having an unprecedented relationship is to have an unprecedented relationship with yourself. As we discussed that is one where you relate to yourself; you've expressed yourself. You demonstrate on a consistent basis, which means it is vital that you schedule time to love yourself.

So, assuming you have a strong relationship with yourself first has been met, what is the most significant factor in having a quality relationship with someone else? The most significant factor in having an unprecedented relationship is selection. Now even if you are already in a relationship this factor also applies to you, I promise. Selection means selecting the qualities you need in a relationship.

So if, you are already in a relationship, then this is a factor you will look at as brand-new.

Let me give you an idea, relationships go through several phases.

They go through that, love at first sight, or lust phase. Another phase is one of deep love, and it goes through phases of questioning, where you think to yourself, What in the world am I doing here?

These phases happen in all relationships; it is the nature of relationships. But, what will make a relationship last is if both people share, similar natures. Or if they share natures that will compliment each other. What I mean by nature is whether, your relationship, or your relatedness is based on the moment, or whether it will have a lasting impact.

HOW YOU DETERMINE YOUR ANSWERS ARE BASED UPON YOUR BELIEFS, VALUES, AND GOALS.

Urban Street wear | Vernon Deas & GroupFly Clothing Story

Let me give it to you this way. If you want to hire someone for your job, you want to talk to someone who is exceptionally good, an example I can give you is my old friend Vernon Deas, here is a man who not only inspired me as a teenager growing up, but is still to this day inspiring youth all over this country while building a solid clothing and apparel brand.

Vernon is truly an incredible man. I remember sitting down a few years ago with Vernon, back in Oklahoma City, and asking him, this question. What is the most important thing in your company's success? He said, it was clearly, inspiring these young men to give their all. See Vernon, is not just an entrepreneur, graphic designer, photographer, and founder of Group Fly Clothing, he is a father, husband, an inspirational speaker, and is a role model any man is proud to look up to and aspires to become.

Vernon didn't just start a clothing line, he created a movement. It's funny people hear the word motivation, and they think it is kind of silly idea. But, it's through motivation you achieve the spark to ignite a passion to a progression to become inspired.

The term Group Fly simply means, a group of people reaching a higher destination. Vernon's brand does three things: CREATE amazing product, LEAD, and INSPIRE others. Vernon has used his passion of hip hop, urban culture, graphic design, and clothes to inspire his higher calling to serve his God in all he does, while taking to the Urban Streets and providing at risk youth the opportunity through motivation, hard work, dedication a chance to realize their dream.

Vernon's Brand, Group Fly is an urban graphic design clothing line, much like many other clothing lines across the world, so how did Vernon take an idea from concept, to create a movement by using forgotten talent from the inner cities, and allowing them an opportunity to thrive!

He didn't have any monetary advantages over his competition; he was usually at a disadvantage. His company didn't have a larger advertising and marketing firm handling the launch of the clothing line. So what is it that Vernon had, to create a truly unique and rapidly growing brand? Achieving rapid growth was Vernon's capacity to get more out of his cadets, employees, the crew behind Group Fly. It was his ability to relate to them in a way, where they bond with you, and hence, you're able to move them to a different level of action. Vernon always new another key factor in achieving a higher level of success, he knew that as valuable as motivation is, that selection is even more crucial.

Vernon was using his passion for developing his brand, while simultaneously was giving his time, heart, and talent to a group of kids, that many people today would still not even offer an equal opportunity in evaluating their talent, and skill. Vernon was trying to launch a clothing line, where he began at a major disadvantage, and with decidedly limited capital to work with, he could not afford any mistakes. An image is everything in fashion, and sex sells, so how was Vernon going to hock a bunch of clothes with nothing more than a crew from the inner city?

In order for Vernon to be successful, he had to select the right people. He knew he had to select people who's nature would be to work together. He had to select people who would normally probably give more of themselves, than anyone else would expect of them. He knew that was the most critical task he had to go thru. By going thru those selections Vernon built a veracious advancing clothing brand, inspiring youth in one city and advancing across the nation.

Vernon's Group Fly Cadets, as they are called, are by selection the elite, because they are cadets who can relate to each other and work as a team. Vernon was always a personal hero to me growing up. Today, I find myself saying:

THANK GOD FOR THE DREAMERS! WITH COURAGE & HEART TO SERVE, DREAM, ACHIEVE, AND OPEN THE DOOR TO ALL TO PROVIDE OPPORTUNITY FOR ALL OF GOD'S DREAMERS.

You want to see something noteworthy, then take a moment and check out. (grpfly.com)

Now if, the importance of selection is true in forming a winning team to launch an urban clothing line, then it's positively true in creating a winning relationship. And I will give you another example from business.

When you are going to hire someone in business, there are three factors you are unquestionably going to have to be able to answer. The answer to these three factors will determine if this person will be able to succeed long term. Because everyone succeeds first, just like all relationships first start sensational, they have enthusiasm, energy, and excitement. Now, it is the sustainability we looked for. So in a business relationship there are three questions, you must answer. Can they do the job? This is the first question you need to answer, is whether they can do the job. Now more than likely if you are interviewing them, it means yes; they can do the job, because you have probably already screened them. You have probably already gone through their bio, maybe checked some references, or you've had someone else look at things before they were even brought into have a formal interview.

So when you're in a relationship with someone your considering a relationship with them, can they are your partner, now the chances are if you are at consideration of that possibility, then sure they can more than likely. But, the second question is more valuable than the first, and we want to know if 'will' they do the job? Now when I ask will they do the job, I don't mean today, I don't mean tomorrow, I don't mean this week, this month, I don't even mean for the next six months.

The question comes down to, will they do the job ten years from now, will they do the job three years from now? We are trying to gauge if this relationship will last, whether they do the job in business or not, is based on two things.

Does the job meet they're personal goals? This is the first thing we need answered, does the job meet they're personal goals. If someone genuinely wants to make a billion dollars, and the job they're in will never allow that, then you can pretty well be sure that, however, long they're here it's not going to be long. Because; eventually, their goals will take them elsewhere.

If the job is actually about mastering business skills, and their ultimate goal is to pursue a singing career, then they are more than likely not going to be there long. Even if they stay, they will not perform the job to the highest level of quality that is necessary. Because we all know of a relationship where they have been together forever, they have been together for 15, 20, or 25 years, and sadly their friends. They don't have

The Love Mojo

intimacy, they don't have a relationship called an intimate relationship; they just have this nifty friendship. You have the same thing happen in businesses. You have somebody there that just kind of hangs on, they don't actually grow, they don't expand, and sure, they can do the job; however, are they doing it at the maximum capacity, absolutely not.

The Second Thing We Need Answered Is | Does the Job Reinforce Their Nature?

Now lets first look at this from a business point of view, and then I will relate it back to the relationship aspect. Lets say this person is very much a people person, and you shove them back in accounting, they may be able to do the job, and even if yes they can do the job, but will they do the job long term? And will they perform the job consistently at the highest level of quality, well the answer would be no. Because they want to be around people, it is their nature to connect. And so being isolated in accounting is not what will make them fulfilled so sooner or later, they are either going to quite, or find another job. (*I.e., another relationship*) If they stay, they are just going to hang out and do the sheer minimum. So they will find joy outside the relationship/work. Well this is also true in your personal relationships. If you have someone who's goals are radically different from your own, it could be that they want kids and you don't.

Having kids is a pretty key element. Because if you can't resolve those goals where both parties are exceedingly happy, then you will find there will be continuous conflict in the relationship, including resistance, resentment, and eventually if you stay together, repression, if you don't end the relationship. Secondly if, you are in the position and you are the kind of person who never acknowledges anyone, that's just is not your nature, you're not much into acknowledgement you just assume people know. And if you are partnering with someone who craves acknowledgment, needs to hear how much you love them on a consistent basis, while being praised, and you are not that kind of person, you never have been, you can try to get yourself to do that for a while, but your nature says, that as soon as the person looks satisfied, as soon as the pressure is off, you will go back to your old style. So that, person will not be reinforced in a relationship with you.

But, someone else will come along and stroke them, and tell them how great they are and how amazing they are, and guess what, they will find a great attraction, a great love, a great appreciation for that person. And you will start notice or feel that there is a sense of loss for you, and what is happening is that you are two great people, with two drastically different natures. It's important to note that if your nature is different from the person you are with, and that does not mean you are not attracted to each other, people who have totally different natures can be totally attracted to each other. The problem is they don't have that long sustainability; instead you have a hot love affair instead of a long lasting intimate relationship.

This Is The Third Thing We Need Answered Is | Does This Person Fit With Our Team?

One of the biggest components of whether the person will be a proper fit on your team is values, matching values. I am not saying everyone needs to be identical, that's a lovely recipe for boring; however, I am saying you need to be complimentary. I mean if your goal is to go out and change the world, make a difference in people's lives, and your partner is the sexiest thing on the planet, and you worship the ground they walk on, but they're goal is to get all the way to the top, and that includes stepping on as many people as needed to expedite their climb, things will not work out.

Even if you two have so many other things in common, the fact that your values are extremely different you will be in constant conflict, and when you are constantly in conflict then a relationship is hard to sustain. You will have conflicts if you can't relate to what they value most, and when they can't relate to what you value most. Diversity is compelling in all relationships. However, opposite values are a core aspect of individuals. Your values determine everything about you. The President of (PETA) People for the Ethical Treatment of Animals, could not be in a successful, long term relationships with the President of let's say, the National Cattlemen's Beef Association.

Another key factor is sensuality or sexuality, because what you value in your sensuality is also extremely celebrated in an intimate relationship. It seems never to fail, in so many relationships we find that one partner is trying to change the other partner to make them a certain way. There is an idea that you can fix

The Love Mojo

your partner, well hate to break it to you, but they don't want to be fixed; there is nothing wrong with them. It is in their nature and who they are. How do you fix something that is not broken? See, you can't fix anything, because they are not broken, they just have a different set of values than you do, and there is nothing wrong with that. So just a little fair warning, if you do decide to try your hand at being Handy Manny, the handyman and fix your partner, when you fail you also run the danger of not only hurting your partner but severely damaging their spirit. So, start your relationship with someone who matches your values, you will start on a level playing field, where growth is possible, and you minimize conflict.

You have the foundation for a deep relationship with anyone else. So choose whom you will be in a relationship with, don't react. Don't take what is given to you, merely by the environment you walk by each day. Be clear on what you want, decide how you will make that happen, and then go, and make it happen. You deserve an unprecedented loving relationship. Yes! Occasional challenges will rise and allow you to grow stronger in your relationships. Decide what you want and make it happen.

Remember the purpose of an unprecedented relationship is to magnify the human experience. Don't settle for less than you know you deserve.

In the next chapter, you will learn how to achieve the vitality, to enhance all aspects of your life.

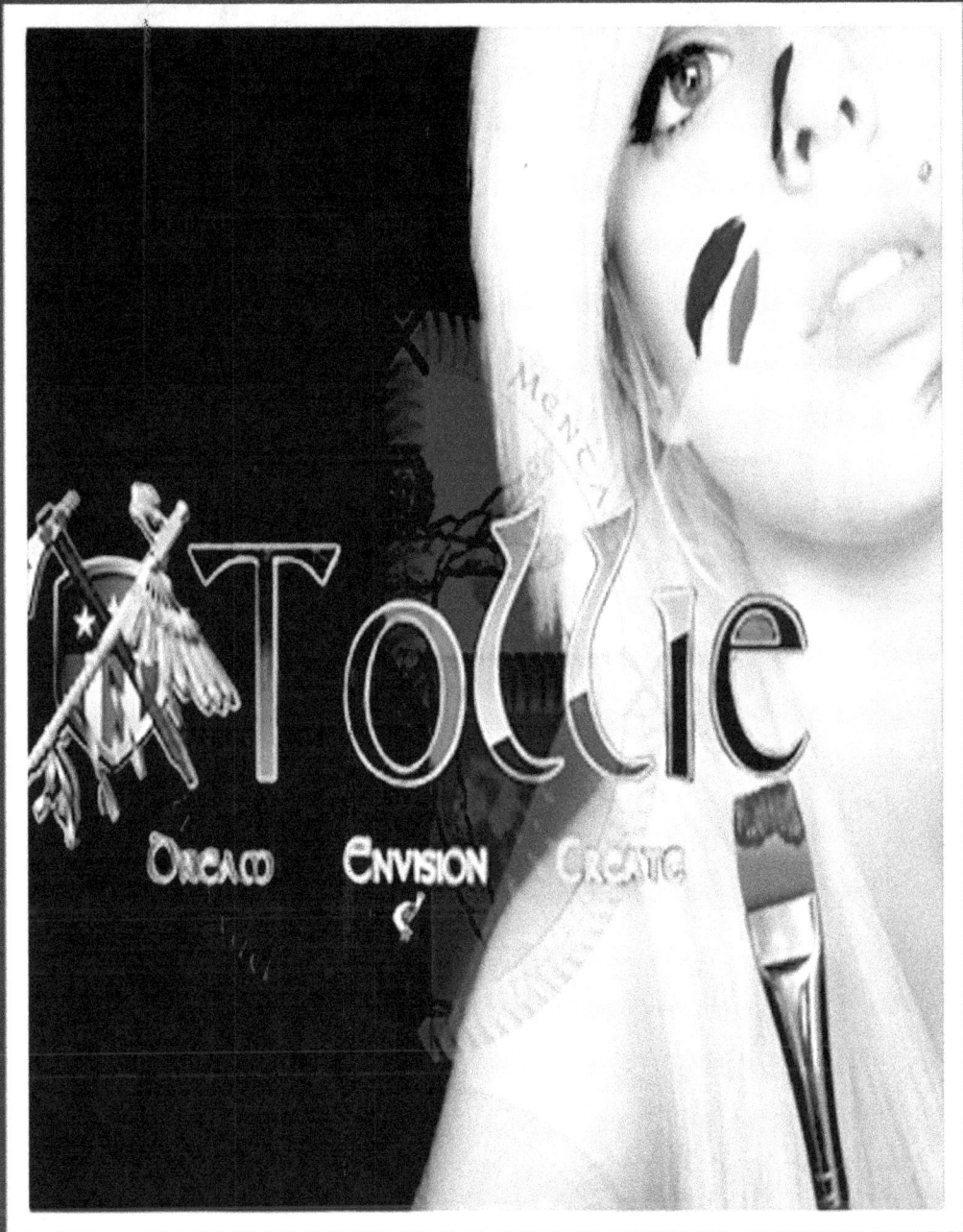

You are the Artist Brush Creating Your
Life's Masterpiece.

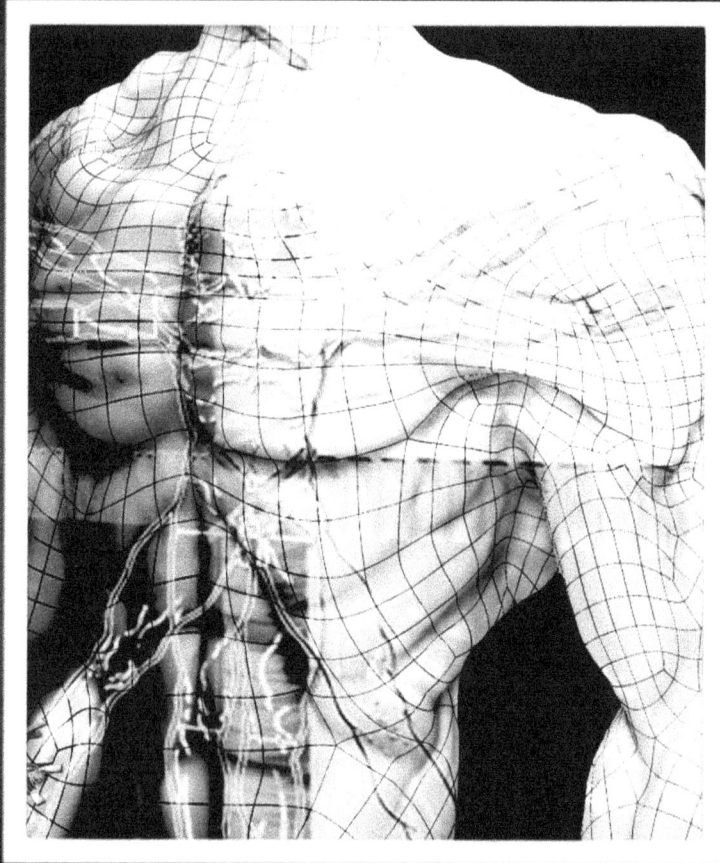

Chapter VI

Body of a Warrior | Spirit of a Dreamer

"AN ACTIVE MIND, CANNOT EXIST IN AN INACTIVE BODY." -GENERAL
GEORGE S. PATTON

Life's | Vitality

This Chapter Is About a Subject That Effects Everything Else In Your Life.

This entire book is focused on the foundations to achieve success in the major aspects of you life.

I hope to instill a belief of greatness inside you, so you will create lasting change and rise inspired. Like we have said most people focus on the petty things in life, rather than focus and change the key things in life. So many people put all their attention and focus into the things don't matter, and they make them more prominent than they actually are, and get stressed out. Let me tell you with complete certainty, that there are particular things in your life that if you focus on them your life expands and propels you forward in terms of your fulfillment, joy, relationships, health, and vitality.

Every aspect of your life is transformed into opportunities which you have up to this point only dreamed about, and now see as possible which allows you to take action because you have become inspired. But, there are certain areas of your life that if you don't focus on them, you get pain. So that brings us to the core aspect of what we are going to talk about in this chapter, which is your energy. When we think of our physical bodies, our vitality, our physical health, we don't stop to recognize that without out or health, vitality and energy to produce, all aspects of our life will not matter if we don't take care of our bodies. No matter what it is you want in your life whether it be you want to improve your relationships, finances, emotions, or career, none of these things matter if you don't take care of your body. So that's what we are going to focus on in this chapter, is our bodies and energy, because it is crucial! But, I've got to tell you, most people do not focus on their bodies because we don't live in a society where most of us value our bodies that much.

The greatest illusion, which we have bought into, is a false value on physical attraction to the body, and we have proved that sex sells, yet we don't focus on the vitality, health, and energy and make it an absolute must in our life.

We have tons of advertising on how to get drunk, end pain instantly through the use of a drug, or anything else you can consume in a super big gulp size. This is one of the reasons my company Tollie International Media Marketing and Advertising has taken a stand to engage in empowering, dream infused advertising and marketing to inspire the individual, not degrade.

In our society, we do things for money all the time, but we forget our bodies, we do things to meet our career needs but we forget about taking care of our bodies. In fact, most people will take care of their kids, they will take care of their spouses, their loved ones, but their bodies are usually the last thing you worry about for most of us. Yet, we try to go out there and accomplish all our goals, we give everything we have to everyone else, but when we don't have the energy or the vitality to do so, boy there is no fulfillment, joy or happiness there at all. Same as in a relationship, how can you give anything when you are empty. So if, you focus on creating wealth and making as much money as you can, its essential to realize your goal is not to become the richest man in the graveyard. No, you want to create wealth, you want to achieve in order to live an unprecedented life, which involves the vitality and energy truly to enjoy every aspect of your life.

You need to focus on your temple, the place where your spirit resides and most people are digging their grave with their teeth. But, here's what is truly powerful, it is the little changes in your body, which produce the massive changes in how you feel and experience your life. So, take it from the guy who weighed well over 500 pounds in my life, that my goal in this chapter is to help you increase your energy so you can propel yourself into an inspired state. Because increased energy means a greater quality of life.

It's About Energy | Vitality

The Body of a Warrior | Spirit of a Dreamer

We always admire people who have charisma, and of course, we do because charisma is energy, and we feed off of energy, it is the juice in life, it's the mojo baby! Look at people who have the ability to get things done, it is not just that they have the willpower its because they have the energy, its there at the end of the day, not just at the onset. I want you to feel life full of energy, it's the mojo, its the juice and there are simple changes you can make to create the energy and vitality. Also, if your overweight and you want to change, and you have tried all the diets, and you've tried exercising until you are blue in the face, there is a reason why all the diets and exercise have not worked.

THE REASON THE DIETS AND EXERCISE HAVE NOT WORKED IS BECAUSE OF ACID IN YOUR BODY.

Many times people go all out and exercise so much that their body just can not handle, so your body retains fluid it retains fat in order to protect the body from these acids which you will learn in this chapter. So if, you were looking to lose 5, 10, 15, 25 or even 50 pounds this chapter is the ticket, and it is different than things you have tried, and believed in the past. The reason I love this so much is that it is profound knowledge, and what makes it profound is it's simple. Simplicity makes doing things much easier to use, making simplicity a beautiful thing. Now I have tried, read and studied almost every single diet, or recommended food choices out there today. The reason I believe in what I am writing in this chapter is because, not only will you agree with the common sense behind the principles and examples but also it is based and proven by science.

When you start to understand the Acid Alkaline Balance in your body, and how it effects your energy, how it effects your flow of oxygen, how it effects the amount of fat your body retains, how it can even affect cholesterol you will be blown away by the process. The acid alkaline balance exceeding opens the door to a lot of the answers we don't have yet about the overall health and disease prevention. Let me tell you right now, you are going to hear about some real life examples of people who's lives have been drastically changed because of this research. Now, unlike a diet book, I am not using examples of how people lost all this weight, and now are wearing a size 0 and they feel just super duper fantastic and fabulous, until they gain the weight back. No, instead how about You hear about real life examples of people who exhausted all medical means to cure their cancer and were given months to live, are today cancer free and in the greatest shape of their lives and medically considered, a miracle. I hope this little teaser will give you the appetite to continue reading, because I feel so passionate about this subject, that I urge you to give yourself

The Body of a Warrior | Spirit of a Dreamer

this gift and not stop reading because you feel your already in perfect health. Sadly, there is so much research on nutrition, that so much of it gets lost in the shuffle.

For years, the original research studies on acid alkaline were done by Dr. Neil Solomon, M.D., Ph.D. years ago at John Hokins University. Dr. Neil Solomon focused his research solely what he could find in clinical nutrition that could massively improve the energy of an individual and the overall homeostatic balance in our body. What is homeostatic balance?

Homeostatic Balance Is Your Body's Natural Ability To Heal Itself.

Since that time, many people have done the research on acid alkaline balance and its impact. So I am going to share with you some of their findings and how you can take pieces and apply it your life today. Now, what I share with you is only the propellant, in order to have sustainability I encourage you to learn more on the specifics, and also try and disprove or defunct what we learn. One man we will learn from is Dr. Alex Guerrero, who studied chinese medicine and acupuncture, and to me embodies the term genius.

I started learning about him, and as I did my research I found it humorous all the negative things written about him online. If you google Dr. Alex Guerrero, and maybe google this term (*Dr. Alex Guerrero SCAM*) you will come back with a laundry list of articles, everything from scam artist, con artist, witch doctor, the list goes on. The negative's which you see on Dr. Alex Guerrero make a massive claim to the fact that since he is not a traditional Medical Doctor that he must be ridiculed and shamed so he can be silenced, because our society has forgot that all doctors Practice Medicine, it is not the Science of Medicine.

Dr. Alex Guerrero is known for his ability to create change in two extremes, he specializes in the peak performance athlete's who have started to burn out, and turns them around. But, he also specializes on taking care of patients that traditional doctors think are terminal and are inoperable, or there is nothing that can be done, and his statistics are astounding. He has cared for 400 terminal patients designated as untreatable by their physicians, five years later approximately 85% of them are still alive and thriving. This man has unquestionably discovered some tools which can be used to shift a person's health in a remarkably short period of time, even those who felt there was no hope.

The information you will read in this chapter has the power decisively to transform your life in a way you have never imagined. It has helped turn terminal patients (*people labeled soon to be dead with no hope*) into lively, thriving, and healthy individuals. It has cured cancer, arthritis, brittle bone disease, and countless other chronic conditions for millions of people around the world. And it has transformed the energy levels of people to the point where they never get sick, and they're full of unprecedented energy on a daily basis.

So, my hope is to deliver it to you in an easy to understand way, but also in a way that will have a tremendous impact on you, so you remember it, and use it to change your life. So the first thing, I want to do is free you from fear. So many people walk around everyday, afraid someone is going to sneeze on them, and they are going to get a cold or the flu.

Myth Buster | Illness and Germs

In Our Society | Sickness & Disease Is Something Entirely Out Of Our Control... Really?

We walk around all day, and we're constantly bombarded with evil germs and viruses, knowing their only purpose and deep desire are to ruin our day and make our life as difficult, short, painful, horrible, and depressing as possible. This is altogether not true, and anyone who believes in this can't blame anyone but their own mind for accepting these beliefs as obviously true, in an earlier part of their lives.

Before I share with you exactly why this isn't true, and why we're led to believe these things, can you think of some of the things others around you might have told you in the past to make you think this way? Your parents? Your friends? Things like:

- "Don't go outside without a sweater, you'll catch a cold!"

- "Stay away from germs and dirty places, or you'll get sick."

- "Don't eat food off the ground, it's infested, and you'll get a disease"

- "If you don't eat your vitamins you'll get sick or die sooner!"

- "Don't stay out in the sun too long, or you'll get a heat stroke."

And on and on, and on... Most of the time this advice takes the format of *"Don't do X, it's out of your control, something terrible will happen to you..."* Further more we're constantly pumped by the media which brings us reports of deadly viruses around the world which are responsible for killing thousands of people.

All these things presuppose that our health is something entirely out of our control and that our outer environment is filled with dangerous and mysterious things that are out there to KILL and destroy us!

The Flu and NYC Similar When There is a Trash Strike in the City?

Isn't it odd that in life we most often get advice from people that have no clue about that specific subject? Why on Earth would we need advice from someone about Health, if they weren't healthy themselves? If you wanted to become wealthy, would you go into the world and study poor people? Or would you go and study rich people, and try to figure out what they're doing, and how they got rich? Of course, you would learn from the person who consistently creates wealth.

Let me give you another example, that certainly helped open my eyes. Have you ever been in New York City, during a trash strike? Luckily it hasn't happened on a reoccurring basis, but the cause and effect is a powerful visual for our bodies. Trash piles up on every road, the smell is disgusting, and what you'll notice is that there are rats, everywhere! You wouldn't go to NYC, and if you experienced this firsthand, you would not be saying to yourself, Wow! Look at all the trash these rats brought. Of course, you wouldn't be thinking that, because the garbage piling up on the streets provided the perfect environment attracting the rats. All the garbage provided the rats everything they needed to survive and thrive.

But this is how so many of us approach our health these days! We're all looking for the Germs, the viruses, the rats which are the cause of disease and illness. The reality of it is, the only reason why those germs and viruses ever invade your body is, because you created the waste necessary in your body first, to provide the germs and viruses to exist and grow.

In order to get rid of the rats, you must clean the trash first. In order to be entirely healthy, pumped and juiced, you must cleanse the junk in your body, and create a healthy environment you can sustain. At this point, you may think *"Tollie, that sounds so new-age, I've heard it before, give me a break."* I'm not going to give you a bunch of new age beliefs and let you run with it. There is actually a qualifying science to what I'm about to teach you, so hang with me. You see it is the backwards philosophy on health in most of our lives that creates the confusion, the sickness and disease. Most doctors are trained to look for the cause of the disease, to look for the viruses, to kill the viruses, bacteria and the germs.

THIS IS AS FUTILE AS TRYING TO KILL ALL THE RATS IN A TRASH INFESTED CITY.

The Body of a Warrior | Spirit of a Dreamer

Lets take the United States as a benchmark for an example. If the above backwards healing philosophy of treating symptoms worked remarkably well, then why would 1 out of 2 people die of heart disease in the US? And 1 out of 3 from cancer? More and more doctors now recognize that the former health model system doesn't work, and they're turning to other holistic methods of healing and curing disease.

When I say holistic I don't suggest a new age mumbo jumbo, I am referring to new, intelligent and scientifically proven, recently discovered information which more and more people are becoming aware of.

Before I go on, I want you to understand this: Your health is not some highly complex phenomenon which you can't gain complete control over. You don't have to hand over your health to an expert who will know what to do with it. All you need is profound knowledge; profound in the sense that it is straightforward and immediately relevant to your life. Your views of health will affect you more in your life than any pill, any disease or any doctor you see, and my aim is to help you develop a new, empowering and optimistic belief system about your health by delivering you this information.

The reason why so many of us have such whacked beliefs about our health is because most of the things we learn about health we learned as kids and we usually learn our health beliefs from people who aren't necessarily healthy and energetic at all! We're subconsciously taught that symptoms are the cause of disease and that the world is an evil place full of viruses and germs out there to ruin our lives.

As a result, most of us end up in life styles where health is a deep mystery, and we never pay any attention to our bodies. Unless, of course, we get a 'dis-ease,' then it makes sense to go rushing into the doctor asking for a remedy. As you read this, and begin to form these new understandings.

I WANT YOU TO DEVELOP A NEW BELIEF:

Your body, is your temple, it is where your soul resides, it is the single most important thing in your life and comes first before anything else. Because, without your energy, vitality and stamina, you won't even be able to use your love mojo...

Your Inner Electrical Plant | The Acid-Alkaline Balance

Why Do We Actually Get Sick? Why Do We Get Pain?

What exactly is it that creates energy, vitality and unprecedented health in us? There are of course a thousand answers to this timeless question, but what I want to introduce to you here is the concept of acidity and alkalinity in your body, it is a concept so profound and unpretentious that will put everything you have ever learned about health in your life into a crystal clear perspective. The answer is, it's in your blood. What keeps us alive, is a perfect question to start us off. What makes all the cells in our body flourish for 100 or more years on this planet? Most people don't know that your body is one enormous Power Plant which works on electricity. If you were to imagine a dimmer switch in your room, that you can turn up and down to control the light intensity in your room. Think of that dimmer switch in your body for a second.

All the cells in your body communicate thru a remarkably sophisticated system of nerve signals, which are decidedly, electrical signals, driven by electricity in your body. All the food you eat is broken down into micro particles called colloids. These colloids are moved thru your body by electricity. What would happen if this constant electrical charge in your body went down? Would your energy levels go up or down? What if this electrical charge went thru the roof? Would your energy and health go thru the roof, as well? You bet, and you'll learn more about it and how to control this charge in a moment. What makes this constant electric life given current in your body possible? In order for you to live, there is a delicate chemical balance

The Body of a Warrior | Spirit of a Dreamer

in your blood, which produces this life giving electric force in your body. This balance is between two primary forces Acid and Alkaline.

Let's take a stroll down memory lane for a moment and recall what we learned in high school chemistry. Do you remember that acidity and alkalinity is measured by a pH scale? Yes, I know it's been a long time, and if trying to remember days past, where stories of our parent's walking 30 miles to school in 50 feet of snow, with no shoes is all the your memory will allow you to recall, let me refresh your memory. In school, we learned how acidity and alkalinity is measured on a pH scale, where 1 pH is absolutely acid, and 14 pH is absolutely alkaline. The pH balance point is 7 pH. The operative level your body needs to produce proper currents in your bodies pH is a level of, 7.36 pH (*which is slightly more alkaline*).

7.36 pH is essential, if this number would shift by just 1 pH you would die instantly.

Because your cells could not function, also all the organs in your body would shut down. This pH balance takes place in your blood. Your blood is the river of life, the force which keeps you alive your entire life even though you're not even aware of it. Your blood is constantly running through every cell of your body. It is also your blood, which carries oxygen throughout your entire body, keeping you alive. It's noteworthy you understand how acid and alkaline balance affects your blood.

All of your blood cells have an electrical charge of their own. The electrical charge enables your blood cells to travel freely throughout your body. The center of a blood cell has a positive (+) electrical charge. The outside of a blood cell has a negative (-) electrical charge. The reason why your blood cells have a negative electrical charge on the outside is so they can repel each other. (*Two negative charges repel each other.*) The negative charge prevents blood cells from sticking together. We all know that when blood cells stick together it can ultimately lead to death. Fully charged your blood cells travel quickly through your blood vessels and arteries providing the oxygen your body needs to stay on the ball. In just a moment, I'll explain what acid is, how your body produces it and the overall effect on your health. Yes, there is more to acid in your body than just indigestion. Let's understand at what happens to your blood when this unique balance

The Body of a Warrior | Spirit of a Dreamer

is out of whack. I am going to explain the principal reason why we get sick. I'll tell you why we are tired and zapped of all our energy. Also, why we get diseases and why so many of us have a sluggish feeling all the time in our daily lives, and it's because of our blood.

Our blood is the river of life, blood is the source of energy throughout our entire body. It is blood which keeps our entire internal electrical power plant working.

When the pH balance in your blood shifts out of balance, it turns more acid, the acid level in your blood strips the negative charge around your blood cells. This causes the repelling force between your blood cells to dilute dramatically. This creates a lot of problems for your blood cells, your blood cells begin to clump and stick together. Think of this as if your blood is turning to a creamy sludge mixture when your blood cells start sticking together. Your blood cells clog together and have trouble getting through to all your blood vessels. This causes your blood to move slower, and many cells in your body will not get enough oxygen, and your body will begin to suffocate. When red blood cells are stripped of their negative charge, they stick together. Do you think these cells have difficulty carrying oxygen to all parts of your body? How do you think this affects the electrical energy in your body?

As these cells clump together they slowly get less and less oxygen to the point where you're fatigued all the time, your energy levels drop super low and the probability of getting sick becomes super high. Here, what's intriguing: as acid increases in your body and keeps attacking your blood cells in this way, your blood cells literally explode. When your blood cells explode, they release acids of their own into your blood stream. At this rate, you begin to compound acid into your blood stream as more and more blood cells begin to explode from the lack of oxygen and increased acid level in your blood. These cells are decidedly unhappy, they cause cancer, depression, sickness and disease.

Create a Body Where Disease Can Not Even Survive

If you're reading this chapter and right now you're suffering from disease, sickness, or if you're tired all the time, this is what's happening in your blood. Does this type of environment in your blood make it easier for germs to grow and prosper in your body, or does it make it more difficult? The answer is obvious: You're creating a waste environment in your blood stream! If someone had this kind of trash in their blood, would it be any surprise if they got sick 6 times per year? Would it be a mystery if they got a terrible disease like cancer?

When the life giving balance in your body becomes more acidic, your body goes thru tremendous strain, you've seen this so far in the pictures of blood cells above. However, if your body simply continued to compound the acid in your blood stream, you would die very quickly. As I said before this pH balance in your body, is so vital, if it's altered by just very little its life threatening to your body. Your body needs this balance to keep the electrical current in your body running you would simply die without it. So what does your body do when your environment becomes more trashy (*Acidic*) like with everything that goes on in our body, our body is designed to deal with emergencies so it takes a few measures to:

- A) Re-establish the Acid – Alkaline balance

- B) Protect other parts of your body from Acid

Your body is designed for re-balancing the level of acidity and alkalinity in your blood, to do this it uses alkaline from the food you eat. However, most of us don't eat food with alkaline in it (*as you will learn quickly*). As your body runs out of alkaline from your diet, it begins to use your alkaline reserves. Your body has reserves of alkaline it uses at acid emergencies. However, these reserves don't last terribly long. When the acidity in your blood continues to increase your body runs out of alkalinity reserves and you, reach an alkalinity deficit! This is when most people get a significant DIS-EASE. (*i.e.: Cancer*) When you have an alkalinity deficit, your body will start doing are breaking down the calcium in your bones to use as an aid to this problem. This is why most people shrink when they get older!

There is no actual reason why people should shrink when they get older, it's just because of this alkalinity deficit that most of us go thru, completely unaware of it.

Your body will also begin to break down a lot of your proteins to deal with the alkalinity deficit, which is why most people end up shrinking and looking mighty flabby when we grow older. This is a process most of us call aging.

Your body stores acid in fat cells and when you blood is more acidic, your body will store acid into your fat cells. The reason your body will store acid into blood cells is an attempt to protect your blood and your vital organs. When your body Stores acid in your fat cells it makes it difficult for you to lose weight. This is why so many people struggle to lose fat and even when they do, they most often gain it right back very quickly. We'll explore this in full detail very soon. Also, your body moves acid into vital organs, once alkaline reserves are gone. When the body has no more alkaline sources to re-balance the alkaline/acidity equation, it will concentrate acid into the weakest parts of your body. I.e., Your kidneys, liver and your colon. For most people, this is a time when cancer is most imminent.

When the acidity level in your blood is high, this is a vital emergency for your blood vessels and your arteries. What do you think acid does to your arteries? If your body didn't do anything about the acid in your blood, it would burn a hole in your arterial walls. Living with holes in your arteries obviously wouldn't be fun. Your body searches for a binding agent, and uses cholesterol to protect the arterial walls from the acid in your blood. This is quite natural, and all our bodies use cholesterol in this fashion. However, the problem arises when we get into an alkalinity deficit and when the acidity level keeps rising. Cholesterol keeps building up; your blood is already clumped together due to acid and has even more trouble getting through your arteries with all the cholesterol built up in your blood vessels. Compounded with the effect of your blood clumping together as it's stripped of its life giving negative exterior charge, and the extra

The Body of a Warrior | Spirit of a Dreamer

acidity in your blood as your blood cells explode. It's not a pretty picture! But it does give you a better perspective of why so many people suffer from heart disease.

"Okay Tollie, you've told me all about acid and how it works, but what exactly is acid? What am I doing in my life that could be producing acid, and how can I obtain a level of health in my life where my acidity / alkalinity level is always balanced?" Let's get to that right now...

If you think about it, cancer cells are actually cells that are struggling so hard persevere and adapt to their trash environment that they multiply by the hordes. What you may notice is that your acid / alkaline balance is actually a reflection of your life and your inner world. The life giving balance of acid and alkalinity in your body is determined by two things. Your diet how much alkaline you take in and the energy, or megahertz you take in. Also, your lifestyle plays a significant role, your emotions, thoughts and your actions will have a direct impact on your bodies alkalinity. What must take place in order for our fragile acid/alkaline balance to get disturbed?

THE ANSWER IS: MOST OFTEN, THIS DISTURBANCE BEGINS WITH A DISRUPTION IN OUR LIVES FIRST.

The primary reason why so many people have a high acidity level in their blood is because of what they eat! And yes, I know you've probably heard about nutrition a million times, and you've heard people ranting to you about eating vegetables and all that other crap. I'm about to summarize for you a large chunk of what this whole chapter has been leading up to so far. We all talk an immense deal about eating properly, but most people never honestly do it. So I hope that this chapter has opened your eyes up. I hope you will be encouraged to the point actually to use what I'm about to show you here, and experience the many incredible changes in your life. I promise you if you use this information, your energy level, and your health will shoot through the roof!

The Body of a Warrior | Spirit of a Dreamer

What Foods Produce Acid In Your System?

Before we list some of these foods, we must examine a bit more about energy. Then this will become plainly visible. As you recall, your body operates on an electric force your whole life which is possible through the delicate balance of acid and alkaline in your blood. The state of your blood is also incredibly pertinent to this life giving electric force.

THE ENERGY, WHICH YOUR BODY OPERATES ON, IS MEASURED IN MEGAHERTZ (MHZ) -

* 1 Megahertz is a measure of vibration or energy.

* 1 Megahertz is equivalent to about 1 million vibrations per second.

How much energy (*megahertz*) does your body need to maintain to function and live at a healthy, operational level? The answer is about 70 MHz. Your body operates on a 70 MHz Range.

In fact, scientists have measured how many Megahertz's each one of our vital organs roughly operates on, here's a brief list:

* Your Brain 72 to 78 MHz

* Your Colon 58 to 65 MHz

- Your Liver 60 to 65 MHz

- Your Stomach 58 to 65 MHz

CAN YOU SEE HOW MOST OF YOUR BODY OPERATES ON THE 70 MHZ RANGE?

This is the energy level your body must stay at to remain healthy, vibrant and energetic. The challenge is most of the foods we are eating do not provide this energy. What happens is we eat foods that provide us with less energy than we actually need.

THESE LOW ENERGY FOODS ARE ALSO HIGH ACID FOODS WHICH CAUSE OUR BLOOD ACIDITY TO SKY ROCKET. FOR EXAMPLE:

- Chocolate Cake has 1 MHz of Energy

- Big Mac has 5 MHz of Energy

HERE, IS JUST AN EXAMPLE OF SOME LOW ENERGY FOOD AND DIETS WITH HIGH ACIDITY:

- High Animal Protein Diets

- High Sugar Diet

- Alcohol - Alcohol is the absolute maximum acid product you could intake.

- Spicy and Hard to Digest Foods

- Saturated Fat Products

- Chips

- Cookies

- Hot Dogs

- Nachos

The Second Element | Which Produces Acid In Your Body, Is Your Emotions.

All types of stressful, negative emotions produce a spike in your acid levels. Some of the emotions that will produce acid are anger, resentment, worry, and frustration. If you think about it, can you remember the last time you felt any one of these emotions? How does you body feel, when you are in a state of anger or frustration? We all can accept when you are in a state of resentment, it feels terrible, and your mojo is in a funk, it can feel like a deep churning pressure in your stomach. That stomach pressure is part of the acid which is building up in your blood as you indulge in these emotions, and you thought it was just gas...

Honestly, most aches and pains are just part of the process of the body trying to detoxify itself, and remove the build up of acid in your system. Our body cleanses itself and some of the signs this process is taking place are a headache, migraine, muscle pain, and fatigue. These are all signs of your blood being clogged up due to you having too much acid. Let's look at two examples, which will put everything we have discussed so far into a perspective so that you will be able immediately to implement this extensive information in your life.

Let's take the Flu Season as our first example. Often times we hear doctors and media referring to the flu season. As if, the flu virus had a favorite time in the year to come and mess things up for people. Let's take a closer look at the flu season, and why so many people get sick at this time. In most cultures, the holiday season is a period of extreme temperature hot or cold, depending on which hemisphere you live on. Since we know stress can increase acid in your body, is there more stress during the holidays? Definitely! All the added responsibilities, all your existing responsibilities, family members coming into town, in-laws coming into town, extended communication with other people, worry, frustration, and often anger.

We also talked about how food can wreak havoc in your body. What kind of food do we eat during the holidays? Is it healthy, nutritious, is it what we consider balanced food? Heck no! Think of the things you eat during the holidays, turkey, gravy, potatoes, pies, and don't forget the icing on the CAKE! All these foods are extremely low in MHz and high in acid. You create an energy deficit and an alkaline deficit. Oh oh… look out, here comes dis-ease. What about toxicity, do we add toxicity more during this time of the year? Sure we do, especially alcohol, think about all the Christmas parties, and then rolling right into New Years. Add the stress, food, extremes in temperatures, and throw in alcohol, we know have the total product of decay making it a recipe for disaster.

Most people combine all four of these elements together during the holiday season and create a significant alkaline and energy deficiency in their blood. Is it a mystery why they get sick? Knowing what you now know of course not! But most of us are trained to look out for the flu bug.

In reality, the flu isn't the basis of the flu season any more than the rats are the cause of all the trash in New York during the trash strike. It's just all about the environment we create in our blood. Here, is one more example.

Mr. X's *"Ultimate Weight Loss Plan"* Mr. X is over weight and has been struggling with his weight all his life. Finally, he gets so frustrated, so determined, so angry with himself that he decides to make a change:

"This is it! I have had it, I am going to lose 50 pounds, I am going to get a personal trainer, I am going to eat right, I am going to look good! ARRGGHHH GO, GO, GO!!!"

Mr. X gets so determined that for the next 2 weeks he relentlessly works out till he's almost dead at the gym. He over works his body and adds even more acid due to the high intensity physical stress. He gets stressed out whenever he sees a Big Mac and becomes deadly serious and hostile about everything he eats.

"I'm going to do all this correctly, right now! I am dead serious about this!"

Well, what Mr. X doesn't know is that he's creating significant acid in his system through his emotions, and his frigidness about everything he eats. He's become so serious, so rigid and so stressed out and worried about his weight and about losing it that his blood begins to become more acidic. As a result, his body stores acid in his fat cells, making losing fat extremely difficult for him to get rid of. After three weeks Mr. X gets so frustrated, he's noticed that he's actually gained two pounds. Out of frustration he gives up and heads for a tub of ice-cream devouring all of it in front of the TV. Have you ever known someone who tried losing weight and was so frigid about their diet? Yet they never lost weight? This is why so many people fail at losing weigh and achieving the body of their dreams.

Here, are the easy steps to alkalize and energize your blood. So now that you know how the acid / alkaline balance in your blood affects your health, your energy levels, and your life, you're probably dying to know exactly what you must do to make sure you re-establish your balance, keep your blood healthy, and the electric force in your body at maximum output.

The method to do this is painless and breaks down into three steps. If you follow this advice and implement it into your life, the results you'll experience will be nothing short of extraordinary. You must alkalize and energize your body.

The Body of a Warrior | Spirit of a Dreamer

Your first step is you must super hydrate your body.

If you've read anything by me before then, you probably know that I usually preach a lot about drinking water every day. Most people who just hear something about this subject think:

"Oh no, another guy who's going to talk about drinking 8 glasses of water per day!" "That's right!... so if you know this already? Why aren't you doing it?"

If you're not drinking at least 8 cups of water a day, chances are you are creating a water deficit in your body. If you have a water deficit your blood suffers extremely, as water provides a crucial source of alkalinity in the body. If you're dehydrated your blood will clump together, and everything we've talked about above will be accelerated.

HERE, IS A BREAK DOWN OF HOW MUCH WATER YOUR BODY USES EVERYDAY:

- Your Intestines use about a half a cup of water each day.

- Breathing uses about one and a third cups of water every day.

- Your lungs use about two cups of water on a daily basis.

- Your skin uses about two cups of water every day.

- Your kidneys use about Five and half cups of water every day.

Under normal conditions, the body loses approximately twelve cups of water every day! The main effect of dehydration is seen in your blood, your blood clumps together and can't carry oxygen to all parts of your body. As an effect, you'll feel tired, low on energy, and your immune system will be lowered. Studies show that most people are so dehydrated they mistake the body's natural demand for water for hunger! Most people find difficulty drinking eight cups of water a day, as too much of a chore. However, this is usually only because your body has adapted to severe dehydration. Once you start drinking more water and give your body the message that *"Hey, we have water! We can have all we want! We're not in a desert after all!"* it will get the point, and you will actually feel thirsty more often.

The challenge for our bodies is that we're constantly presenting drinking fluids that aren't part of what our bodies were meant to take in naturally. Our bodies cope with it and adapt. The moment you start giving your body what it truly needs and deserves it will thank you for it, and it won't want to go back to the other crap! Also if, you tried drinking water before and your story was: *"Well… water just makes me feel sick…"* It's not the water that's making you feel sick. If, you feel this way after drinking water, it means you are super over acid and in a substantial alkaline deficit. As you drink water, your body tries to remove the acid from your system with the life giving source you're providing for it, this results in you feeling ill as the acid moves through your blood stream and out of your system. You will feel this way only briefly and will begin to love water after only a couple days.

If you take this message to heart and decide totally to hydrate yourself once and for all, here's a quick method: Buy a 2.0 Liter Bottle of Pop of your choice (*Coca Cola, Pepsi, Sprite...*) take the bottle to the bathroom and pour the contents down the toilet as you do this, say to yourself. I'm not drinking this crap anymore! Clean out the bottle and fill it with drinking water. This is approximately how much water you should be drinking every day. Carry this bottle with you around the house and whenever you feel like drinking/eating some junk, take a sip of water. Your goal should be to finish at least half the bottle in a day. Also, keep a glass of water by your bed when you go to sleep. When you wake up, drink the whole glass before you set off on your day.

THE NEXT STEP IS YOU MUST EAT FOODS WHICH ARE HIGH IN ALKALINE AND ENERGY (MHZ).

The essence of this entire chapter comes down to this last part right now. If, you learn nothing else here, take this honest advice your energy level will skyrocket. Your goal is totally to alkalize your body. Foods which are high in alkaline, is usually foods that grow out in the sun like, vegetables, and fruit. The reason for this is that the chlorophyll in these foods captures the energy in the sun, which is essentially the source of all life. Now you may say:

- *"Oh no, another guy who's going to talk about eat vegetables"*

OR

- "I've eaten vegetables all my life, and I still get sick, and I'm low on energy."

First of all, there's, a reason why eating normal vegetables has little effect, secondly the reason is: Most of the foods we buy today are chemically processed. This includes fruits, vegetables, and everything else. Food processing takes an enormous chunk of this energy away and often adds a ton of crummy stuff, as well. The alternative is to drink green drinks. I rarely promote any kind of supplement but, please bear with me as I introduce you to this concept.

You may recall I mentioned someone by the name of Alex Guerrero. You may have seen him on TV; Doctor Alex Guerrero was one of the various doctors who massively investigated and researched this acidity / alkalinity concept, and he's the recommended expert in this today. Since the popularization, of the acid concept many people have formulated green drink supplements. You can find these in the nutrition segment, in any grocery store. A green drink is essentially an assortment of various green foods, wheat grass, spinach, carrot, and tomatoes. All these foods are powdered down into teaspoon servings you mix with water. (*Just one of these drinks has over 350 MHZ of energy.*)

Listen, if you're fatigue, or if you have a low immune system please take this advice and use it. You will see a massive boost in your energy and health. These drinks are made from unprocessed foods, and they super alkalize and energize your body. Rush to your local grocery store and go into the nutrition section, and get one right away. Then go an on a three day cleanse (*Described below in detail*), to alkalize and energize your body. I promise you, if you do this for just three days, you won't believe the change you will make in your life.

The Third Step Is You Must Become Aware Of Your Emotions.

Look, it is essential for you to know that you don't have to be afraid of your life going to hell in a hand-basket because of your health. You have full control over your health. The belief I have is that your body and health is something driven by your mind and spirit. You don't have to believe this, but you are welcome to adapt and try on this belief in your life if you want. But, please understand this, if your life and your emotions are messed up, chances are your health will be too! This has been preached by countless self improvement and new age authors, but now that you've read this chapter you know the acid truth of it.

Stress creates acid, acid gets you out of balance which messes up your blood, which messes up your energy, which messes up your health, which in the end messes up your life!

I encourage you to start becoming more aware and conscious of what's undoubtedly going on in your life. Sickness and Disease are merely Symptoms of what is certainly going on underneath in your life; getting rid of the symptoms will not fix your life.

Here, is how you can apply this information quickly into your life. So far you've heard me rant on and on about using this stuff, well I'm going to keep on doing it! Not because I'm a maniac, but because I honestly care about you. I also know and understand that most people who make a decision change their life or read something interesting usually do nothing about it, or they say *"I'll do that….tomorrow…"* and they put it off. Why do most people fail to make a change in their life? Because they never get started! That's why it's absolutely massively crucial that you get started immediately and create momentum. Don't leave the sight of this chapter with out taking some action to implement this new information in your life.

Seriously to get going on this I highly recommend you get going on a minimum three Day, Alkalizing and Energizing Body Cleanse. Follow this advice for three days straight, and just do these three easy things.

- First thing is you need to drink 8 glasses of Water per day.

- Second, drink at least 2 green drinks per day.

- Third eliminate foods with high acidity from your diet.

The purpose of this is to cleanse yourself, to feel the new found energy and health you will produce by doing this consistently for three days. I promise you once you feel this energy you will never want to go back. You may think making these small changes in your diet won't affect your life much. If so allow me to correct your thinking about it. These small changes will unquestionably revolutionize your life.

As we wrap this up, here is the secret to all of this. First of all, does it make sense to you that you have to provide your body with more alkalinity to make your body stay in balance? Sure it does, because we all live stressful lifestyles, or acid lifestyles. Remember is you are going to live an acid lifestyle, by the way, you eat, or by your stress or the way your living just remember it takes four parts of alkalinity to balance out one part of acid. If you just create this balance in your life, by drinking more water, by drinking a green drink or wheat grass and giving yourself enough greens the changes can be miraculous. It's a simple addition to your life, yet the improvements in your life are so radical its almost hard to imagine. Let me give you an incredible example, there is a guy I want to introduce you to by the name of Sean.

Sean's story (*Sean Stephenson*) begins as a wish actually, because his life changed because of his Make-A-Wish, which was granted. Sean's wish was to meet Tony Robbins, and so Tony had him attend one of his three day seminars. Sean was 21 years old when he attended Tony's seminar. Sean had stunted growth which was apparent when he when next to Tony and was only knee high. Sean was in a wheel chair when he attended the seminar, his bones were so brittle which meant he couldn't walk obviously, his parents handed Sean to Tony on stage. When his father handed his son Sean over to Tony, he told him:

"Open your hands fully, and don't squeeze him at all, if you squeeze him at all you will break his bones."

Sean was in such a fragile state that even a cough has caused him to break a rib before. Because his bones were so brittle, he was considered by all medical experts as terminal. After the seminar, Tony sat down and had lunch with Sean. Tony asked him what he believed about everything he just experienced. Sean said:

"Well I believe that there has got to be an answer, but no one has been able to give me one."

TONY REPLIED:

"Well, I'm not a doctor, and I can't tell you what to do. I know couple experts, who understand acid alkaline, and I've got to believe that if your bones are so brittle that they are breaking when you cough or sneeze you've got to have an enormously acidic body. I believe that if you talk to some of these people that at least they could make your life more comfortable, and who knows maybe even save your life."

So, Sean went and saw one of Tony's experts, and he ended up staying three days with this person. Sean changed his entire diet, and remember his prognosis was terminal. Tony checked in with his parents on occasion, and they said he felt better and better each day. Then six months later not only was Sean still alive, but he was stronger than ever. He was able to cough and sneeze without any fear.

Within twelve months, Sean showed up at one of Tony's seminars to surprise him, and he rolled up onto the stage in his wheelchair, and said to Tony, *"Let me show you what I can do now."* Sean got out of his wheelchair and did pushups, and pulled up his shirt and showed Tony his six pack on his stomach. Sean is now lecturing all across the country. He has been written up in various newspapers and magazines as this wonder kid, and he is telling everyone what you can do to transform your body. He is explaining how you can transform your body by understanding what your body needs, and his prognosis is no longer death. Here, is a young man who literally has his life back.

You see most of the changes in our lives happen so gradually, we never even notice the difference until its too late. It's kinda like if you put a frog in boiling water it will jump right out, but if you put it in cold water and boil the water slowly, it will boil to death. In the same way, most of us walk around dead and low on energy not even knowing the potential we could be truly living.

I promise you if you take my advice for a minimum of three days, you will experience a massive boost of energy in your life that you will only be able to compare to a time when you were a little child full of unmeasurable energy.

WE LIVE IN A WORLD WHERE THE LAST THING WE USUALLY LOOK AT IS OUR HEALTH AND OUR BODIES UNTIL IT'S TOO LATE.

I hope this information has been a wake up call for you, and if you already consider yourself at a measurable level of health, than I hope you will still apply this and watch as the level of energy in your life shoots to levels you never felt before.

Remember stop looking for the rats in your life and your body.

Seek out the methods to clean up the environment that invited them over in the first place.

The Body of a Warrior | Spirit of a Dreamer

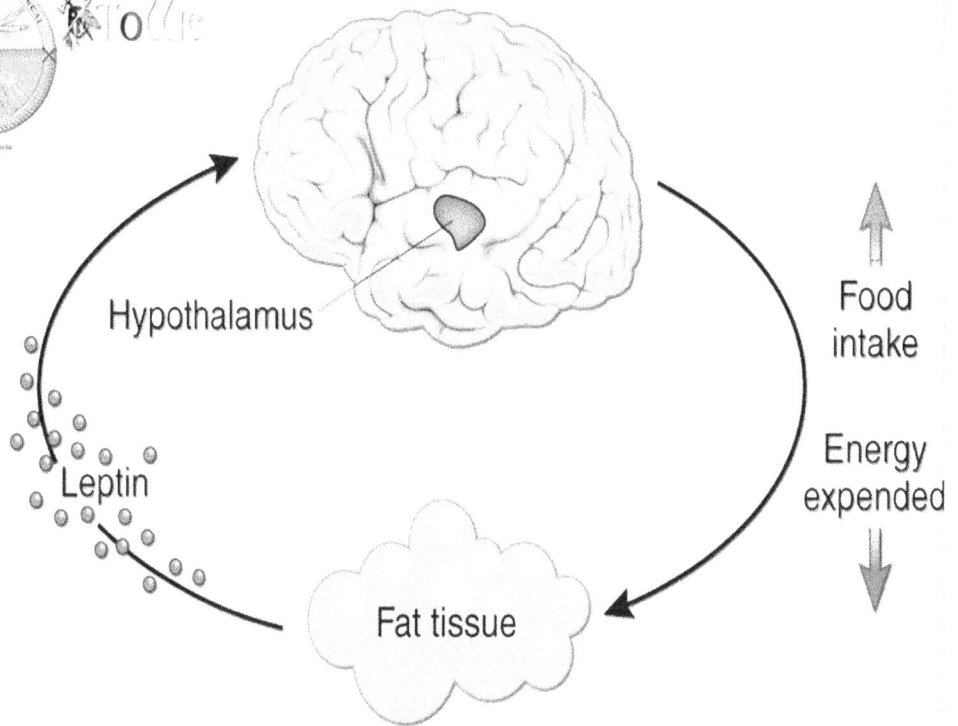

Homeostatic Balance

Homeostatic Balance

U.S. 2012 Chart
Leading Causes of Death

	15–24	25–34	35–44	45–54	55–64
WHITE	1 SUICIDE · 2 CANCER · 3 HEART DISEASE	1 SUICIDE · 2 CANCER · 3 HEART DISEASE	1 HEART DISEASE · 2 CANCER · 3 SUICIDE	1 HEART DISEASE · 2 CANCER · 3 SUICIDE	1 HEART DISEASE · 2 CANCER · 3 RESPIRATORY DISEASE
BLACK	1 SUICIDE · 2 HEART DISEASE · 3 CANCER	1 HIV · 2 HEART DISEASE · 3 SUICIDE	1 HEART DISEASE · 2 HIV · 3 CANCER	1 CANCER · 2 HEART DISEASE · 3 HYPERTENSION	1 HEART DISEASE · 2 CANCER · 3 HYPERTENSION
ASIAN/PACIFIC ISL.	1 SUICIDE · 2 CANCER · 3 HEART DISEASE	1 SUICIDE · 2 CANCER · 3 HEART DISEASE	1 CANCER · 2 HEART DISEASE · 3 SUICIDE	1 CANCER · 2 HEART DISEASE · 3 HYPERTENSION	1 CANCER · 2 HEART DISEASE · 3 HYPERTENSION
HISPANIC/ALL RACES	1 SUICIDE · 2 CANCER · 3 HEART DISEASE	1 SUICIDE · 2 CANCER · 3 HEART DISEASE	1 HEART DISEASE · 2 CANCER · 3 HIV	1 HEART DISEASE · 2 CANCER · 3 LIVER DISEASE	1 CANCER · 2 HEART DISEASE · 3 LIVER DISEASE
NATIVE AMER.	1 SUICIDE · 2 CANCER · 3 HEART DISEASE	1 SUICIDE · 2 HEART DISEASE · 3 LIVER DISEASE	1 HEART DISEASE · 2 LIVER DISEASE · 3 SUICIDE	1 CANCER · 2 LIVER DISEASE · 3 DIABETES	1 HEART DISEASE · 2 CANCER · 3 DIABETES
WHITE	1 SUICIDE · 2 CANCER · 3 HEART DISEASE	1 CANCER · 2 SUICIDE · 3 HEART DISEASE	1 CANCER · 2 HEART DISEASE · 3 SUICIDE	1 CANCER · 2 HEART DISEASE · 3 HYPERTENSION	1 CANCER · 2 HEART DISEASE · 3 RESPIRATORY DISEASE
BLACK	1 HEART DISEASE · 2 CANCER · 3 HIV	1 HIV · 2 CANCER · 3 HEART DISEASE	1 CANCER · 2 HEART DISEASE · 3 HIV	1 CANCER · 2 HEART DISEASE · 3 HYPERTENSION	1 CANCER · 2 HEART DISEASE · 3 DIABETES
ASIAN/PACIFIC ISL.	1 SUICIDE · 2 CANCER · 3 HEART DISEASE	1 CANCER · 2 SUICIDE · 3 HEART DISEASE	1 CANCER · 2 HEART DISEASE · 3 HYPERTENSION	1 CANCER · 2 HEART DISEASE · 3 HYPERTENSION	1 CANCER · 2 HEART DISEASE · 3 HYPERTENSION
HISPANIC/ALL RACES	1 CANCER · 2 SUICIDE · 3 HEART DISEASE	1 CANCER · 2 HEART DISEASE · 3 SUICIDE	1 CANCER · 2 HEART DISEASE · 3 HIV	1 CANCER · 2 HEART DISEASE · 3 HYPERTENSION	1 CANCER · 2 HEART DISEASE · 3 DIABETES
NATIVE AMER.	1 SUICIDE · 2 CANCER · 3 HEART DISEASE	1 SUICIDE · 2 CANCER · 3 LIVER DISEASE	1 CANCER · 2 LIVER DISEASE · 3 HEART DISEASE	1 CANCER · 2 HEART DISEASE · 3 LIVER DISEASE	1 HEART DISEASE · 2 DIABETES · 3 LIVER DISEASE

SOURCE: Centers for Disease Control. NOTE: These are the most likely causes of death for each race, sex, and age range in America, excepting homicide and accidental death. A collaboration between GOOD and Way Shape Form.

Causes of Death in America

pH
Balance
Guide

10 FOOD
Green vegetables,
Cirus fruits

9.0 Mushrooms
Soy Milk

8.5 Tofu
Nuts & Rice

pH Alkaline

8.0 EMOTIONS
Joy

7.5 Peace
Love

Neutral pH **7.0**

6.5 FOOD
Sugar
Artificial Sweetners

6.0 Alcohol
Coffee
Meat

Acidic pH

Dairy products
Bread & Cakes

EMOTIONS
4.0 Anger
Stress

3.0 Tiredness
Fear

pH Balance Guide

Acid/Alkaline Food Comparison Chart

EAT LESS　　　　　　　　　　　　　　　　　　　　　　　　**EAT MORE**

◁◀◀ MORE ACIDIC　　　　　NEUTRAL　　　MORE ALKALINE ▷▷▷▷

Soft Drinks	Popcorn	Most Purified Water	Fruit Juices	Most Tap Water	Apples	Avocados	pHresh gre
Energy Drink	Cream Cheese	Distilled Water	Most Grains	Most Spring Water	Almonds	Green Tea	Spinach
Carbonated Drinks	Buttermilk	Coffee	Eggs	River Water	Tomatoes	Lettuce	Broccol
	Pastries		Fish		Grapefruit	Celery	Artichok
	Pasta	Chocolate	Tea		Corn	Peas	Brussel Spr
	Cheese	Sweetened Fruit Juice	Soy Milk		Mushrooms	Sweet Potatoes	Cabbag
	Pork		Coconut		Turnip	Egg Plant	Cauliflow
	Beef	Pistachios	Lima Bean:		Olives	Green Beans	Carrots
	Beer, Wine		Plums			Beets	Cucumbe
	Black Tea	White Bread	Brown Rice			Blueberries	Lemon:
	Pickles		Cocoa			Pears	Limes
	Roasted Nuts	Peanuts	Oats			Grapes	Seawee
	Vinegar	Nuts	Oysters			Kiwi	Asparagi
	Sweet & Low		Salmon			Melons	Kale
Processed & efined Food	Equal, Nutra Sweet					Tangerines	Radish
						Figs	Collard Gre
						Dates	Onion
						Mangoes	*Raw / Unco*
						Papayas	

Acid/Alkaline Food Comparison Chart

Chapter VII

The Emotional Code

"I KNOW THAT MAN IS CAPABLE OF GREAT DEEDS. BUT IF HE ISN'T CAPABLE OF GREAT EMOTION, WELL, HE LEAVES ME COLD" -ALBERT CAMUS, THE PLAGUE

Last chapter we talked about the power and importance of energy in your body. But you can have a lot of physical energy in your body and have it shunted, by investing that energy in emotions, that pull you down. We all have times, when we feel frustrated, overwhelmed, depressed or even angry. We also have times we feel euphoric, joyous, and excited about our lives. The secret is not ever to feel the negative emotion, because that's not fair, this is not about positive thinking or denial. It's about using the power of your emotions as action signals.

See, pretty much every emotion you have felt in your life, is actually a call to action, and what I want to show you in this chapter is how to make that happen.

Can you think of anything more important than how you feel? We kind of touched on this earlier in the book, so let me use some similar examples to kick start you memory. Any time I speak or do a seminar I will always ask people in the audience this question, *"What do you want?"* Now after, I ask the question, I always get an array of answers, anything thing from losing weight, to making loads of money or creating more time for loved ones or being of service to people through charity.

I follow up by asking them, *"Ok, and when you achieve what you want, how is that going to make you feel?"* They will answer:

- "Well I want to lose weight, because I will feel sexier, and create more joy in my life."

- "If I had enough money then I would feel peaceful, and not have to worry about Finances anymore."

- "If I had more time to spend with my loved ones, I would feel like I mattered, and my life had meaning."

But, the reality is in the end, they don't actually want the money, or any of the tangible items, what they truly want is the 'feeling' they hope to achieve, they want to feel better! They want to change the way they feel, they want to change the emotional content of their life, in that moment.

The Emotional Code

I think it's real beneficial for us to take a new look at emotions, because I think maybe you will see that some of the emotions we feel are negative, or the emotions that we feel cause us the most pain, are actually our best friends. Because, these types of emotions maybe giving us signals that we need to make changes. Now, if we heed these emotions, if we utilize them, we can change the quality of our experience and our life immediately. So I want you to see that emotions are the ultimate power, they start wars.

Emotions cause us to get married, and they cause us to get divorced. Emotions cause us to have children, and emotions can cause us to be ill or they can cause us to be healthy.

In essence, the history of your life, history of your world is the history of emotions. Emotions are the core that call us to action and change our entire life.

So, where do emotions come from? What are the real purpose of emotions? What are some of the most intense emotions, we experience on a daily basis, which shape our destiny? And finally, how can we master our emotions and utilize them to shape our lives? In essence, these are the questions I want us to answer in this chapter, but let's start with an easier question. How do you deal with your emotions right now?

I have found that people deal with emotions in primarily one of four different patterns. The first pattern is people avoid their emotions, they literally try and not feel. They try and not have to feel, the emotion of rejection. The problem with this pattern is that is you are always trying to avoid rejection, you are never going to succeed. Because anything in life, that requires you to deal with other human beings on a massive scale when you are taking a step forward, and you are trying to create change exposes you to a point where someone disagrees with you, or rejects you. It is the ultimate fear of rejection keeps people out of relationships they never get to have the feeling they do want which is love. People will never feel intimacy, or a feeling of connectedness because the fear of rejection keeps them out of it, so you can't ever truly avoid negative emotions because they are part of life. Also, negative emotions cause us to grow.

Some people don't try to avoid their emotions; instead they move into the, *"I'm going to endure my emotions,"* phase. Or they go a step further, and they will endure the negative emotions and then deny it. The people who try and endure their negative emotions will try and disassociate themselves from those feelings. You will hear them say something like, *"Oh it doesn't feel that bad."* However, during the whole time they keep stoking the fire inside themselves while thinking about how terrible things are. Or how someone is taking advantage of them. Or how they do everything right, but things just still turn out wrong, and why is it that this always happens to them. In other words, they never change their internal dialogue. They never change their internal focus, or physiology, they keep feeling like crap, but they try to pretend it's not there. They will either deny or dissociate it, and inevitably these erupts. Because the more you don't listen to the messages in your emotions, the more intense they become. You emotions keep hammering on the door louder and louder, trying to get through to you. All of a sudden you feel worse, and worse and worse.

The third thing I see people do is they try and use their emotions for competition. I call it the nursing home olympics, *"you got it bad, let me tell you how I feel," "you think that's a sore, let me show you a real bed sore!"* They think this is going to in some way make them feel better, but this is never going to make you feel better, consistently focusing on negatives. *"You think your job is horrible, let me tell you how bad my job is,"* and they keep competing to make their emotions even worse.

People will compete with others over how they feel, so that they make themselves feel even worse about their own lives. Stay out of this competition, it is not one you want to win. I hope you choose the fourth way to deal with your emotions.

The fourth way to deal with emotions is to learn from them and deploy them. So where do emotions come from? Do emotions just attack as, sitting out in the water hearing the soft sounds of the jaws movie soundtrack, than when the time is right they attack us! Is our emotions like a virus, where all of a sudden we just feel something? Well the correct answer is like we already know, emotions come from other people.

For example, if you feel loved, it's because of what someone else did, they came over and said, they love you. They showed love by hugging you, touching you a certain way, they gave you a kiss and you feel loved.

Do you feel loved because someone came up and touched you in a loving way? No, the truth is the reason you feel love is that you chose to represent the feeling of love when they touched you in that way.

You allowed yourself to feel that way, to have those sensations and feeling of love. You have some rules, criteria that say, when x, y, z happens then I get to feel loved. And then at that moment when all those criteria are met, somebody hugs you, or kisses you, says they love you, etc., you then in your own body create these sensations that you call love. You realize those sensations, you put yourself in that physiology at that moment. Conversely if, you feel crummy, if you feel angry, overwhelmed, depressed, frustrated, and lonely all of these emotions are also created by one person, and that is you. The emotions you feel are due to what you choose to focus on. Emotions are the meaning you attach to any experience in life. Let's repeat that so you remember it, because it is essential.

HOW YOU FEEL, AT ANY MOMENT IN TIME IS REALLY THE RESULT OF THE MEANING YOU HAVE GIVEN TO YOUR EXPERIENCE.

Let's say a man opens the door for a woman. How does that woman feel about that? Well, the answer is it has nothing to do with the actual event, but rather her interpretation of the event. What she chooses to label that event as meaning. Some women feel demeaned by the process. *"How dare you, you male Chauvinist pig!"* You can imagine how some guys look back dumbfounded, thinking, *"What in the world just happened?"* Because what it meant for him was, respect, or to him maybe it meant he was doing it out of appreciation, or love, or even just simply caring. See, what we feel is not based on our experience, but again on our interpretation of our experience. It is the way we represent our experience that determining how we feel.

Look again at that word, represents it means if we spell it out, re-present, in other words something just happened, and now that it just happened we take it in through our five senses, and you make a re-presentation, another presentation of what happened, inside your head.

The way you represent those events will determine how you feel. So in the case of our previous example, the women took the simple act of the man opening the door with a smile on his face and she represented it, inside her head as:

- "He's trying to take advantage of me."

- "He's trying to make me less than him."

- "He's trying to dominate me in some way."

We must be exceedingly careful in the meanings we attach to things. Because, those meanings that we attach to any experience will determine the quality of how we feel about our lives. We must make sure the emotions that we feel, are appropriate. In essence, we want to make sure our emotions are empowering us, and not disempowering us. There are no negative emotions, there are no bad emotions, every emotion serves us, as long as we interpret it in a way that adds a powerful meaning to our life. Something that moves us forward instead of backwards.

Now let's go a step further, and let us analyze the difference between two emotions, by just experiencing them. Stop reading right now, and I want you to think about something you want to happen in the future, and I want you to hope that it will happen. Just take a moment, and close your eyes and hope it will occur, with your eyes closed visually see the event take place in your mind, and just hope, notice how this feels.

Now, I want you to notice, do you see like two different possibilities when you hope? I'm curious, do you see your future event working out, or maybe not working out? But more importantly, how does it feel to hope? Now, that you have opened your eyes, take a moment and change your state a little bit get your mojo flowing by moving your body around some change your physiology.

Now, secondly I want you to consider another emotion. Just for a moment I want you to close your eyes, and think about what you hoped would happen, however, this time I want you to expect it to happen. Put yourself in a state of absolute, expectation where you know it will happen. As you expect, this will happen and as you know this will happen you create that conclusion in your body. Notice how this feels, and notice how this belief is different from hope. As you open your eyes, I want to know what was the difference?

Now, when I ask people in a speaking event, the same question here are some of the answers I get. One of the first differences people will tell me, is that when they hoped, they saw two different examples of their future event. They saw their future event working out and they saw it not working out. So when they would hope for a particular event to occur they held two different options available to them in the future. And they didn't feel tremendously sure when they hoped for a particular outcome. When I asked them which one they liked better, without any question they liked the feeling attached to expecting the event to take place.

IN ADDITION, THEY WILL SAY THINGS LIKE:

"Well I felt like when I was hoping, that I was passive. But, when I was expecting, I was active and felt I could move forward. I felt an intensity to take action and to achieve my goal."

So, what I began to perceive was the difference in these emotions for a lot of people are the way you represent them. Maybe that means you focus on both outcomes or possibilities when you hope. But when you expect something to happen, then you focus on only one option, this is what is going to happen, and it is all you picture, it's the only option and outcome. Additionally, there is this movement when you expect, this sensation, this tension, but it is a positive tension. All emotions have different components. We will learn

The Emotional Code

how to use those components in order to intensify our positive emotions and to minimize our negative emotions.

Now, I had you do the quick exercise for a couple reasons, and I want to reinforce something.

Were you able to hope, your future event would take place a moment ago?

Were you, in fact, able to expect what was going to happen in the future, were you able to feel that difference in your body?

Then once again, I proved to you that you do control your own emotions, don't you.

There was no reason to expect it, nothing I said changed the content of whether or not you would succeed, I just told you to choose to expect, something would work out and you did it. And you did it, and it felt better, right!

So remember, you are always in control of how you feel, nothing in the environment controls you, it is the way you interpret the environment, the meaning you give, the rules you have which determine which positive or negative feelings you give yourself.

What is the Function of Emotions

So why do we have emotions in the first place?

What is the value in emotions, especially painful emotions?

People look at positive emotions and easily see the value of feeling great, and they see negative emotions as some sort of punishment, kinda like a point system. Well, I think it can be kind of like a point system when it comes to our emotions. When we don't follow our own rules, and we don't live by our own values, and by our own life standards, then we certainly give ourselves pain as a way to keep ourselves on track. And it helps us stay on track because we want to avoid pain.

I THINK NEGATIVE EMOTIONS SERVE AN IMMENSELY POWERFUL AND POSITIVE ROLE IN OUR LIFE.

That reason I had already alluded to when we started this chapter. Negative emotions are a signal, that a change is needed. So let's think about how negative emotions signal change. When you feel an emotion like fear, which is an emotion people will try to avoid like the plague, at all costs. We will also seek to avoid any emotion along the same lines such as, worry, concern, or even terror. When you feel anyone of those emotions, you want to recognize there is an embedded signal. Rather than just trying to avoid the feeling, you should listen and notice the signal and utilize it.

The signal of fear is, you must prepare. Now that is a valuable signal, and it is in your body for a reason, it's saying that something may be coming in the near future and that you are going to want to be prepared for it. Either it is a warning to be able to cope with what is coming or prepare to deal with the event, and that's valuable information. We don't want to deny that feeling, we don't want to avoid that emotion and pretend it's not there, thats how Niagara happens.

This is how people get into trouble, emotionally, physically, financially, and in their relationships. They don't want to feel the fear that their relationship isn't working out so they pretend it's still going swell. Until one

The Emotional Code

day, they find themselves five feet from Niagara falls in a boat with no oars, saying oh shoot! and it's to late, and they take an emotional fall. Make sure these emotions serve you.

Emotions Carry Messages

Make Sure These Emotions Serve a Purpose

The way to make sure these emotions serve a purpose are from realizing that every emotion has a message for you. Don't make it wrong, or try and avoid it or even freak out about it as if it is a dreadful thing you feel.

INSTEAD, I WANT YOU TO DO SIX THINGS:

- **NUMBER ONE** | IDENTIFY WHAT THE EMOTION IS.

- **NUMBER TWO** | ACKNOWLEDGE & APPRECIATE THE MESSAGE THE EMOTION IS OFFERING YOU

- **NUMBER THREE** | IS TO GET INCREDIBLY CURIOUS ABOUT THE EMOTION AND WHAT IT IS OFFERING YOU

Do you need to change the way your looking at the world? Do you need to change the way you are acting? Do you need to change the way you are communicating? Use the curiosity to ask yourself how you can use the emotion in a way to make your life better, or stronger, or is this something you genuinely want in your life.

- **NUMBER FOUR** | GET YOURSELF TO FEEL REASSURED BY SEEING THAT YOU'VE WORKED THIS OUT IN THE PAST, AND YOU'VE MADE IT THROUGH THIS EMOTION BEFORE.

- **NUMBER FIVE** | GET YOURSELF CERTAIN THAT YOU CAN HANDLE ANYTHING LIKE IT IN THE FUTURE BY REHEARSING USING THIS EMOTION AS A TOOL OF EMPOWERMENT.

- **NUMBER SIX** | IS TAKING ACTION WHICH CAN CHANGE YOUR WHOLE LIFE.

Those six tools I just went through real fast are in essence what we are going to learn and utilize.

Now we aren't just going to learn how to change how we feel, but using how we feel, even those negative feelings to make our life better. Now, I want to say something, while working with people I have learned so much about emotions, and I have been intrigued by the power within any given emotion. I will tell you one thing I have noticed going through hearing how so many people describe all the emotions they feel on any occasion.

There is one common theme I see with all people, and that is their ability to draw in extraordinary detail their negative emotions, and not their positive ones. I get to learn about how people get frustrated, insecure, lonely, bored, sad, angry, impatient, annoyed, anxious, unsure, guilty, unworthy, depressed, disrespected, humiliated, can you believe I do this. But, the bright side is this, I get also to learn about how they have joy, love, success, abundance, contribution, flexibility, creativity, power, impact, curiosity, wonder, beauty, spirituality, respect, sincerity, integrity, kindness, confidence, ecstasy, and you name it! We have lots of pleasure we can have in our lives too.

The Challenge Is That Most People Spend Their Time In the Negative

People spend more time trying to avoid negative emotions instead of using the emotions to their advantage.

So what I have tried to do is sit down and see how there are all these ways to describe each emotion. The question is do enough emotions fall into a group or categories that we can chunk them down. In other words, you might say:

"Well I'm really feeling concerned or worried, or anxious or scared or terrified."

And well all of those are just a form of fear.

So this is what I want to do, I want to create a model for each other. A model that I have created is primarily where I fit all emotions into ten categories. Now the challenge is that we all have different labels, with what each emotion means. So yours may not agree with the ones I am putting down.

But just for our ability to have a conversation, and for the ability to deal with our emotions, we are going to say there are ten types of emotions.

Here, are the ten emotions, and I want you to jot them down, on a piece of paper. So write down the ten categories of emotions, and here they are.

The Emotional Code

The Ten Categories of the Emotional Code

So again the ten categories are:

I. UNCOMFORTABLE EMOTIONS

Uncomfortable Emotions: Which is a pretty sizable category. I am primarily describing in this category emotions that don't have a tremendous amount of intensity, but they do bug you, bother you. Feelings of boredom are a perfect example, or being impatient, uneasy, distress, or even mildly embarrassed would fit under feeling uncomfortable for most people.

2. FEARFUL EMOTIONS

These feelings could be, concern, apprehension, worry, anxiety, feeling scared or even terrified. These are all different types of emotions that we are going to relate to fear.

3. HURTFUL EMOTIONS

Any kind of feeling you would link to hurt. And we are going to talk about how most of our feelings of hurt comes from a sense of loss.

4. ANGER EMOTIONS

Anger again has a large variety of feelings, everything from mildly irritated to angry to livid, to resentful, to furious, to enraged. Any of the emotions in this category, we are going to talk about as an anger emotion.

5. FRUSTRATION EMOTIONS

These are any emotions that you linked to being held back, or hindered in your pursuit of something.

6. DISAPPOINTMENT EMOTIONS

Anything that makes you truly sad and/or defeated as a result of something you expected but it didn't work out well.

7. GUILTY EMOTIONS

Maybe another way of describing guilty emotions would be emotions of regret.

8. INADEQUATE EMOTIONS

Any emotion you've experienced which caused you to feel as if you were less than or unworthy, would fit in this category as well called inadequacy.

9. OVERLOADED OR OVERWHELMED EMOTIONS

Now, I am using the word overloaded to make it soft, but what I mean is, you feel as if you are overwhelmed, hopeless, depressed, anything that makes you feel as if there is more than you can deal with. Then those emotions would go into the overloading category of emotions.

10. LONELY EMOTIONS

Anything that makes you feel alone like you're lonely like your apart from or separate from would fit into this category.

Ok, it is a extensive set of categories, but here is the reasoning behind my madness. I want to train you, and myself because I just started using this technique myself because I just came up with it, and it's super-duper in a far out kinda way if I do say so myself. All of these emotions, these categories of emotions are there for a reason, and they are to give us a message. They are giving us a message that something in our life needs to change. Now one of two things have to change when we feel any of these emotions which you are about to learn so stay with me.

At any moment, you feel any emotion, the first step you are always going to want and take is to identify the signal. What I mean by identifying the signal is to figure out which one of these categories does it go into. So real quickly, let's take a look at how this might work.

Let's say something happens between you and a loved one, and as a result, you feel rejected. So as your looking over your list of ten categories, you see that rejected is not a category. Well, when you feel rejected you can be feeling a vast array of feelings about that rejection. You might feel uncomfortable, or you might feel actually hurt by the rejection. Maybe you are just feeling angry about being rejected, or perhaps because of the rejection you felt lonely. What you are going to try and do, is get down to the core emotion that is actually controlling you, rather than this giant word called rejection. Because, rejection is obviously not the essence of what you felt.

First off, I know you are not proficient at this list of ten categories yet, and how could you be it is brand new. But you will become skilled at recognizing emotions and being able to place them into a category which best fits how you are truly feeling.

Now what we are going to call them from now on are action signals, because that's exactly what they do. These emotions are signals to make us take action, to reevaluate the way we are perceiving something or the way we are preceding. The way we are communicating our feelings to other people or the way we are behaving around other people or situations. In other words, these emotions are going to signal us to change, in order to get what we truly want. This is what these action signals are all about, they are not negative, they are not bad, they are there to serve us. But for now lets come back to the example.

We said step number one was to identify the signal. So in this example we said that rejection actually was just uncomfortable for us. Maybe what happened was you turned to kiss your husband or wife, and they were busy reading or writing something, and they didn't really reciprocate. So it made you feel a little uncomfortable, because you didn't honestly feel lonely, you didn't feel hurt, you didn't feel angry, you just felt a little uncomfortable. The signal being uncomfortable is calling to your attention a message. The message of uncomfortable feelings is, you need to change your state first and foremost.

Because right now, no matter what happens in the state your in, you are not going to appreciate it. You are not going to be resourceful in understanding what things downright mean.

FOR EXAMPLE, YOUR FEELING IN A STATE OF BEING UNCOMFORTABLE ABOUT THE KISS, YOU WILL START TO HALLUCINATING:

- "Well gosh, my husband or wife they weren't very loving to me, does that mean their not interested in me anymore..."

- "Does that mean that our relationship isn't as strong..."

We tend to hallucinate when we get into a un-resourceful state. But when you feel uncomfortable, the first message from that signal is, to change your state. Then, the second message from that signal is to clarify what you want. Immediately you need to clarify what you want, because that's what this signal is trying to tell you. It is a message saying:

"Yeah your uncomfortable, so what do you want?"

If you want your wife or husband to be closer to you, then be clear that's what you want. And once you have become clear on what you want then step three is immediately to take action in that direction.

The way to take action in that direction is to communicate your desire or do something that expresses it. Make sure you do something until you achieve what you want and you are no longer uncomfortable. It is honestly that simple, because the last thing you want to be doing is sitting around thinking all the worst case scenarios in your head, which only drives you crazy, which is a whole other signal you will need to deal with. Feeling uncomfortable, is giving you a signal so you can immediately change your state, clarify what you want and number three take action in that direction. If you do that, you will conquer that emotion immediately.

Let's say you felt rejected to the point where you called it hurt. You genuinely felt hurt inside. Well, what is the message of hurt? When you feel the sensations of what you call, hurt feelings that signal is giving you a different message. The message you are receiving is, your feelings are hurt, and that there is an expectation you have which has not been met. You have a sense of loss. This sense of loss is why the feeling of being hurt is more intense than just being uncomfortable. You feel as if you have actually lost something. As with all emotions, the challenge with this is when you identify the message, you must immediately clarify what has to be changed.

Whenever you have what you used to call *"a negative emotion,"* you are now going to call an, action signal.

You know this action signal is signaling you to change, one of two things, either your perception or your procedure. Let me clarify what I mean by all this.

Your perception might be, for example, a feeling of hurt. You feel hurt, you feel like your husband or wife doesn't love you as much. Because, when you first met, all you had to do was look at them, and they would drop what they were doing and come over and hug or kiss you. Now they don't do that, and you feel a sense of loss, which is hurting you inside. That hurt is a lot more painful than just the feeling of being uncomfortable.

Are these appropriate emotions for us to feel, based on the current situation and time with this person? Really, this is the question we want to ask ourselves whenever we have any emotion. We know when we have a signal of hurt, we first need to identify the message being sent to us. Then secondly, immediately we need to appreciate what message the signal's offering. The message being offered is we need to change.

Again, either our perception or procedures must change. So the perception is that this person no longer loves us.

SO WE HAVE A COUPLE MORE QUESTIONS TO CONSIDER BEFORE WE KNOW WHAT COURSE OF CHANGE IS APPROPRIATE.

- Do we need to change our perception?

- Do we have some rules that are inappropriate in this situation?

To be entirely honest the answer in this particular example is probably yes, I hope you agree. This person is just wrapped up in whatever it is they are doing, and they are just immersed , it doesn't mean they love us any less. What this emotion is telling us, is we need to change our perception, because otherwise we are going to feel pain for no reason.

You might also look at the same situation as a signal with a message that you need to change your procedure. Procedure means the way you are proceeding with this information. This may be a signal to you, that you are not actually communicating your needs to your husband or wife in the most effective manner. So if, you are not communicating in the most effective manner then maybe what you need to do is change your procedure.

INSTEAD OF FEELING HURT, OR UNCOMFORTABLE, INSTEAD TURN TO YOUR HUSBAND OR WIFE AND SAY:

"Honey I know your wrapped up in your work and I know your totally immersed. I know your trying to do stuff that supports the whole family here. But, I just need three minutes here just you and me. Because, Right now I just need to feel loved by you, and I need to hold you, to feel connected."

Now if, that person starts getting upset, obviously you're getting feedback. The feedback may be telling you that your procedure still isn't working. Maybe you need to be a little more flexible, a little more creative, or maybe you need to be a little more loving in the way you do it. Also, you may change the timing in how you go about doing something. Also, another way you might change the procedure is that the message being sent is telling you, the way you are communicating to your husband or wife doesn't create the desire to make you feel loved right now. Maybe your present behavior is turning them off.

For example, let's say your feeling rejected by your spouse. Because, when you walk in the door, they don't rush over and give you a hug, they are immersed in something else. So how do you respond to that?

Well, what a lot of people do when they feel rejected is they become uncomfortable with the situation. They feel hurt, or some people will become angry, when they feel rejected. Now what's the message of anger?

The message of anger is you have a standard for your life. Something that is critical to you, and it's not being met by another person or maybe not even being met by yourself. Sometimes we get angry because we are not living our own standards. So let's say, as a result, one of your standards, is that people who love you run up to greet you at the door, which did not happen today. You feel angry, because you feel one of your standards has been violated. Something you feel is crucial is not happening, and now you are angry about the situation.

How do you respond to your spouse who doesn't even know what's going on?

The Emotional Code

Maybe you give them the Old Stink Eye, giving them that no so subtle look of anger, displeasure, and/or indigestion. Maybe, you make some snide remark, or you find something wrong with what they are doing and point it out. Maybe, as a result, this person will purposefully reject you. Now when your feeling this rejection, hurt or anger you will first identify what message this signal is telling you.

NOW YOU SAY TO YOURSELF:

- "Ok this anger means I have a message here."

- "The signal here is that I need to change either my perception or my procedure."

Maybe you don't need to change your perception, maybe they undoubtedly are rejecting you deliberately. Maybe the procedure is not only how you communicate but also how you are behaving.

MAYBE YOU NEED TO LOOK AT THE SITUATION AND SAY TO YOURSELF:

"Im not treating this person in a very loving way. No wonder they are giving me this feedback, and what needs to change is me."

Are you still following me? Let's recap what is going to happen in each situation we receive an action signal. We are identifying the signal, appreciating the message the signal has given us, and we know the message is telling we either need to change our perception or our procedure. In other words, the way we are communicating or the way we are behaving. I realize at first this may sound complex, but if you re-read this chapter a couple times, you will get this down.

I want to change either my perception or my procedure, the way I am communicating to this person or the way I am behaving. Maybe it comes down to how I looked at the whole darn thing.

Now I need to look at things, communicate or behave in a new way. Because, in essence that is the message of pain. Let me say that again, because I think you'll get this one. If your feeling pain, it's a message that you need to change the way your looking at the situation and, therefore, what it means to you. Or change the way you are communicating your desires or needs to someone, especially if the pain involves somebody else. Or change the way your behaving, the way your treating others and that will get you a new response.

That in essence is the basis of all these action messages. They are telling you that you have gotten to set a new outcome and move in a new direction. Otherwise, you are going to stay in pain. And let me mention something real quick. If you ignore a message, if you ignore one of these signals, an action signal, whether it be the signal of feeling hurt or fearful, angry, frustrated, disappointed or overloaded that signal will not go away it only intensifies. If you ignore a signal, you will feel hurt even more. If you ignore the message the action signal has sent, you will feel even more angry.

THE SIGNAL INTENSIFIES UNTIL ONE DAY, YOU GET SMART ENOUGH TO SAY:

- "Hey I've gotta change something here!"

- "I've got to change my expectations, the way I'm evaluating things, the way I'm looking at things, the way I feel about it or the way I'm communicating what I need, or I've got to change the way Im behaving."

- "I am going to keep feeling these things until I make one of those three changes!"

The Emotional Code

Action Signals Decoding Your Emotional Triggers

Before we go any further, let me review with you what each message is giving you in each of the ten action signals.

We have already said that if you are uncomfortable, then the message is clear, you need to change your state, clarify what you want, and take action in the direction of what you want. Immediately you won't be uncomfortable anymore.

And if you feel an emotion of fear, concern, apprehension, worry, anxiety, scared, frightened, or even terrified no matter what intensity the emotion is you feel there is only one message being sent to you. The message being signaled in a fearful state is, we need to prepare ourselves to deal with something or to avoid the negative consequences of something that is coming up. Basically fear is get prepared, get ready to deal with something, and that is a powerful message.

Now here is the problem for most people, they become fearful and they deny the message and pretend they are real strong, which only makes the message and feeling grow stronger, as well. Or worse they just surrender the fear, and they don't get the message, and so they get wrapped up in the emotion and become more and more scared, and they amplify it. So rather than prepare and focus on what they need to do, they think about the worst that can happen. People have a fear of failure, and that's a valuable fear, it's simply saying get prepared so you don't fail.

You might have a fear because the IRS is coming to visit you and you get a little note in the mail, which sets off a feeling of panic and anxiety. Having a fear of the IRS is probably an extraordinarily useful fear. It's probably saying, you need to go get all your paperwork in order, and if you didn't have that message, or that fear you might have just blown it off and not been prepared when they show up and cost you a lot of money and antacids. Same can happen is someone asks you to give a speech, and you get a little fear inside you, and then it grows into anxiety. As the intensity grows, the more we tend to surrender to the emotion, rather than get the message.

So it makes sense that maybe we ought to change the signal fear and say instead that I'm a little concerned. So then you might say:

"I'm a little concerned about this speech, so I need to prepare so I can do the best possible job and I will feel confident instead of fearful."

With each of these emotions, we want to hear the message being given to us. Now you may already be prepared, in fact, you are as prepared as you possibly can, and you can not prepare anymore.

Sometimes we prepare so much and then we just need to have a little faith. And at that point you might just have to say:

• "You know what, this is a message saying that I need to change my perceptions, not my procedures."

• "I'm prepared by my procedures, I know what I'm doing, and I know how to do it."

• "Now, I need to stop focusing on this thing being the worst possible situation, and I need to decide to become confident now!"

Category Number Three | the Feeling of Being Hurt

When you feel hurt, the message is that your expectations have not been met which creates a feeling of loss. So, you expected him/her to keep their word, and they didn't and that hurt your feelings. Or you expected someone that you shared something intimate with and they told others, and now you feel hurt, and a sense of a loss of intimacy or trust. It is that sense of loss, which creates a feeling of hurt inside of us.

So when we feel hurt, what do we need to do? Immediately, the message is we need to assess if there actually is a loss. Again do we need to change our perception? Maybe we didn't communicate to this person clearly that when we told them our secret, we wanted them not to tell anyone else.

So maybe you haven't lost anything. It is possible you just need to change how you communicate your needs. It is also highly likely you need to re-evaluate your behavior.

Category Number Four | the Feeling of Anger

Remember in this category we can have emotions like irritation, livid, furious, enraged, or resentful and all of these emotions fit into the category of anger. All of these emotions are merely signals which are giving you a message. The message here is that an important rule that you have in your life has been violated by someone else or maybe even by you. See when we think something is extremely important and somebody violates that rule we get upset about it. How we deal with being upset, is profoundly determined by how much pain or pleasure we genuinely experience in our lives. Also, it is determined by how close we get to people or how much we push them away from us.

So if, someone violates your standards, then that's the message. What your supposed to do with that message is real simple. Communicate that you have a standard. Communicate that you know its only your rule, and it's not necessarily their rule, but you need their help. If we use the previous example where you shared something in confidence with someone, but you didn't explain it was in confidence, you just expected them to know that. And you didn't just feel hurt, you felt angry about it.

So the bottom line is, rather than beating that person up you need to go to that person and communicate a different way. You need to change the way your communicating. You need to change your procedure. And you say:

"I know you didn't know this was supposed to be private, but this is really important to me."

And you need to communicate and deal with it as quickly as possible. Anger usually grows from being hurt. When your feeling hurt you have a feeling of loss, something you expected didn't work out. When your angry, it's because something you feel is extremely crucial wasn't handled correctly. Or you have a lot of hurt that has built up inside you. However, you have not expressed or communicated that hurt to them. So anger is usually a signal that something you believe is extraordinarily significant has been violated by someone or yourself. Or you have a lot of hurts that you have not expressed, and they have built up until they became anger.

So how do you deal with it? You change your perception, because maybe this person wasn't trying to hurt you at all. Change your procedure, communicate better what your real needs are or change your behavior. Tell people upfront:

"Hey this is private, promise you won't share this with anyone because it's real important to me."

The Emotional Code

Either method you will get out of your anger quickly, it's a signal that says you need to clarify to people what your rules are and get them to agree to meet them, or you need to compromise them possibly. Some things you are going to get angry about are things you are going to get angry about the rest of your life, so you better identify those things. Also, you need to realize that those are just your standards, and they are not everyone's standards. So if, you go around always upset because everyone is not playing by your rules then you are going to be upset your whole life. So again maybe you need to change your perceptions, change your rules so life is a lot more straightforward and a lot less painful for you.

Category Number Five | the Feeling of Frustration

These action signals are telling you to change your approach to achieve your goal. What ever your going after, your not going to get it, by the way, you are doing it right now, and that's why your frustrated. You keep trying to get a different result by doing the same thing over and over again. There was a definition given a long time ago about insanity. Insanity is attempting to get a new result by doing the same thing over and over again, it will never work. So you need to change your approach. When you feel frustrated just know that's a message that you need to change your approach, you need to be more flexible in the situation.

Category Number Six | the Feeling of Disappointment

If you start to feel disappointed, that's a signal. And that signal is bringing you a message, and that message is you need to realize an expectation you had, an outcome your going after are not probably going to happen unless you change your expectation and make it more appropriate for the situation at hand. Maybe you wanted to have something happen in too short a period of time.

Overcoming Frustration| Business Partner & Coach Chris Hughes

A few weeks ago when my business partner Chris Hughes knocked me out of a pattern of disappointment. Chris is a guy who is much stronger in the area of setting realistic goals and then creating a viable plan of action with measurable steps to take in order to achieve the best possible outcome.

My problem is sometimes I shoot past the moon without ever designing the aircraft to reach my intended target, so Im just jumping towards the sky, becoming more and more disappointed when I just can't seem to reach my goal.

So, I remember being together with Chris and saying to him, Chris I hope you can help bring a few things back into focus for me. I told Chris, I've been doing everything I know, listening to every podcast, reading every book, and nothing seemed to be working. I told him how I felt no matter what I tried, I could not get off the ground. I told him how I was doing everything I've learned, and I've been trying to create attainable goals and cast appropriate dreams, but nothing is working.

Chris looked at me with a little schmuck grin on his face and said, *"Well do you want some help?"* He didn't say that, in a harsh way, he said it to break my pattern and interrupt my thought process. So I looked at him with a dumbfounded expression on my face. Chris just continued to smile, causing me to start laughing a little bit, suddenly my state changed, and my mojo started to come back. Chris knew I was being ridiculous in what I was saying and feeling. See this is where working with Chris is a perfect combination, because he is a master at creating measurable goals and putting a plan into action which provides the necessary steps in order to achieve those goals. It is something Chris has been doing for small business owners and internet marketers for years and is the reason why his Brain Smart Success is so popular with many small business owners.

CHRIS THEN SAID:

"Listen, you need to realize the reason your disappointed is that your getting feedback. Disappointment says that you set some pretty strong goals within a certain time frame, and you didn't meet those. So you need to change your goal a little bit, you need to make it a little more appropriate for where you are right now. Just make it a little more realistic for where you are right now."

What he said reminded me of something I heard a long time ago. God's delays are not God's denials. He then went on to say:

"You see you may just be in lag time, which means that if you go out right now and plant a seed, you don't go the next day looking for a plant. You don't expect all of a sudden to reap your reward the next day."

If you plant a seed, and then return the following day, asking the soil: *"Hey soil where's my plant?"* The soil will just laugh at you saying, are you new? Tollie, it doesn't work that way. You have to work through all the different seasons and stuff, how can you be disappointed all ready? But some people tend to do that, so Tollie you may just be in lag time, sometimes you put a seed in and plant something, and it takes a season for you to get the reward. See, your still in Spring time and your expecting it to be fall. What Chris reminded me of is that disappointment says you need to change your expectations, you need to change your view of things and come up with a more realistic outcome for the time you have involved and the people involved and circumstances.

The Emotional Code

So you see what Chris reminded me of, was the message of disappointment, and how to use it. See no matter what you personally know, sometimes you need that partner, that coach to kick you in the butt and remind you how to look at things differently in order to achieve your goals. I would encourage you also either to find a partner in any aspect of life you need someone to help keep you accountable in and use them when you start to feel disappointment.

Or if you don't have a coach, and in that case, I would recommend a few, but especially I can vouch personally for my business partner and coach Chris Hughes, and I encourage you to see how Chris and his companies can help you achieve your goals. (brainsmartsuccess.com and also whoischrishughes.com)

Category number seven | the feeling of guilt or regret

When you have feelings of regret or guilt, you may listen to those people who say, don't feel regret or guilty about anything! Let me tell you that kind of advice is complete nonsense. Guilt serves you if you hear the message. Because the message of guilt is ultra super duper & simple, it says you violated one of your own standards. It is telling you that you must do something immediately to insure your not going to violate again in the future. That is why you feel the pain of guilt.

Now most people either deny the guilt, and take themselves out of it and don't feel guilty at all. But if you just dismiss the guilt and don't get the message then the guilt is just going to come back. Now you know, that guilt will come back unless you take action. When your guilt returns, you will also feel immense pain again, and it is this pain you are trying to avoid. So, get the message the first time and take action to make sure it doesn't happen again. Because, if you ignore the message, you will find yourself feeling overwhelmed or surrendering to guilt, which is the other extreme that will happen. People just walk around and allow themselves to feel inferior for the rest of their lives. They feel so ashamed about what they once did, and that is not the purpose of guilt. Guilt is to make sure you clean up your act. Guilt is to make sure you don't violate this again. Guilt is the cattle prod to zap you in the butt in order to make things right when you screw up.

This is important, remember sometimes you can't make up for something you did in the past, and you are hanging on to a guilty feeling. Maybe what you feel guilty about is something you did to someone who has since passed away. Maybe there is a situation or event in your past which you have been holding onto that guilt, and you can't go back and change or fix the situation. Remember the only thing you can change is your present and future behaviors, and when you do that you can let go of the guilt. That's the message it offers you. And again when you immediately feel the signal what do you do, you identify the signal and you realize your feeling regret or your feeling guilt, and secondly you appreciate the message which is telling you to change something, either your perception or your procedures. Maybe your feeling guilty about something you shouldn't feel guilty about at all.

Have you ever felt guilty about something that you shouldn't have felt guilty about in the first place? I know I have, I felt guilty one time because I didn't make someone feel happy enough. I used to run around and try and make everyone feel happy, and if I didn't make them happy then I would actually feel guilty about it, and how stupid is that! Look, we don't want to fall into that category you might want to change your rules or your perceptions. Or you might need to change your behavior in the future, change the way you are going to communicate to that person or people like them. Any one of these three changes will immediately eliminate the guilt, and then the guilt has served a noble purpose, hasn't it. The guilt kept you on track, and helped you move forward, and it has made you a better person, so gold stars for everyone!

THAT'S WHY GUILT IS THERE, UTILIZE IT, DON'T WALLOW IN IT.

Category Number Eight | the Feeling of Inadequacy

When you feel inadequate, those are any of those emotions again that make you feel less than. It would be an emotion which makes you feel unworthy, for example. Whenever you feel this emotion, or an emotion like it get excited and appreciate its offering you a message.

The Emotional Code

The message it is offering you is clear, it is telling you that you need to do something in order to get better at something in this category right away. It doesn't mean you have to be perfect at it, inadequacy just says you have to do something, don't sit on your butt anymore.

Your feeling of inadequacy is because you haven't done anything to become exceptionally strong in that area.

Now the first thing you've got to do as you go through this process is ask yourself is this truly an appropriate emotion? You need to ask yourself:

- "Am I really inadequate, or do I need to change the way I am perceiving things?"

- "Maybe I have some rules that say that in order to be adequate I have to go out on the dance floor and be able to out do, Usher."

See that's probably inappropriate perceptions, so you need to change the perceptions, or maybe changing the procedures. So maybe you need to be saying:

"I need to prepare myself by doing something right now in order to get better."

One easy thing you can do is just go practice. Another thing you can do is go out and initiate some communication.

So inadequacy is a message to get up and do something to become better, or to change your criteria. To look at what you are doing and make it easier for yourself to feel adequate, because you've probably got rules for yourself that are too harsh.

Category number nine | the feeling of being overloaded or overwhelmed

This is one of the categories which I feel immobilizes and destroys more people's lives than virtually any of the other categories combined. I used the word overloaded in order to make it simple, because if you use the emotion depressed you immediately build much more intensity than if you say I'm overloaded. The key here is to realize that this is a signal. When you feel hopeless, depressed, overwhelmed, or overloaded the message it is offering you is that you need to reevaluate what is most pertinent to you in this situation. Sit down right now and decide what is undoubtedly vital, and what is a necessity to you, versus what is a desire. Write down all the things that are most pertinent to you to accomplish. Then the second step is to put them in order of priority. Then the third step is to take the first item on your list and do something about it.

It is the same thing with depression, it is the same thing with feeling hopeless. Sit down and instead of feeling hopeless you first need to change your state that's the first step. Then after, you change your state, the second thing you do is to clarify what is most pertinent to you and write it all out. After the first two steps are complete, then you move onto the third step and place your list into an order of importance then step four is to take your first item on your list and go and handle that item immediately by taking action. The minute you go and handle anything on your list and you deal with one single issue your brain can handle it. And as soon as you handle that situation you will like you are in control of your world. You will not feel overloaded, overwhelmed, or even depressed.

Your self esteem grows when you take steps in order to gain control of events, instead of allowing events to take control over you.

All you have to do in order to take control of events is to chunk them down, and choose one thing and master it. Go down your list to number two and master it and so on and so forth. The message is clear, you are trying to do too much in too short a period of time. You look at the whole world expecting everything to be perfect over night, and your feeling like you can't handle it all. Coming in at number ten we have a decidedly lonely category of emotions. Have you ever felt extremely lonely? Seriously, I don't think there is anybody alive who hasn't. But what does it mean when you feel lonely? What is the message you should get from that signal of loneliness? I think the message is quite straightforward, what we honestly need at that moment is a certain connection with people.

Now the challenge with that message is a lot of times people take the word, (connection) or the idea of a need for connection, with another human being, and they make it into a sexual connection. Or instant intimacy I guess is another way of saying, getting it on, horizontal style. However, they still feel frustrated because even when they have the sex, they still feel lonely. What we certainly need to do is identify what kind of connection we truly desire. Maybe you do need an intimate connection, maybe you need some basic friendship with someone who shares similar interests. Maybe all you truly desire is someone to laugh with, the ability to share a conversation while enjoying the other person's company.

WHAT'S EXCITING ABOUT BEING LONELY IS IT SAYS:

"You really care about people, and you love to be with people."

So you need to find out in what ways you need to be with people right now. And then take an action immediately to go in the direction you want.

IN OTHER WORDS, ALL 10 OF THESE EMOTIONS ARE A MESSAGE TO OUR BRAIN TO RESPOND:

The Emotional Code

"Hey what you're doing right now isn't working, and you need to change it."

You either change your perception or change what criteria you're using. Or change the way you're communicating, because you're not communicating in a way that people understand your needs or you need to change your behavior. What you're doing isn't working, so change your approach. Maybe it's an emotion like regret, where your brain is communicating, something you did isn't working and you broke your own rules in a way that doesn't work for you. Either you simply didn't break the rules, and your perception is unfair, or you did break your rules and you need to change them. You need to do something to ensure you never break these rules again.

Once you change your rules, you will never again suffer through this kind of pain, because it is not appropriate. In a sense, this is how we want to deal with these 10 emotions and what you want to do is get to know all 10 emotions.

REVIEW THEM OVER AND OVER AGAIN. SO THE NEXT TIME, WHEN YOU SAY:

"Oh my gosh I'm feeling jealous."

You will first identify the signal, because you will know which of these 10 categories it falls into. Then you can ask yourself the relevant questions.

- "Well gosh, jealous what is that?"

- "Am I feeling angry feelings or am I feeling fearful feelings about this jealousy?"

So the first step is to determine if there is a need to change my perception or my procedures. You then ask yourself:

- "What is the meaning that I should take from this message?"

- "Or maybe the fact that they said hello to this other person, means I need to change my perception. Because that's not so bad, and I shouldn't be feeling jealous."

Then you start to build a new perspective with allows you to consider the event in a more resourceful state.

"Maybe that was an unfair rule, and it was an unfair way of looking at things?"

NOW, YOU BEGIN TO INITIATE AN IMMEDIATE ACTION YOU NEED TO TAKE.

- "I need to communicate my needs, to this person so that they know and can respect my values, so they can respect what my needs are."

- "Maybe I can change my behavior, so when I feel jealous, I can go and just share more intimate feelings more passionate feelings with this person, then maybe it will change the whole quality of the relationship right then and there."

So know that we understand the 10 messages let's take a look at the six steps, and I've given you the first two over and over again just so you remember them.

The Emotional Code

THE FIRST STEP IS IMMEDIATELY TO IDENTIFY THE SIGNAL.

THE SECOND STEP IS TO APPRECIATE THE MESSAGE.

Let's say the message is I need to change something, so do I need to change my perception or do I need a change the communication of my needs. Or do I need to behave differently, and what is the specific message? What is the specific question when emotionally I feel hurt? Well there is an expectation that I have, and it's not being met, and I have a sense of loss. Then I go to step three of the six steps.

Step three is I need to get curious.

What I need to do is get curious about what it is that I honestly want to feel. And what would it take to make that happen? See here are the four questions you are going to ask in order to get curious. We have identified the challenge, we appreciate the meaning, and we respect the fact that our emotions are helping us to signal to take a new action.

AND NOW WE'RE CURIOUS, AND HER CURIOSITY IS SAYING:

"Well how do I really want to feel?"

Let's say you felt destroyed, which is actually just hurt, and since I don't want to feel hurt how do I want to feel in this situation?

* "Well I want to feel confident"

- "I want to feel loved"

- "Or I want to feel connected."

As soon as you identify with what it is that you want to feel, you are moving in the direction you want to go. All these emotions are telling you to refocus on what you want and take some new action. So you need to ask yourself:

"What do you want?"

THE SECOND QUESTION YOU WANT TO ASK FROM A CURIOUS STATE OF MIND IS WHAT WOULD I HAVE TO BELIEVE IN ORDER TO FEEL THIS WAY RIGHT NOW. SO MAYBE YOU WOULD ANSWER:

"I want to feel close friendship instead of pain."

SO THE NEXT QUESTION YOU WOULD ASK IS:

- "What do I have to believe in order to feel that way?"

- "Well I'd have to believe that nothing could ever violate my sense of friendship with this person, because they really do care about me and that feeling is really there."

AND THE THIRD QUESTION IS WHAT AM I WILLING TO DO, TO HANDLE THIS RIGHT NOW, IN ORDER FOR ME TO FEEL THIS WAY RIGHT NOW.

- "Well, I'm willing to believe that I am willing to trust and have faith to trust"

- "I am willing to communicate to that person that I love them no matter what"

- "I am willing to ask them what can I do in order for us to create a lasting friendship"

- "I am also willing to take the necessary steps to ensure I am never in a position where I feel destroyed, by the way, someone communicates."

AND NOW THE FOURTH QUESTION IS WHAT'S SIGNIFICANT ABOUT THIS, OR WHAT CAN I LEARN FROM THIS? WHEN YOU ASK YOURSELF THIS QUESTION YOU MIGHT SAY SOMETHING ALONG THE LINES OF THE FOLLOWING.

- *"Well one of the things that I learned is that I contributed to these feelings by my rules and, by the way, I look at things, or by my intensity."*

- *"So what can I learn from this, so in the future I never have to go through these feelings again?"*

Again, if you can get curious about your emotions and what created them and what you can learn from them and how you can make sure you don't have to go through the pain again. Then sure enough, you can accelerate your growth in life experience a lot more pleasure and a lot less pain. Now in step four you become confident. And how do you become confident? You reassure yourself that you can manage these emotions right now, by remembering times when you handled them in the past.

Are you following me on this, have you ever felt jealous before in the past? And when you had a jealousy from the past, you got over that insecurity didn't you. Can you remember a single time, or have you ever felt destroyed or seriously hurt, but you got over it? I want you to go back and remember a specific time when you genuinely felt hurt, and somehow you got over it.

Maybe, at the time, you didn't think you were going to be able to get over that hurt, but maybe you communicate with the person or maybe you changed your state. Or maybe you asked yourself a fair question.

"What else could this mean maybe this person isn't trying to destroy me, and they are not trying to hurt me. In fact, perhaps they are stressed out, and it's not even about me. Also, I believe people are doing the best they can with the resources they have."

When you are trying to gain confidence in order to overcome a negative emotion, here is an easy tip. Remember, a time when you were able to deal with an emotion, and this will create confidence so you can deal with a current emotion.

Step five | To Get Certain

What I mean is to be certain you can handle this emotion now. I want you to stop reading right now, and in your mind imagine coming up with different ways of handling this emotion. I want you to come up with three or four different ways where jealousy came up, and you communicated your jealousy to someone else in a way that they were able to hear you. Now, if the first way you tried to communicate your jealousy didn't work, then you need to try another approach. You rehearse it in your mind, several times, where you see yourself maybe expressing it one time as this:

"Well you know, I'm wrong, and I had this misperception."

AND MAYBE ANOTHER TIME YOU MIGHT SAY WITH A SMILE:

The Emotional Code

"I'm a little crazy at times, but you know, at least I'm being honest. And honestly, this is how I felt at that moment."

MAYBE ANOTHER TIME YOU CHOOSE TO COMMUNICATE SIMPLY BY GIVING THE PERSON A HUG AND WHISPERING IN THEIR EAR:

"I need your help."

See, the key is to look at all the different ways you can communicate your emotions and how you felt. By doing this, you deal with it, and you rehearse how appropriately to respond, and communicate the feeling behind the emotion. You rehearse it enough times where you feel confident that you have lots of ways to express your emotions in a way that empowers you in your relationships rather than disempowers you. And finally we come to step six and you get excited, while taking action.

You need to do something right away which will reinforce that you can handle this emotion. Go communicate to that person that you want to manage how you feel right now, so you don't stay stuck in the emotion. Go and express your emotion in some way that reinforces, what you have rehearsed inside your mind.

Remember what you got curious about, and the new distinctions you made, certainly do work for you. You deepen your confidence by changing the way you feel, and you are doing so right now. So we have six easy steps and ten emotions, which now you can recognize. So let me ask you, how do you get proficient at anything? You practice of course, and as much as I do not like the word practice, since it sorta implies, your not particularly skilled at something, I prefer do it.

The way you get proficient at something is you do it. Every time you do it, you try and do it even better. Here, is an incantation I heard years ago. Good, better, best, never let it rest until my good becomes my best! You don't ever practice, because you are always going for it, full throttle and having fun with it, as well. Remember, the best way to deal with an emotion is to kill the monster while it's little.

Make sure you deal with those anger emotions, when they are still at the level of being only a minor irritation, and not when you are enraged. If you handle them at the level of a little irritation, they are a lot easier to deal with.

ALSO, REMEMBER THE TOOLS YOU HAVE ALREADY LEARNED. WHEN YOU START TO FEEL ENRAGED, CONNECT YOURSELF AND SAY:

"Well maybe I'm not enraged, maybe I'm a little annoyed. Or I am a little inconvenienced by this conversation."

And that connection, will allow you to break your pattern and make it easier for you to hear the messages of those emotions, and take new actions. Now, you will take action against your negative emotions, instead of being caught up in those emotions, or even worse surrendering to them. The worst case scenario is being defeated by your emotions.

Remember, the emotion is there to serve you, but it's up to you, to hear the message and act upon it.

In case you haven't already figured it out, the best way to achieve what you want is by focusing on it. In other words, you want to experience it, and plant it. Think of your mind, emotions, and your spirit as the ultimate garden. The way to ensure you harvest what you truly want is never by practicing planting seeds of disappointment, or fear. Because, you never want to become the farmer who brags about how skilled they

The Emotional Code

have become harvesting plants of disappointment or fear. Instead, you want to be the zen master planting the bonsai trees of love, warmth, and appreciation.

In fact, I am going to give you ten emotions, that if you will plant these emotions daily and you cultivate these emotions, it will hold you to a unprecedented standard. By holding yourself to the standard of these ten emotions, you are saying, that every day you want to feel these ten emotions. Your result will be that you have planted the seeds of greatness. You will have planted the seeds to a tremendous and juicy life, where the mojo flows free.

The life you will have created will not need a lot of action signals because you are already acting. You are already living life at it's fullest. See, a weed in your garden is a call to action, it's not a negative or a bad thing, it is only offering you the message to take action. The message the weed is signaling to you is you need continually to weed your garden in order for the seeds of desired emotions to grow stronger.

One of the easiest ways to keep the weeds out is to keep cultivating the kinds of plants you want right there in the garden. Now, the roots of the plants you want become stronger, bigger and so they grow deeper, creating less room for weeds to sprout up.

Increase Your Mojo With These 10 Emotions

1. LOVE & WARMTH:

If you want to create a behavior, the best way to do this is to put yourself in an emotional state where that behavior is automatic. Here, is an example: If you want to have close relationships, then do the things that make you close to other people. The easiest way to do that is to cultivate an emotion of being loving and warm. If you put yourself into a state of love and warmth, you won't be sitting there trying to figure out how to make your relationships work, because, in a state of love and warmth, it will happen automatically.

2. APPRECIATIVE & GRATEFUL:

If you are always feeling amorous and warm and also appreciative and grateful then automatically you will do whatever is necessary to strengthen the people around you. This will cause you to maintain a deep sense of caring.

3. CURIOSITY:

If you seriously want to grow in your life, then learn to be curious. Become curious like a child, or even Curious George, one of my favorite storybook characters from when I was a kid. Children know how to wonder, and that is why they are always filled with happiness and a sense of joy and abundant possibilities.

You want to overcome the emotion of boredom, then become curious, because it's rare to find a child feeling bored. Let's say you are in school, and you are trying to make yourself study more, which is a hard habit to create, but if you are curious then studying is automatic. Cultivate the emotion of curiosity and life becomes a never ending study of joy!

4. EXCITEMENT & PASSION:

Excitement and Passion adds serious mojo to anything in life, because life is Passion! Nelson Mandela once said, *"There is no passion to be found playing small, in settling for a life that is less than the one you are capable of living."* Passion adds to life enjoyment, passion turns anything seen as a challenge into tremendous opportunities. We want to ensure we add passion to our lives each day, and the way we do that is as straightforward as making the decision to feel the passion each day, we allow ourselves to feel passionate.

5. DETERMINATION:

The Emotional Code

What is the key to follow thru with losing weight? The key to losing weight is creating a state of determination. Growing up as the fat kid and trying every diet imaginable, swallowing every diet pill or silver bullet I could get my pudgy hands on I know how hard it is to lose weight. However, I also know that all my attempts ended in failure, which led to my personal weight topping out at well over 500 pounds all because I never understood how to create a state of determination.

Just like most people who never follow through with their weight loss goals, I found myself constantly pushing myself onto a diet, rather than putting myself into a state of determination. If you are determined, you have created a state of determination where there are no excuses. You have no stories being told anymore, you have a resolute, determined state to lose weight. How can losing weight be easy? Losing weight becomes easy because you are in an emotional state of determination where the appropriate behaviors happen automatically.

6. FLEXIBILITY:

The greatest seed you can plant to grow success is the emotional seed of flexibility, because it creates the ability to change and make adjustments in all aspects of your life. Remember, all those action signals or negative emotions, which cause a feeling of pain, are all a message telling you to make changes, be more flexible. You become more flexible in the way you evaluate things, your perception of what things actually mean to you. Once you become more flexible in the way you communicate and more flexible in your behavior your whole world changes for the better.

7. CONFIDENCE:

When you are confident it creates the ability for you to try new things, put yourself out there on the edge. Being confident allows you to experience that one emotion that is talked about in every religious book on this planet which is Faith! One way to become confident and have faith is to use the muscle more often, exercise it, practice it so being confident becomes automatic creating a deep sense of faith in yourself.

How confident are you in tying your shoes? Usually the answer is of course extremely confident they can tie their own shoes, and the reason is because they have done it a billion times. So if, you want to have confidence then the best way to become confident is to exercise it every day, same as you did learning to tie your shoes. Have some faith, have some trust and choose to be confident in a situation and you will discover, you will do well.

8. CHEERFUL:

Being cheerful means that when your happy you tell your face about it. So when your around someone and talking, and you feel happy on the inside your also communicating that happiness on the outside which makes people see your happy and want to be around you. It means your trying to be happy in a way that not only makes you happy, but it also makes those around you happy, as well. Also, cultivating the emotion to be cheerful enhances your self esteem and makes life a lot more fun.

9. HEALTHY:

Feeling a physical vibrancy and health is a powerful way to make sure that anything negative just bounces off you. When I am full of energy, the mojo is flowing, and I'm feeling pumped and bulletproof. I feel as nothing can stop me, challenges are nothing but spit wads bouncing off me, and it's an emotion which makes every day exciting, and full of adventure. It's like those action signals aren't even necessary when you feel vibrant and alive. Cultivate the feelings of being healthy and practice the things you know will make you feel physically vibrant in an ongoing basis.

10. CONTRIBUTION:

If every day you can feel like what you do adds something to others, then life takes on a new deeper sense of meaning. I think we all have a feeling that we want our life to matter, we want to feel that we touched and enhanced the lives of those around us. We want to feel like our contribution or legacy is one that is felt by others, be helped make life better for others.

But, there are little ways you can contribute on a daily basis, and it can be as easy as a smile in passing to a complete stranger. A contribution I cultivated a few years ago has become so automatic that I never even think about it anymore, it is just become and aspect of my character, and who I am. When I'm staying at a hotel, anytime I pass a housekeeper, or anyone working in the hotel, I look them in the eyes, smile and always say, hi or ask how they're doing. And I also notice all the people who won't even make eye contact with them, and this small gesture or contribution makes a face light up and smile! PEOPLE MATTER!

So, now we have our ten seeds, plant these emotions daily. If you plant these seeds of emotions on a consistent daily basis, you will watch your life grow, with passion you can't even fathom. I know I'm dumping a lot onto your brains when it comes to emotions. However, I genuinely think this chapter is one that you will want to read a couple times, so you can get exceptionally skilled at using these action signals.

REMEMBER THE SIX STEPS:

- Identify the signal.

- Respect the message, change your perception or procedure.

- Get curious about what you truly want.

- Get confident, because we both know there was a time in your life where you have already dealt with these emotions and you can do it again.

- Get certain and rehearse and practice all the ways you are going to deal with any emotion you experience.

- Get excited and take action.

Here, is the most valuable thing I want you to remember about emotions. Every feeling you have good or bad is not based on the actual reality of life.

But rather your interpretation as to what things mean. And remember nothing in life has any meaning except the meaning you give it. So if, you don't like the way your feeling, then you need to change the meaning. The way to change the meaning is by asking one question, *"What Else Could This Mean?"* Because at any moment we can choose a new meaning and, therefore, choose a new way of feeling and a new way of behaving. The truth is we are never going to know the absolute true meaning of anything. Choose meanings that will empower you in life, rather than assuming disempowering meanings, which will only cause you pain in life.

REMEMBER PEOPLE ALWAYS DO THE BEST THEY CAN, WITH THE RESOURCES THEY HAVE.

And once again, nothing in life has meaning, except the meaning you give it. If you don't like the way something feels, choose to create a new meaning. Have fun with your emotions, play with them and learn from the ones that used to be painful. Choose to live and enjoy and experience the emotions that create for you tremendous pleasure.

The Emotional Guidance Scale

1. Joy / Knowledge
Empowerment
Freedom / Love
Appreciation

2. Passion

3. Enthusiasm

4. Positive Expectation
Belief

5. Optimism

6. Hopefulness

7. Contentment

Upward Spiral

Emotional Guidance Scale Upward Spiral

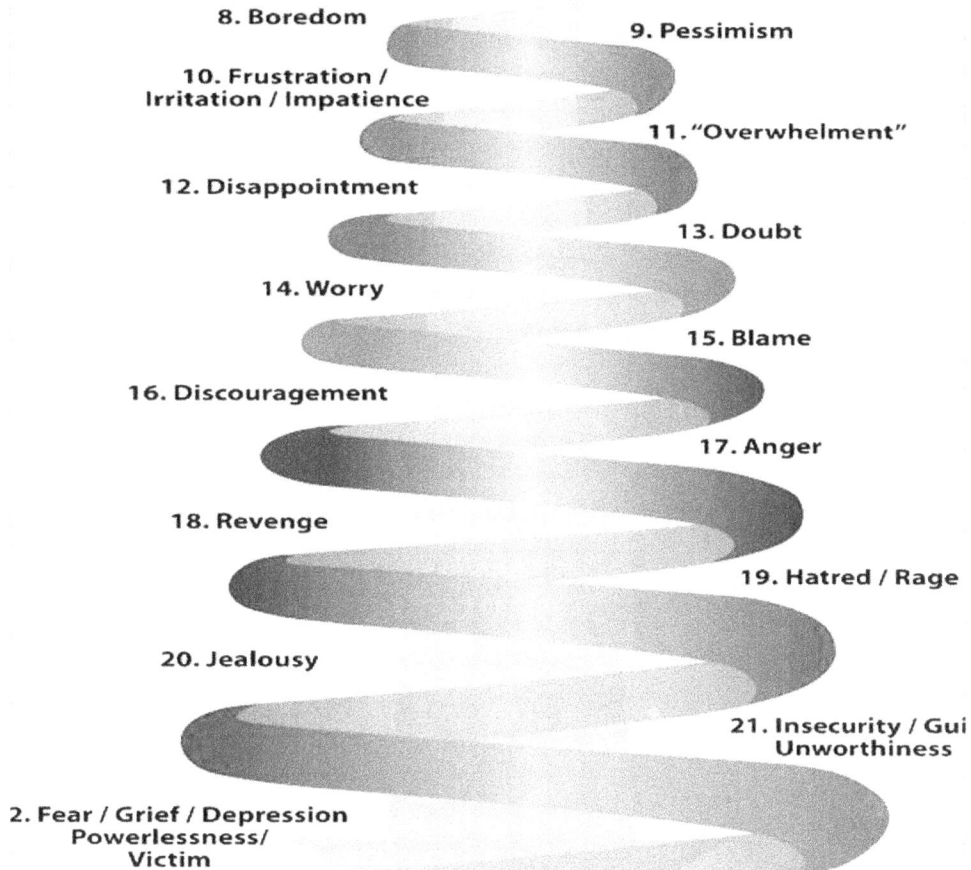

The Emotional Guidance Scale

8. Boredom

9. Pessimism

10. Frustration / Irritation / Impatience

11. "Overwhelment"

12. Disappointment

13. Doubt

14. Worry

15. Blame

16. Discouragement

17. Anger

18. Revenge

19. Hatred / Rage

20. Jealousy

21. Insecurity / Gui Unworthiness

2. Fear / Grief / Depression Powerlessness/ Victim

Downward Spiral

Emotional Scale

Level of Control	Responsibility	Emotions	Thoughts	Appearance
Full Control	It's MY doing that things are good.	Joy/ Knowledge/ Empowerment/ Freedom/ Love/ Appreciation/ Passion/ Enthusiasm/ Eagerness/ Happiness	I can do it! I WILL do it! I can't wait to get out there and do it!!! I love myself! I love my life!	
	It's Fate's doing that things are good.	Positive Expectation/ Belief/ Optimism/ Hopefulness/ Contentment	Things can get better. Good things do happen in the world. If other people can do it, maybe so can I.	
	Neutral.	Boredom	Neutral.	
	It's Fate's fault that things are bad.	Pessimism/ Frustration/ Irritation/ Impatience/ Overwhelment/ Disappointment/ Doubt/ Worry	Bad things just happen. That's just the way it is. The world is a bad place. Might as well accept it.	
	It's THEIR fault that things are bad.	Blame/ Discouragement/ Anger/ Revenge/ Hatred/ Rage/ Jealousy	It's all their fault. If other people weren't so selfish, I could have more. Why does nobody care about me??	
No Control	It's my fault that things are bad.	Insecurity/ Guilt/ Unworthiness/ Fear/ Grief/ Depression/ Despair/ Powerlessness	It's all my fault. Nobody loves me because I'm unlovable. There's nothing I can do. I hate myself.	

Emotional Scale

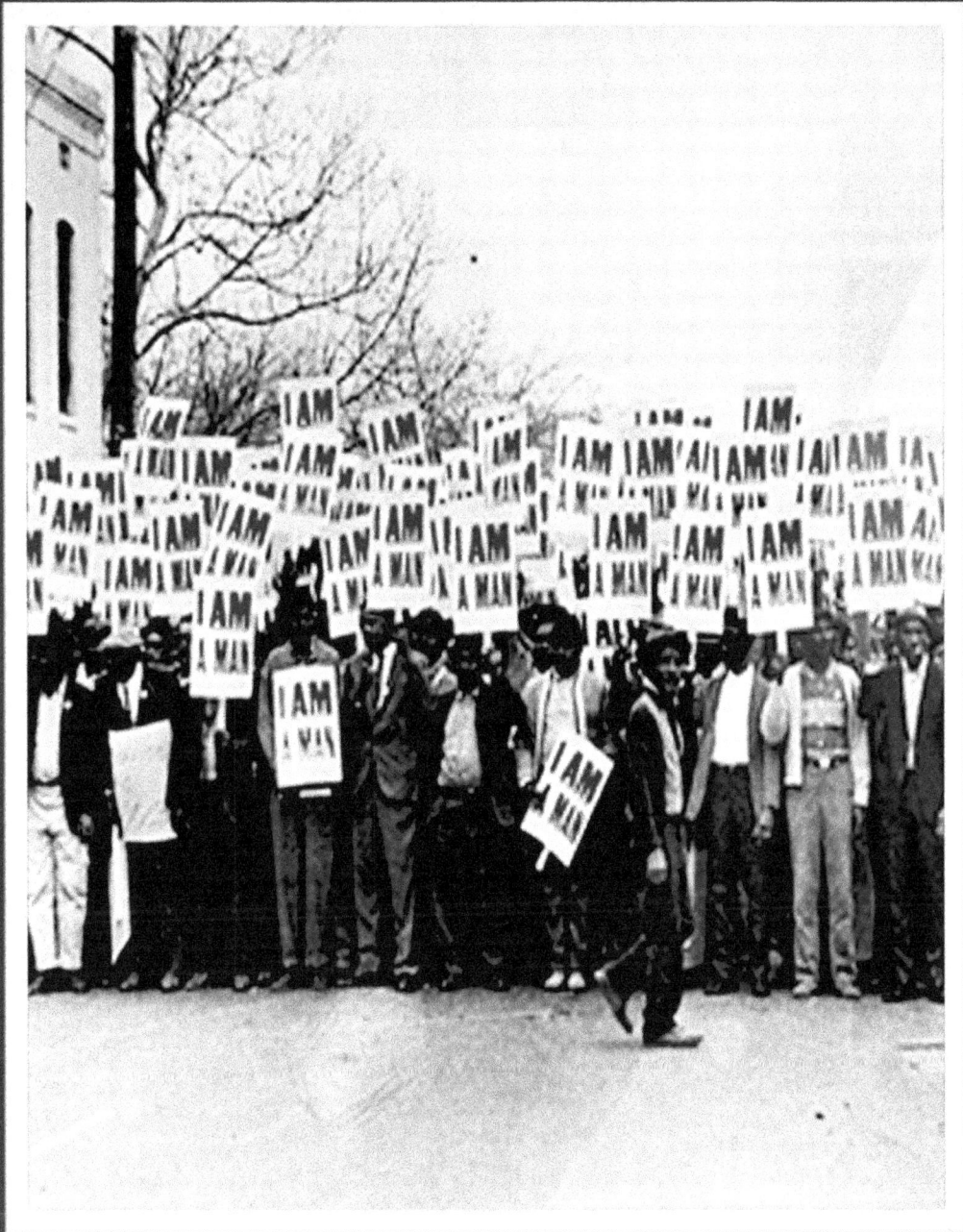

Impossible is Nothing! Regardless the Challenge

Chapter VIII

The Purpose of Life

"BE FAITHFUL IN SMALL THINGS BECAUSE IT IS IN THEM THAT YOUR STRENGTH LIES" -MOTHER TERESA

After all those emotions, and taking you through an in depth look at the breaking the emotional code, you stuck with me, and welcome to Chapter number 8. Honestly, I want to congratulate you, because as I have pointed out earlier in the book, so few people ever follow through. So for, you to be here already in chapter number 8 says to me that you undoubtedly have made some quality changes in your life, or at least begun the journey to become inspired.

I want to thank you for allowing me the opportunity to be with you. So if, we took a moment to recap we would quickly discover that what we are missing is time with ourselves. And I don't mean the quality time you spend in private while sitting upon the porcelain throne in the bathroom, mentally debating the greatest arguments of our time. But I mean the quality time with ourselves simply to allow us to think, and connect with ourselves.

We have also talked about creating the time for our daily mojo. We have also talked about how you can change anything in your life by being honest with yourself. We have talked about the purpose of relationships and how truly to define where you are in your relationships. Also, we discussed how to transform those relationships and take them to the next level. We have gone through and dissected the emotional code.

We discovered which emotions are designed to call you to take action, and how to use negative emotions to serve yourself. We have gone through your physical body and discussed how you can create more energy to allow you truly to become inspired and live your life with even more passion. After all this knowledge, what do we do with all these powerful changes we can create in our life, what is the purpose of our life?

We have to look at what actually makes you do what you do. Everything on earth has a purpose, and so do you. That purpose provides an inner drive that once you tap into you will give your life immense fulfillment. Also, knowing what your purpose in life is, will give you certainty. Because right now we live in a world that is changing so rapidly, that virtually every time you turn around you hear about something else that is changing.

The Purpose of Life

Working with people from all walks of life and ages has allowed me to share in their excitement about all the new opportunities available, and also worry about things changing to quickly. We have all talked about changes happening so rapidly now and paradigm shifts that all that stuff has been so overused it's become passé. However, even though it has become passé and we have become numb to the idea of rapid changes, nevertheless it is abundantly true.

Never in the history of the world has things changed so rapidly. So you need to find something that is eternal inside of yourself, that no matter what changes on the surface this part of you does not change. This piece inside of you is the part that grounds you, provides your compass, guides you. It is the part that truly makes you fulfilled, or in a entirely cheesy way it becomes the wind beneath your wings. And this part inside of you, that we are going to discover will become your purpose.

When the collapse of the housing market happened and many Americans retirement savings disappeared instantly, while millions lost their jobs, purpose gives you a way to find the good in virtually anything.

Finding Her Purpose | Erica's Story & Joyful Music & Dance Studio

Once you know what your purpose is in life, it is available to you 365 days, 7 days a week and 24 hours a day, just like 7-11

The Purpose of Life

But before we get to discovering your purpose let me back up and lay a foundation and understanding. Remember my close friend Erica from earlier in the book, the one who allowed me to attend Jase's The Bridge event. Well Erica is someone who truly had learned what her purpose in life is, and trust me when I say it wasn't a smooth ride for her. Erica was working for Jase and running his entire company. Erica was in her early twenties, owned her own home, was recently engaged to her high school sweetheart, and was extremely successful and making lots of money.

Erica had it all, she even had her fairy tale wedding inside a castle, as she said, *"I Do,"* to Alan, the love of her life.

Alan's dashing and devilishly charming best man (*aka 'me'*) handed over the rings, proud of his best friend, mainly because it was one of the rare occasions Alan was allowed to wear the pants in the relationship, the best man overheard whispers from the audience expressing envy for Erica. But within a year Erica felt burnt out and was ready for a change. Over the next couple years, Erica had some challenges, and some painful emotions, but what she learned was her purpose. Erica knew her passion in life was kids. She had no idea what she was going to do, and a little background with children, aside from Mission Trips she took working with orphans. All Erica was clear about was she wanted to do something with kids, and make a difference. See, Erica learned her passion, and so her mindset was focused on serving and loving kids, once she focused her mind on what she wanted, her brain found a way to make it happen.

ERICA IS NOW THE OWNER OF AN AMAZING PLACE FOR CHILDREN TO GROW AND NURTURE THEIR CURIOSITY, AND LOVE OF THE ARTS.

Erica operates a remarkable place called, Joyful Music & Dance Studios featuring Kindermusik. She took her previous skill set of managing a successful business and infused with her life's purpose of serving kids. Today, Erica works harder and longer than ever before, loves every minute and lives a life of passion. What I truly love about her business is their phenomenal work with special needs children, and speaking the language of Autistic kids thru music and the arts. For any of you in the Orlando Metro area, if you have kids, its an unbelievable feeling knowing they are in a place of imagination, curiosity, learning, around people who will love on your children as their own. I can not tell you how proud I am of Erica and her success, but most of all that, over the years, I have been grateful and blessed to have her and Alan and their entire family as a part of my own. Maybe your purpose in life is children, Let Erica's story inspire you at (joyfulmusicanddance.com).

In each moment, we must be able to find some sense of meaning for our lives, something that is significant or useful. We all know this, Im not bringing up a new conversation. But as your reading this book I feel you are allowing me to share with you as friends. As a friend, I'd like to draw your attention to some things that maybe you already know but haven't thought about for a while. Maybe what I bring up will trigger you to focus on one of the most valuable parts of your life which is enhancing meaning. All of us in life must have a reason for being here. If all your doing here is going out and trying to achieve goals and then you succeed and achieve those goals, and you then say, Now What? As I have said many times throughout this book, the reason for goals is not to achieve the goal, rather what it makes of us as people, who we become.

Ultimately we need to have a sense that who we are becoming has some kind of meaning. Because, without meaning in our lives, there's not a reason to live, there's not a reason to get up in the morning. What is unquestionably controlling most people's lives is fear! When people say their cynical, pessimistic what they're actually screaming out to you is I'm Scared Out of My Mind! They are afraid to dream again, because they live in a state of past failures. So that fear stops them from ever putting themselves out there again, they are afraid to get in a new relationship. They are afraid to put themselves out there and open a new business. They are afraid to cast a new vision of hope and service to others, because a past failure is their current mindset. Maybe they have tried it several times, and it didn't work, and all they got was pain, and more pain so pretty soon they moved away from the pain and stopped dreaming. They stopped envisioning, they stopped coming up with meaning and instead they try to avoid the pain by saying, well there's no meaning at all anyways.

But sadly this gives you the ultimate pain, because it gives you a life without meaning. And no one can live a life that's fulfilled without a sense of meaning. We have been put here for a reason, the question is why. The answer I believe is different for every one of us. Everyone one of us has been put here, everyone of us is unique, different and distinct, and I believe our creator, or I'll use the word God, if I may, God has put us here for a reason, and the question is to find out why.

GOD DOES NOT CREATE THINGS WITHOUT A PURPOSE, EVERYTHING ON EARTH SERVES A PURPOSE.

- Why are you here?

- What are you here to do?

- What are you here to become and to create and give?

These are some of the most significant questions you can answer in your life. And even when you answer them, I am sure that, as your life expands, you will come up with other questions and answers.

SEE WHERE CURIOSITY GETS YA! LIFE IS GOOD...

What are the 3 Decisions That Will Shape Your Life?

This is the essence of what I am hoping you understand after going through this journey with me, and rise inspired.

I want you to know there are no mistakes. I want you to know that every little thing that you do has a consequence, and it can be a positive consequence if you choose it. The most powerful thing that has a consequence in your life though is your decisions. As much as you may think I am beating a dead horse at this point, I can not reiterate how powerful your decisions are when it comes to the quality of your life. The first decision is deciding what to focus on, because where your focus goes will determine how you think, how you feel, what you do and ultimately what you are able to contribute in life. Essentially, we must find an inspiring focus out of any situation.

The second decision that shapes the meaning of our lives is the decision about what something means. Meaning is after all something we call the shots on and decide. Having full control over deciding what meaning we give to events in our life is truly exciting and also scary at the same time. Of course, the third decision we need to make is what are we going to do when something happens. So much of the fear that we encounter in life comes from the fact that most of us don't believe we are in control. We are running around like control freaks constantly trying to control every single event in our lives.

Every single one of us is going to experience various situations in our life, that no matter how skillful we are we can not control the event. You can't control every event especially those that you didn't even initiate. Any time your dealing with other people you won't be able to control the event. Also, we know we can't control the events of Mother Nature. Most of us in life are so afraid that something is going to happen that we can't control, therefore, were going to experience pain, and we try to avoid those things we can't control.

We try to influence every aspect of our lives, such as where we spend our time, who we spend our time with, what we do within environments we feel most comfortable in. But all this accomplishes are it limits the shape and quality of our lives, we have got to be willing to put ourselves out there.

REMEMBER THE ADVICE GIVEN BY THE FAMOUS ECONOMIST CHARLOTTE WHITTON SAID:

"Action makes more fortune than caution."

The Purpose of Life

The reason it is so essential to put ourselves out there is to discover what we are truly capable of, when we are put into environments where we don't know what to do. It's in those environments where we grow the most, it's in those environments that we discover more of our true purpose as human beings. It's in these environments that our character is shaped. So many times we set goals or we have dreams and plans, and we work our tails off, and it doesn't come out as we want. Many people come out of these situations disillusioned or angry, resentful, frustrated looking to blame others. But you know sometimes I honestly truly believe that not getting your goal is part of the design. Not reaching your goal as planned causes you to dig inside and discover more of yourself. When you dig deeper you actually begin to use your full capacity as a human being, those traits, which are within, you only expand when their challenged.

I truly believe that God is not so much interested in our convenience as he is in our character. I also believe because something hasn't happened in a way that you wanted it or designed it to work out doesn't mean it's not going to happen. It's an assessment of how committed are you, it's a test designed to make you more, God's delays are not God's denials. If you don't do your part, then of course, what you envisioned will never come to be. But we have to continue to commit ourselves forward, and no other events will show up that we can't control.

- How do you have a sense of certainty in a world that's changing all the time?

- How do you live in a world where something can happen and take away your entire business?

- What about if a storm comes and takes away your home?

- What do you do if a calamity comes along and takes out your whole family?

- What about a new virus attacking our communities, or someone close could die?

- How can we have a sense of certainty?

Yes, I have heard all these questions. The answer is you have to know the one thing you can control is non events, and what you can control is what they mean to you.

And there within comes the secret in life. Because no matter what happens in your life the meaning of what has happened is yours, you own it. You get to determine the meaning as long as you are conscious and you don't allow the people around you to teach you what to think. And as long as you don't just go on to automatic pilot and allow your nervous system to make up connections that are false.

Let me give you an example of what happens to people.

Certainly by now you realize that what you do as human beings is primarily driven by your need to avoid pain, in your desire for pleasure. All of us have learned through life that certain things mean more pain than others. So, some people are driven by their fear, because to experience the emotion of fear is the most incredibly painful thing that they could ever imagine so they will do anything to avoid being in a fearful situation. Other people are driven by their desire to feel the sense of adventure. Obviously they make decisions differently they focus on different things in life, they can walk in the same room as someone who lives in fear and they are going to notice different things. They are going to sit in a different place, they will want to try a different vacation then someone who's trying to focus on how to be secure.

SO THE QUESTION YOU NEED TO ASK YOURSELF IS:

- What drives you?

- Are you driven by guilt?

- Are you driven by your past?

WHEN WE USE THE WORD DRIVEN THE WORD DRIVE IT ACTUALLY MEANS TO GUIDE, TO CONTROL OR TO DIRECT SOMETHING.

- So what's guiding you?

- What's controlling you?

- What's directing your behavior?

- What's directing your focus?

- What's directing the meaning your pulling from your life?

- What is it that gives meaning to life for you?

- Is it your parents?

- Is it the competition you have with someone else?

- Is it wanting to prove someone wrong?

- Is it your desire to contribute?

- Is it your desire for joy or happiness?

- Or is it a sense of purpose that's driving you?

Do you feel a sense that there's something out there for you to do, there's something your designed to evolve into, to become, to share, to give, or to create. And even though you have no idea what it even is, you are still willing to trust that each day more of it's going to come out. See, whatever drives you, then that is, what's shaping your life.

The challenges we face is never consciously decided by us. Many of us never know what is ultimately going to drive our life forward, we simply give up the controls and are along for the bumpy ride. Were not stimulus response animals but, we CAN be stimulus response animals.

Our nervous systems are designed to help us, they are designed to be a source of decision making, they are designed to help us quickly, when we have an experience to figure out what is the source of that pain, so we can avoid it in the future.

Our nervous system helps us discover our source of pleasure in any event. Then using the previous event as a reference, our nervous system can assist us in seeking out even more pleasure in the future. But when we don't think things through in an inspiring way we don't have faith that there is a higher meaning. Instead, we tend to settle like animals for the lowest meaning that we can find.

WE START TO TELL OURSELVES THE SAME RIDICULOUS STORIES THAT HAVE NEVER PUT US INTO A RESOURCEFUL STATE.

- "Well this is happening because I'm a bad person."

- "Well this is happening because there is something wrong with me."

- "Well, this is happening because I am just destined to fail."

Very often in life we don't consciously think things through; instead our nervous system just makes quick decisions for us.

EVERY MOMENT WHEN YOUR ALIVE, WHENEVER YOU HAVE A SIGNIFICANT AMOUNT OF PAIN YOUR BRAIN SAYS:

"Hey what is the source of this pain?"

And your brain uses three criteria in order to determine what the source of your pain is. Your brain will look for something that is happening about the same time that you had the pain, and is unique. Because, after all, you weren't feeling pain a few moments ago, and you are now, so what's unique about this situation? Your brain looks for something that is recent something that is happening about the same time as you have pain. Your brain will also look for something that is consistent. Your brain will look for something that whenever you have had pain in the past, this has also been a factor in that situation.

Let me tell you how these three criteria can help you. Let's take an easy example, you go out one day as a child, and you touch a hot stove. And you feel some pain, and you pull your hand back quickly from the hot stove.

YOUR BRAIN SAYS:

"Ok what was unique to that moment that gave me that pain?"

YOUR BRAIN LOOKS AROUND AND SAYS:

"Aha, this burner!"

YOUR BRAIN SAYS:

"What was happening about the same time I felt the pain?"

The Purpose of Life

Then your brain concludes at the time you were touching the burners. Then the brain takes the third step and asks, what is consistent about the event, well maybe nothing in this situation. So maybe you do it again, or maybe another two or three times, but hopefully only once if it hurt enough, that is if you attached enough pain to the situation. But if you end up touching the burners on a hot stove a second, or third time, then your brain will find consistency in that third step.

IT'S LIKE WHEN SOMEBODY SAYS TO YOU:

"You always do that."

OR IT'S LIKE ONE OF MY FAVORITE COMEDIANS BILL ENGVALL WOULD SAY:

"Here's your sign."

Look human beings can make one time constant, if it's painful enough. It's like back in the day when families had the old 900 pound television sets, sitting on a TV tray in the living room, and little Billy strolled up, tugged on the electrical cord, and that TV landed smack dab on top of his head. Well, Little Billy will never go pulling on electrical cords attached to TV sets resting on an unsteady TV Tray again. Heck for that matter Billy won't be able even to spell his name correctly after taking a hit like that.

Ok, so what's the bottom line here and what have we learned? Your nervous system has already learned you don't grab hot burners. You just don't do that, Their freak'n HOT! So now in the future when you are trying to make a decision about what to focus on, and what things mean, and what to do and your going by a stove with hot burners, one of the options is not to go grab that baby, just for fun. Now, as basic as this lesson is, we failed to realize that this straightforward system that assists us so much in making decisions because it helps us discover what is the source of our pain or our pleasures. And this system helps us to avoid the pain and gain more pleasure in the future. This basic system can be misguided or misinterpret information.

This is how it works, and I'll give you an example. I was in Cabo San Lucas, doing a seminar at the American Leadership Academy, and several people had considerable challenges in their life. And one of the guys just couldn't get himself to have any meaning in his life. As I kept digging, digging, digging the real problem he had was he felt lonely because he felt disconnected, because he wanted to have someone he could share his time with while away at college. But he couldn't get himself to do that. Why would you suspect someone couldn't get themselves to be able to share their life and time away at school with another person? Not hard to figure out is it, and the answer is PAIN. The person clearly as I had guessed had a painful relationship in the past, which he had, and it was so painful that he linked up in his head that a relationship equals death.

A past relationship which caused you pain might cause you to undermine yourself and not get involved in a real relationship.

Now how did his brain do that? Well, he said he was in this relationship, and it was so enthusiastic, but after they had become intimate this girl became controlling, paranoid, jealous, and even after ending the relationship he had to deal with a serous stalking issue. But what certainly made things worse was after ending the relationship, and dealing with her stalking, then she threatened not only his life, or any possible future partner but also threatened to take her own life. And this was his first and only long term relationship. So, you can see how he linked up that relationships equal death, and death not only to me but also possible loss of life through suicide by my ex girlfriend.

IT'S NOT TO HARD TO FIGURE OUT THAT IF YOUR BRAIN SAYS:

"Why am I feeling this intense pain?"

MEANWHILE, YOUR BRAIN LOOKS FOR SOMETHING UNIQUE AND SAYS:

"Well because I'm in an intimate relationship."

AND THEN YOUR BRAIN LOOKS AROUND AND SAYS:

"What was happening around the same time, I felt the pain?"

What was consistent around the time of the pain, well it's an intimate relationship, so pretty soon your going to avoid another intimate relationship, right! But it doesn't stop there, his brain also linked up that the cause of his pain was something else, and that was women. After all, what was unique?

AND YOUR BRAIN IS ANSWERING:

"I had this women around, I was in an intimate relationship with a women."

NOW SECONDLY YOUR BRAIN IS TRYING TO FIGURE OUT WHAT WAS GOING ON:

"Well about the same time I felt the pain I was with this women."

And sure enough what was recent? This women right, around the time I had the pain she was there. So sure enough all of a sudden after two or three dates, he's ending the relationship and avoiding any kind of connection or commitment with all women. But it didn't stop there, he also linked up that the reason he felt this pain was because he trusted.

SO AS A RESULT, HIS BRAIN LINKED UP UNCONSCIOUSLY:

"If you trust then you will die."

Now, in his case I would say the opposite would actually be true. If you don't trust then you will die, because you certainly will not be living. Because if you don't trust, if you don't have faith, then you instantly die internally. You may not die physically, but you die emotionally. Because, anything that's worth living in life requires faith.

An Inspired Life requires trusting, it requires faith, it requires knowing you can get out of the chair and walk on this floor. Without hesitation, you trust when you step out onto the floor you don't need to stop, analyze and assure yourself whether or not you can do this. You don't think about your weight and the structure of the floor and what's underneath it because of your faith. You just trust, otherwise you'd be immobilized, you have to trust to drive a car. You have to have faith to enter a relationship, you need to have faith to start a business.

YOU NEED TO HAVE FAITH WHEN ALL OF A SUDDEN SOMEONE AT YOUR COMPANY SAYS:

"These 35,000 people are gone."

You need to have faith that if your one of those 35,000 who lost their job that there is a better plan for you. You will quickly act on that faith and take swift action discovering a better plan, a better solution for your life.

You've got to have faith in order to create an inspired life, a life full of passion and adventure. When you lose trust, you lose meaning. When you lose meaning, you lose your life, and maybe not physically but certainly emotionally. And when you lose your life emotionally, the physical loss of life is not that far behind. Medical researchers are now proving the mind body connection is not some psycho mumbo jumbo, but a physical reality. That the way, we think and the way we feel about our lives effects us physically.

The Navajo indian elders always believed this was true. When they were ill, and death was imminent they would go off on their own to die, away from their families. The Navajo Elder would sit alone under a tree and while praying would pass on. My Grandfather, sat my dad down one night, and said many things he never told him before, and then ended the conversation telling my dad, that his work on earth was done, and God was calling him home, he passed away peacefully the next day. And most recently, I truly believe that, after the massive scandal and devastation that engulfed Penn State and Joe Peterno, the legendary football giant died of a broken heart.

Massachusetts studied what caused people to die of their first heart attack, under age 50, without a second chance at life. Researchers wanted to know what was the number one risk factor involved. They assumed someone who would die from their first heart attack, would be a person who just had so much cholesterol in their body, that their heart wasn't able to recover. Researchers found out that this was not the number one risk factor. So they thought diabetes and some form of a genetic factor. Once again the research disproved their belief.

What the Department of Health, Education and Welfare for the State of Massachusetts's concluded in their study shocked everyone. In their published findings, the most prominent risk factor determining if someone will die from their first heart attack, with no second chance, is what researchers called job dissatisfaction. You have got to have a deeper meaning for your life, than just some function, life is not about the hours

The Purpose of Life

you spend on that grindstone, or burning the midnight oil. Life is not scraping by until you can retire, grab a beer, sit around the bar, while the jukebox plays the working man's anthem, take this job and shove it, in the background.

No wonder so many people in life turn to alcohol, drugs, or television for some kind of release or diversion. Even then, they can't find something to entertain themselves, but they still don't recognize any fulfillment because a distraction never creates a life of significance. Distraction does not create joy. Distraction will not give you what you are seeking. Drugs will not change your life, perhaps they will only end your life. The only thing drugs will do is hurt you, they will produce pain, and there are all kinds of drugs. Anything that doesn't expand you as a human being or allows you to share more love and joy with others in a natural process that enhances your physiology and your mind and your emotions and your spirit are probably something you don't need.

Your life needs to grow, you need to expand, and you need to contribute. You need to know as a human being that you are here for a purpose, and no mistakes were made in your existence on this earth. There is meaning, even if you have not found it yet, it just means you have to discover it. For most people, they don't discover meaning for their life, until life is over. What a sad place to be, when you are told you have a life threatening illness, or someone extremely close to you, who you love very much is about to leave the earth's bonds. You don't have to wait for the pain to discover the meaning. You need to decide what the meaning of life is for you, then you discover it, but first you must define it, because you can always refine it later in life, but first you must discover meaning for yourself.

COMMUNICATE WITH YOURSELF:

• "This is why I am playing the game of life."

• "This is what it's about, if every day I'm just being this way, if I'm just doing these kinds of simple things with other people, or with myself then I know I'm on track and I know there's a reason for my existence."

Have you ever heard the story of Viktor Frankl, he's the man who wrote the book, Man's Search For Meaning. Here, is a man who was in a Nazi Concentration Camp, and with pain everywhere around him and knowing at any moment he could be gassed or maybe spared. When he was spared from the gasses that day, he had the unique privilege of removing the remains of the other dead bodies out from the gas chambers. Then he had to bear placing the bodies into the big ovens to discard of the remains. Talk about intense, but somehow in the midst of all that pain he found a deeper meaning. The meaning was that even though he was in pain in that particular moment, somehow someday he would survive. And he would come to share the story, so this story would never happen any other people in the future. Viktor couldn't find meaning in the moment, he found a meaning in the future.

For most of us, the meaning we want for our lives is here today, and it's preparing us for an even greater meaning in the future. If we just use all of our life's experiences, the pain and pleasure. To become more! And prepare ourselves for whatever it is that our creator has brought us here for. To prepare ourselves for when at the moment of truth when we are needed, we will deliver. And my real belief is we are going to be delivering all along the way. It isn't something that some day you are going to do, it's something you will do every day.... or ARE DOING.

Let me say this, if you are driven by anything other than your love, your spirit and your desire to contribute, to grow and expand then maybe it's time to free yourself. And the way to free yourself is to decide, consciously decide what you want your life to be about. Decide consciously what is the purpose of your life, something simple that you can experience every single day. When I look at people's lives, and I see the people who have so much difficulty, I think the number one reason why people fail to experience the joy in their life and experience life as a win, and it isn't because their life isn't a win. Because the win could be just reaching out and touching someone around you. The win could be just telling someone that you love them. The win could be just taking care of your body, respecting God's temple. The win could be just stopping and feeling grateful. The win could be anywhere, you don't have to land on the moon, to take the win, and of course, you can enjoy landing on the moon, as well. But how much better enjoying the process, because we are going to spend most of our life in the process towards the achievement of our goals.

I'm not saying don't go do things, and I'm not saying don't have massive dreams, and I'm not saying don't do those things at all. Because, our lives are better because people dream epic dreams and they have made

The Purpose of Life

them happen. What I am saying is, do not pursue them at the expense of not appreciating what's true along the journey.

Granny's Story | An Eternal Love

More than a decade has come to pass, whereas she rendered her farewell

She was small in stature, her spirit unvarying to that of a GIANT! Same as mixing propellant into rockets set alight a mystifying sky, she illuminated the hearts of all, with her mixture of love and compassion. Her smile ever so magnanimous as if measuring several Counties wide. She's a little piece of heaven, within a town plucked from pages of a Norman Rockwell design, doors wide open, *"Ya'll are welcomed, so C'mon and stay a while."* Neighbors were family and strangers are cousins. This women, she welcomed all, the front door never opened. Because the back door never closed. No sign was ever needed, her smile and Spirit affirmed it, we welcome one, we welcome ALL. Always inviting, and coffee always brewing. Good Morning! this gal declared, as the aroma from her cooking lured us all.

From daybreak to sunset and into the night it was this women's love which was felt many miles wide. All hours of the day her home was a beacon of light and filled with family and friends, seeking warmth and a piece of pie. This amazing women was known far and wide, known for her love, warmth, compassion and maybe a hint of small town gossip.

Her beloved husband passed a few years earlier, a great man to all, his name was Tollie, and that says it all. A man of character, and values who I aspire to affirm. Continuing a legacy of service measured by the namesake I'm proud to call my own. Just before first light on a tranquil morning-tide as light gently pierced the Oklahoma sky, Gertie May Daniels lay in waiting for her final eternal passage. We will never forget her smile spanning from ear to ear as we said goodbye and she *"Slipped the surly bonds of earth"* to *"Touch the face of God."*

When my Granny passed away it was a really tough time for my mom. This was the women who raised her for the largest portion of her childhood. The passing away of a loved one is an event you can not control. God knows we tried. Granny Daniels was diagnosed with Alzheimer's years before her final goodbye. Many questions continue to surround Alzheimer's Disease.

There's a gapping spectrum of time, between someone diagnosed, up until their eventual passing. With Granny, she was a stubborn one, and spent years timelessly perfecting all the phases of Alzheimer's. And today I look back at those years with a new perception, because I understand the mind and body connection. If someone decides that, because they have some DIS-ease, they will in effect, translate that meaning into a one of demise. So in their mind, it means they're going to die. What you focus on, is what you receive so focus on dying and of course your nervous system will communicate to the rest of your body and you will die.

Fortunately, I don't think she ever understood what her diagnosis meant. As time passed, she was no longer in our world. I can only imagine the special place she created in her mind. Like I have said earlier in the book, it is important, in times of great challenges, we look for the good in all challenges. As for my Granny Daniels, finding the good was *Easy Peasy Lemon Squeezy*, She embodied, if not overflowed, with the feeling and meaning of goodness. She left me with many special life lessons, and observations, all of which, have become the greatest gifts she passed onto me. I hope you will extend me the honor and allow me to share with you my Granny's final gifts.

I am not sure the exact date that Granny learned of her Alzheimer's. Nevertheless, I do recall the early years and onset of her symptoms. It started off slow where she would ask the same questions over and over, and you could tell her memory was fading. One thing the family did, was to insure she remained

The Purpose of Life

focused on an encouraging future. A future where she had a sense of meaning, a variety of things that she was needed for. I remember even as a kid, how amazing it was to see how Granny would respond simply by being surrounded by those she loved.

To discover a meaning for Alzheimer's, I knew I needed to see the reality in what was happening. I believe by faith, that in every situation, no matter how dismal it may seem, there is good to be found. I was trying to find meaning and searching for that good, during the last couple of years. I look back, taking away a different meaning for the situation. If someone is terminally ill, by understanding the mind body connection we are able to, consistently reinforce a compelling future, with your loved one. Talk about all the things you expect their help with, vacations, the kids, grandkids, and ANYTHING to give them a purpose for living.

All human beings have a need to feel significant and appreciated. You want your loved one to feel a purpose and discover a sense of meaning which makes living compelling! Help them see only a bright future ahead of them. Now with Granny, it was a different situation all together. See, it was an undeniable fact, she was slipping further away. Granny began forgetting recent events and small details about her personal history. All of these are common in the early stages of Alzheimer's. Too quickly she was unable to recall her own address and her telephone number. She even forgot the high school from which she graduated. Time seemed irrelevant, and just like that, a spectacular lady lost all awareness of her recent experiences, including her surroundings.

It was at this time, everyone knew that that this awe-inspiring women who gave so much, now needed more than we could provide. The disheartening truth was it became necessary for her to be placed in a nursing home. It's in these moments when finding an empowering meaning is challenging. Your mind is racing with all the ways you want to justify what you know is right and needs to be done.

Can one ever justify taking a someone who always was there constantly caring, loving, encouraging and protecting everyone else, while asking for nothing in return? The best you can do, is conclude that if anyone else tried to care for her, could they provide the same 24 hour care, by trained caring professionals? The answer is more than likely no. So the meaning in this event is, to show love by insuring she has the best care for her specific needs.

As I am writing at this moment, I can not recall a time when I saw my Granny Daniel's during her time in the nursing home. The last memories I have of her, was after my Granny Gay moved back to Oklahoma, to care for her mother. I remember the first time we were back home in Healdton for a visit.

The first time walking into the room Granny Daniels lived in was emotionally hard, physically difficult. Young and immature, the concept of trying to discover meaning, in this particular situation never crossed my mind. In that moment and time it was distressful enough just trying to process the reality of the moment. Through the skewed lens of reality, in that moment, my only perception was, MY Granny was bed ridden, confined to her room, and even worse her bead she was in pain! She entered the final severe stages of Alzheimer's, losing the ability to respond, forfeit control over her own movements. She was unable to communicate verbally and physically.

What tore me up inside at that moment, was having full knowledge that she had no idea who I was, where she is, and no way to communicate.

In perpetuum, flowing through my mind, was a sense of fear and confusion, she must be encountering. Powerlessly, she opens her eyes, without the ability to speak, or to communicate yet her physical body awakened suggesting her awareness but not her state. Never wanting to go back in that room, I didn't want my presence to cause her fear or discomfort. All I was linking to this moment were emotions of fear and inevitable hurt. I recall through my research, learning how most people experiencing Alzheimer's rarely lived from onset to final stage as many years as Granny.

I longed for her to be at peace, my observation was that of only helplessness and consequential pain. We were helpless to care in the way she easily cared for all of us. As if overnight something changed, and there was a new meaning to the situation, it was Granny's final purpose on earth, her eternal gift. I'll never forget our final visit, before Granny shared her closing goodbye, it was an experience I'll never forget. Trying to avoid pain, I didn't want to go into her room, I just couldn't bear witness to her laying in confusion while she glared towards the ceiling, thinking to myself how frightened she must be. Angrily, demanding to know, why won't she just let go, I was prescribing to the notion that my Granny needs to succumb. Finally, and with no sense of haste I came to terms and entered her room. I slowly opened the door. This time as I entered Granny's room I felt a calming peace, no apprehension, no negative feelings what so ever. Surveying the room my eyes veered towards her bed, as she came into focus my eyes filled with tears.

I was received by a remarkable, radiant ever so vibrant smile, elated in awe I thanked God! Here was my Granny, with a whale of a smile, her gracious love, and warmth beaming from her soul. She needed no words, because words would fail to express a feeling that true. Granny communicated from a simple smile, upon the face of a simple lady, down home in a simple town, within a simple home. Granny's smile was infectious, allowing me to feel at peace. I know wherever she was mentally, it was someplace special and a place not short on love. Granny set the meaning of it all, her message was clear as long as you share love and happiness with others, and simple smile can start it all.

Granny Daniels final gift embodied who she was; constant and true to her character. The gift of a smile, many times overlooked in our day to day lives but when you pause and notice the little gifts we encounter each day, when you can appreciate the feeling of a loving smile, and when you connect on a deeper level with another human being it magnifies the human experience. Things come and go, they go from in style to out of style, they are life's greatest distractions, and as much as we may feel a temporary feeling of happiness or joy, they will pass the test of time, when you close your eyes on a lonely cold night and you see that beautiful smile, the darkness becomes a calming peace, and you become engulfed in a lasting familiar warmth called love. These are the gifts we remember. These are the gifts that give meaning. These are the gifts which make life worth living and her gift was the same as the day she was received on earth as it was when she said her final earthly goodbye.

Her gift was love, joy, faith, and that family is anyone you allow into your heart to share life's simple joys. One woman who touched so many, and steadfast to her purpose she never left until she gave her final gift.

AND I REMEMBER AS MY MOM HUGGED HER FOR THE LAST TIME, AND SAID:

"Granny, we're ok, we will be fine, you don't need to protect us anymore, you can go home, we love you it's time for you to be with Grandaddy, he misses you and is waiting at home for you, we love you!"

Shortly after Granny said goodbye, and went on home, but she left her love, she left her smile and warmth, and when I feel a sense of loneliness all I have to do is close my eyes and I see the greatest gift as her smile is as vivid today as it was when she first gave it to me.

As the family felt the end was starting to come there was more pain and tears and we felt it all. At the same time we reminded ourselves that we were creating the meaning of loss because of our short term thinking about this woman. Her body and her presence but her life will live on beyond her physical presence here. And for Granny, it probably means love, love of her final gift a lasting legacy of love through the small things, the important things which came to be Gertie May Moore Daniel's purpose in life. For her it's a chance to be with her husband my Great Granddaddy, Tollie Clarence Daniels. This is another meaning that could give you joy at a time your feeling pain.

She died in her sleep, out of pain on the day she decided her work was done, her smile was her final goodbye. She created in her family a greater sense of courage, to look at life in a new way. She left us with a greater sense of dedication to give even more. She added to our drive, she added to our commitment to be givers in life as she was to any soul who had the privilege of coming across her path. I also hope it makes you think about what's most important in your life.

I remember a quote by Michael Landon the actor from Little House on the Prairie and Bonanza he gave to Life Magazine just before he died, he said:

"Somebody should tell us right at the start of our lives that we're dying, then we might live life to the limit every minute of every day. Do what I say, whatever it is that you want to do, do it now. There are only so many tomorrow's."

If you and I are going to live our lives fully then maybe sometimes we can take the experiences of those around us and learn from them. We can learn that in all our lives we are either warnings or examples. Granny Daniel's life was an incredible example. She didn't feel anything in life was insignificant; not a flower, not an animal, not a stranger passing through or the smile they can share with each other. She lived her life by example and she showed us that life is meant to be happy, to be a joy, to appreciate the little things as well as the big things, to appreciate one another to be givers and be lovers of life.

I remember when my mom received the phone call that her Granny had gone home, there were a lot of emotions and tears. But at the same time my mom felt an incredible since of peace for her. It's amazing how instantly our focus could change simply by changing what we were focusing on. We couldn't control the event, but we could certainly direct our own minds, by thinking beyond ourselves and into something deeper, which is a deeper meaning in life.

I remember going down for Granny's funeral, held in Healdton a little town in Southern Oklahoma. As many times as I have visited family in Healdton this trip, I was seeing the town in a whole new way, a town where my families roots are deep. Granny was a simple girl, with simple values and a simple mission. When I got there and looked around and Granny never explicitly said what the mission of her life was and the purpose of her life. As I arrived at the small rural Baptist church I was overwhelmed with the amount of people there to say their goodbyes.

The couple of days leading up to the funeral I was inspired by the fact that this woman who has been in her own special world for a few years now, still breathed life into the hearts and minds of so many around town. Every place we would go from the flower shop, restaurants, grocery store, city offices, everyone shared their love for my Granny. I took the time this trip to actually listen as strangers shared their stories of love and admiration for Granny, and for my Granddaddy Tollie. I felt the joy and happiness as the stories of remembrance before and during the funeral changed to stories of laughter at the gathering after the funeral.

I remember meeting my cousin Travis for the first time, the only man I met who carried around cans of beer in his pant pockets, and as he popped the top on another warm beer hearing my mom holler out:

"Travis, you know Granny be turning over in her grave now, if she knew you were getting drinking during her funeral."

He, just replied in a slow slurred Texas draw (*Yes there is a difference between a Southern draw and a Texas draw*):

"Aww Becky Joe, You want one?"

Everyone shook their head laughing, as loving families do, and exactly how Granny would want it to be.

I heard from people who talked about their memories of my Granddaddy Tollie. They told me at his funeral people were standing outside the church to pay their respects because no one else could fit inside. People from several counties came to pay their respects for him and to my Granny. It was at this moment I discovered a new meaning, a profound meaning that has shaped my life and all my actions since that day. I found a new meaning for Legacy, and what is a true Legacy anyone can leave behind. I looked around at all the people laughing, loving, sharing and reminiscing.

The true meaning of the word legacy to me was people and love. Granny and Granddaddy never had any buildings named after them, never had much money either, no endowments were given, or trusts set up in their names, not a single In memory of, or In remembrance of, was ever etched upon any public display. Grandaddy did have a small county dirt road named in his honor, but that was it. So, why was there so many people who went out of their way to not only pay their respects but share their love, admiration, and stories of gratitude for these two simple people? Simple. Legacy is not a monument, building, or a name etched in honor of.

Legacy is not an endowment in the memory of or even a wing, study, or garden named in someone's honor. No, a true legacy is so much more, it can't be bought, just as it will never be sold. A true legacy is not stationary, nor is it vulnerable to being reduced to a pile of dust.

The True Meaning of Legacy

Because a true legacy breathes, it has its own life, it is a feeling, it is a standard or guide of measurement, it is passed on from generation to generation, it is a verb because it's always fluid and it's an action, a True legacy is the product of Love + People and Service to ALL.

Legacy gives a meaning to the most powerful question and idea any man or women could ever ask, What Could Be... Legacy is the answer turned into action when a man or women Rises up Inspired and proclaims, Let It Be... A true Legacy which my simple grandparents left me, are a testament to the historical fact that one man, one woman, of all backgrounds, faiths, circumstances, ethnicity, color or creed can and do make a difference.

The monuments proclaiming a Legacy of greatness to Lenin and Stalin have all but disappeared, but the Legacy of one women, a world away, living in poverty, surrounded by disease and famine, asked the question, What Could Be... and with Faith she went to serve when others would not, she was unreasonable when she decided to rise inspired and declare, Let It Be... And this one women with no means, special training, or support steadfast in her Faith that God was her compass and Love + People and her purpose to serve ALL ignited a ripple effect of understanding, compassion, service, and renewed a resolute commitment to caring with love and good deeds across the world. But Mother Teresa was an unreasonable woman, whose purpose was to Love ALL and Serve ALL because ALL people matter. And when Mother Teresa was called home by God, her funeral was attended by the leaders of almost every country spanning across every continent and every state on earth. Because its all those little things in life, and along the journey that are so, so, so, immensely important. And I like to feel as if we have always believed that they are important and we always lived as if they are important. I just want to double up the effort, per my commitment to my Granny.

So in her honor I challenge you to do the same. I challenge you to hold yourself to a higher standard. I challenge you to realize that you're here for a purpose, because there is something for you to do and be here for yourself and for others. You can't just do for others and not do for yourself, or you won't be here. So I designed this to encourage you to ask yourself, are you being efficient, are you being effective in your life? The differences between these two questions are as different and unique as night and day.

Being efficient means you are doing things right, but if your being effective you are doing the right things often. Are you doing the things that will bring you the most joy in your life? Ask yourself the question; why are you doing what your doing? Where does your journey take you doing the things you are currently doing? We all need to have what I like to call a Character Oversight. Your character oversight is a set of personal standards to which we set our compass to every day of our lives. Character determines who we will be as a people, the kinds of mental states we will live in. It is through these states that we effect our mojo as well as effecting those around us.

Stop and ponder what's most important, consider why you are here, what is the purpose of your life. It is through this oversight of your character which you set your compass so you can cast your vision, you can step out of the moment and into eternity. When you are feeling insecure, focus on what's eternal. Begin to realize there is something deep within you which began but never ends. Your true character, builds a strong, unwavering and unflinching source of right and wrong. Character is your compass, explaining what

The Purpose of Life

you need to do, where you need to go, and why you are here. You can interpret this as metaphysical, religious, spiritual or attach any term you want, as long as you know, you are here for a reason. Be strong in knowing that you are in this time for a marked reason, and it is within your soul that you and you alone know that reason. Who knows maybe you haven't found it because you have been seeking something huge. It could also be that right now you already are and have been living your purpose, you just haven't recognized it. Maybe what your doing right now is your life's purpose, this thing that you reject most is giving you the challenge to discover something within yourself which will allow you to give and be more.

Life is about two things, being and doing. Who you are today, magnifies in the future. So allow me to propose this question, who are you today? What's your individual resolve to emerge as a human being here on earth? What procedures are you performing to attain your purpose? What are you contributing to enhance the human spirit in others? Contributing! Life's considerable magnification and solace lies within ones ability to contribute in meaningful ways with others. Purpose is a function of honor, it's a gift shared with others, when you bestow upon the many you inherit beyond all measures. A deep comprehension of fulfillment, is derived from a life of significance, it's the lifeblood of growth and contribution. The age old question posed by the greatest minds and philosophers throughout the ages can now be answered.

Why are we here? This question has plagued man from the dawn of time, when the answer is at it's core forthcoming once you decide your destiny in life. In all seriousness these are the meat-and-potatoes essential questions you need to provide answers for. Why are you here? Are you here to live? Could it be also you here to learn? Is your desire to expand, and grow to view life through a lens of an explorer who's journey is life itself? Are you here to share and love in pursuit of service to your fellow man? I'm asking these questions, confident you are thinking, not merely reading random words on a page.

What is the significant plan for you? You forge the destiny to discover the purpose for your own life. I assure you there is a plan, there is something here for you, and it is different from anyone else in the world, it's yours and you own it. The best way to uncover your purpose is to trust your instinct and say, what is it?

MAYBE YOU ANSWER YOUR QUESTION BY SAYING TO YOURSELF THE FOLLOWING:

"I was living everyday and it was simple, clear and I was living every day, so why am I here?"

Because if you never discover your purpose how will you ever magnify your life's experience? How can you truly enjoy your life entirely?

You Control Your Life's Purpose

I look around and see how unhappy and unfulfilled many people are in their lives, and I wonder why.

I think the answer is they have settled for a place of comfort, and they don't want to see life as an adventure or even a game. They feel like the deck is stacked against them, and they will lose they always have and always will. So they choose to pout and take their toys home, never to play in the game of life. I think one of the reason's why people never win in life or experience winning, experience joy and fulfillment is because they have no clue what is the purpose of the game. I mean if you don't know the purpose of any game, then what's your chances of winning?

You will never get to cross the finish line, feel that sense of fulfillment or joy, happiness, or passion and all the things you honestly want at the deepest level. If you don't know the purpose of the game, if you don't know the goal then it's pretty hard to set up your game to win, you will never pass go and you will not collect $200.

After a while, you start doing things that will never bring you fulfillment. If you continue doing things that bring no fulfillment, you will end up living in the shadow. You'll end up living in the shadow of someone else, rather than directing a life of your own. You must become clear on what you really want. What are the things in life that drive you? What excites you in life? It's funny, when I ask people what do they really want, They tell me all the things they don't want, it is a list that rolls right off their tongue. I will always concur that all the junk clogging up their life are things I wouldn't aspire for either.

However, as bad as all that seems, it still does not negate the need to answer the intent of my actual question. Telling me all the things you don't want in your current life, and expanding on all the frustration you feel, will not produce any relevant changes. You don't need me to feel pity for you. One more sympathetic ear will not empower you to make the changes required for you to evade imminent pain and irritation. It's not because I don't care, in fact, it's the farthest thing from the truth.

Truth of the matter is, my personal past is a testament to the outcome of pity and self-loathing. Empathy and melancholy can manifest itself into directing your butt to the nearest couch to lose yourself in a distraction in lieu of defining your life's purpose. To be a victim is to become complacent. It can result in physically not being able to walk down the driveway or having to stop to catch your breath at any minuscule activity, as it was in my case.

Self-repugnance precedes the self inflicted shame of not fitting behind the steering wheel of your car, or the crappy awareness, knowing you can't travel by air, without booking 2 seats. I implore you to not submit to the stories we tell ourselves, listing all the reasons why we can't do something, or why we bear no responsibility in our choices. As a result of the stories I told myself, I weaved a web of deception, convincing myself that things were not as bad as they seemed. 500 pounds later, you respect your own influence and storytelling that could make you believe status quo, was not that bad.

Please recognize, you will never bring about life altering powerful changes in the absence of unconditional and direct honest communication with yourself. Bluntly put, stop lying to yourself! Compassion is NOT me letting you repeat your excuses or stories of what you don't want, can't do, feel like, etc., The only thing stopping you are the stories you tell yourself to never try. Now, let me ask you because if you have read this far, it's because you have been honest with yourself, you have already made changes and experienced the possibilities. So now with all the possibilities opened wide for you, without any limitation, fear, or excuses.

WHAT DO YOU WANT? REMEMBER, BE SPECIFIC AND DON'T PLAN IN GENERALITIES, SAYING SOMETHING LIKE:

"I want to be financially secure so I can retire."

Great, do you know the statistics about retirement? According to studies done by insurance agencies, statistically on average three years after a man retires, he dies! Here's a new meaning, to retire is to die. Seriously, when you start thinking about what you want, remember to be specific. As nice as it sounds to say you want to be financially secure to retire, that's not what you REALLY want.

What is it about retiring that is exciting for you? As you form that list or things like being more involved in your children or grandchildren's lives, play more golf, to travel etc., now we are getting down to the true desires and wants. Retirement is not going to bring you happiness, you must have a purpose. You have to realize what your purpose is, you've got to decide what your purpose is now, and know that your vision will continue to expand.

The second reason people fail at the game called life is because even though they don't know the purpose of the game, they have tons of rules at how it must be played. It's amazing they even know how to even play, yet they have an abundance of rules which to live by. Not only do they have all these rules for themselves, but they have rules for everyone else around them. Rules for how their spouse should be. Rules for how their boss should be. Rules for how people they don't even know on the street should be. So often in life we get upset with other people, yet it's not about the other people it's about our rules.

The Purpose of Life

They are doing something we know they shouldn't be doing. Wait, no, no they're NOT doing something we know they should be doing. We need to just relax a little bit, stop throwing rocks at glass houses.

We need to realize that whatever people are doing they are doing so because they have a reason. Sure, it may not be the brightest idea from our point of view, but who are we to judge. Maybe it is a truly genius idea by other people's opinion, but you know what, there is a reason. It comes down to how we are wired as human beings. Whenever you see someone and you think they are doing something insane, have some compassion. Are there any stupid things that you have done?

Boy, I could fill another book about idiotic things I have done, and some of the time I did so with full knowledge I was being stupid. It comes down to understanding ourselves and not fully knowing about others and what might be going on in their lives. During one of my trips to Russia, I was talking to Sergei Khrushchev. He told me about a time when he got on the Metro and a man shoved his kids onto the train. His kids were running all over the place, being obnoxious, loud, and just wreaking havoc. Sergei is a very reserved man being raised in the Kremlin and having certain expectations about his behavior being the son of the Soviet Union's Premiere Nikita Khrushchev. He didn't want to say anything, or make a scene yet he was getting more and more irritated and from his perspective the man was just ignoring his kids. Finally Sergei said he had enough, and told the man to control his kids, and the man looked at Sergei and immediately recognizing who he was and apologized. He informed Sergei that they just left the hospital where their mother just died. He informed Sergei he was struggling to deal with the event and the children were acting out to the recent news. Sergei said he will never pass judgment on a situation without knowing all the facts, because a fellow comrade was in need and at first he condemned him, instead of lifting him up. It's an example of how we need to realize that what ever is going on there maybe something deeper also taking place. It made him have compassion, and it gave him less rules for other people in his life.

Why Don't People Succeed at the Game of Life?

The Purpose of Life

- **NUMBER ONE** IS THEY DON'T KNOW THE PURPOSE OF THE GAME.

- **NUMBER TWO** IS THEY HAVE ALL THESE RULES, EVEN THOUGH THEY DON'T KNOW THE PURPOSE OF THE GAME.

How would you like to be in a game, where you don't know the goal and you have a billion rules by which you have to play. You end up feeling like you just sat down to play chess with Stephen Hawkins sitting across from you. Now as frustrating as that may be, and embarrassing let's add in the third reason to the mix.

- **NUMBER THREE** IS BECAUSE THEIR RULES ARE IN CONFLICT.

The third reason why people fail at the game of life is because their rules are in conflict. We have so many rules that we are constantly contradicting ourselves.

One event you're supposed to be one way and then in another event you're supposed to be Dr Jekyll and Mr Hyde! If you have so many rules constantly in conflict, you're going to have pain. You're going to be upset and irritated all the time.

- **NUMBER FOUR** IS BECAUSE PEOPLE WON'T ALWAYS WIN, EVEN WHEN THEY PLAY BY ALL THE RULES.

Here's the fourth reason why people won't win at the game of life, it is because even when the person plays by the rules they don't always win.

The Purpose of Life

So you do everything right but you don't always get rewarded. You gave your all, you put your best effort forward, you put it all on the line and still sometimes it still rains on your parade. Sometimes mother nature unleashes a flood onto your crops and wipes out all your work and planting. And you're stuck standing there looking at your crops destroyed and it messes with your brain.

You start thinking to yourself that all your work, sweat, and long hours were for nothing. Without realizing there's a deeper meaning and there's a deeper plan beyond the moment. You can't see past the event you couldn't control, whether it be a loss of a close family member or the loss of a business or anything that seems to be a loss is a gain if you choose to look for the good in all events.

IF YOU CHOOSE TO ASK YOURSELF:

- *"How can I use this?"*

- *"What else could this mean?"*

- *"If I can't use this today, then how can I utilize it later on?"*

- *"How can I create an opportunity out of this?"*

- *"How can I build myself up and make myself better from this?"*

- *"How can I tap into this pain and use it to shape my spirit?"*

These are the kinds of questions which will support you instead of sitting back and allowing yourself to become a victim. You will never find the answers to move forward, overcome, and conquer with the thinking from a victim's perspective.

- **NUMBER FIVE** IS BECAUSE SOMETIMES YOU WIN BY BREAKING THE RULES.

The fifth reason why people fail at the game called life is because sometimes when you break the rules, you win. Oh my gosh, you do something wrong and you win, you do something knowing you shouldn't and you are rewarded. You throw out your values, and forget your character and allow yourself to be naughty and you get pleasure.

NOW YOUR BRAIN IS SIGNALING:

- "HEY! Hey hey, buddy boy, looks like there's some new rules out here."

- "Maybe I don't have to live by these rules."

- "After all, when I work my butt off and follow all the rules, and held myself to a higher standard, I ended up with someone taking all the credit and felt frustrated. But breaking the rules, felt really good, maybe this is how things should be."

And as crazy as I just sounded, and making the examples completely overblown and crude it is because you also just lowered your standards and what's a win when your standards are so low you become crude and obnoxious. It takes you away from your higher purpose. It takes you away from what's most important in your life. Although you might get some pleasure in the onset you give up that sense of honor and dignity in yourself that says, your doing what's right and good.

Losing your honor is what causes more people to fail than anything else. Because the absolute ecstasy in life requires sometimes a bit of short term pain in order to reach the absolute ecstasy which you become. Also, the experience of life which you create is because of that growth and contribution.

- **NUMBER SIX** IS BECAUSE THERE'S 5.5 BILLION OTHER PEOPLE ALL PLAYING BY THEIR OWN RULES.

The number six reason people fail at this game called life is because in order to win this game you have to work with five and a half billion other people who all have the wrong rules. They also have no clue what the purpose of the game is, and they have also made it very clear that there are certain rules YOU must live by.

We all have different rules, because we all have learned different ways for getting out of pain and into pleasure in life. We need to learn from each other.

- **NUMBER SEVEN** IS IT'S A LIFE OR DEATH GAME.

Finally the seventh reason why people fail in the game called life is because they make the assumption it's a life or death game. Let me be the first to say that this is no practice session or scrimmage, that's why we have to live life at full throttle.

If you think everything is life and death every moment, placing so much pressure on yourself that you truly will not live life, instead you will live in fear, which is no life at all.

Game of Life

How Do You Live Life and Win the Game?

Well in spite of all this stuff that sounds so awful, there are people who seem to be winning, seem to be fulfilled, seem to be making a difference and they seem to have a great deal of joy in their life. They also seemed to be doing it consistently, and they aren't doing it through drugs or alcohol or any type of distractions. They are doing it by living a life of significance. How are they doing it? The first thing these people have done is they have decided the purpose of the game. They may not know what the purpose of their life is, and they could sit around under a tree waiting for an apple to fall and knock them on the head, but instead they just decided.

THEY MADE THE DECISION AND SAID:

"I don't know what the purpose is ultimately, but let me just decide. And for right now the purpose for my life is to love and to be loved, it's to grow and expand while making a difference!"

These people who succeed and find fulfillment took action and decided what the purpose of their life is, in this moment. This is exactly what I want you to do at the end of this chapter. I want to get you started on a mission statement and a statement of purpose for your life. This is a must! An absolute! Because how can you ever aim, when there's no target in sight.

We have all these choices, and all these opportunities in life. You should not be forced to choose between something good or bad, instead you can choose between something good or great. You can never make an easy decision if you don't know what your purpose is, and especially if you don't know what you value most in life. All decision making is value illumination. Without a destination all roads lead to nowhere. One of the biggest challenges in life is choosing, and that means you need to focus on your life, deciding what to spend your time and energy on. When you have a clear defined purpose it will allow you to do that.

The second thing you want to do in order to make your life work is to have fewer rules, and having fewer rules is exactly what those who succeed have. The more rules you have about how people have to be and how life has to be in order for you to be happy is the less happy your going to be. The happiest people are the ones who say, everyday above ground is a great day. The happiest people are the ones who find joy in a smile. They find joy through adventure, or the most simple of actions. See if you can find joy in all the little things, then all the really big things become a bonus for you.

SO WHEN YOU FIND YOURSELF BEGINNING TO REACT TO SOMETHING THAT SOMEONE ELSE MIGHT HAD DONE, THEN ASK YOURSELF:

"How significant is this to me?"

Ask yourself if this situation really is as bad as you first thought. Is it really such a terrible thing for this person to have an opinion different from me.

IN MOST CASES YOU WILL FIND YOURSELF ANSWERING:

"Yeah it is."

Well, what would you have to believe in, so you don't become upset? Does everyone have to live by your rules? Maybe in some areas it is important to you, however it is not valid in other areas of my life. In areas where different rules bare no weight on you, then disregard your rules and you will avoid so much unwarranted pain throughout your life.

The people who win at the game of life have a third thing in common, which is consistency in their rules. Whenever they face conflicts in their lives, they choose to honestly weigh the validity of their anger and if they find no merit communicate to themselves.

"I am a walking contradiction considering I have no issues with this in any other aspect of my life, and I am not going to start adding new ones now!"

People who succeed allow themselves the self satisfaction and a job well done, whenever they succeed. This is the fourth difference between those who succeed at the game of life and those who never even play. They choose to congratulate themselves when they know they have done a exceptional job, and don't look to outside accolades. This is not selfish or conceited, nor is it a form of self-grandstanding. Instead, it's the ability to appreciate your personal good work, without the need to have it reinforced by others. Who are you trying to please in life, yourself or others because not every time you do a good job, will you have it recognized. Just be sure to acknowledge you have done your best, and feel pride in your work. Be sure to catch yourself doing the little things right and allow yourself the gusto you deserve.

If someone telling you how great of a job you did makes you feel all warm-n-fuzzy, its not their words creating that feeling, it's because they took time and said, *"Great Job."* It's the fact that it caused you to stop and think to yourself:

"Oohh... that means I get to feel good."

You send a little neuro-transmitter that allows you to feel warm-n-fuzzy all over. Tell yourself when you do a great job, it keeps you on track. Always reinforce good behaviors, and especially those excellent behaviors you have developed. You reinforce your commitment to a standard of the highest values.

Now, the fifth thing that these people who succeed have in common is personal accountability. When they screw up, and don't do things the right way, and violate their own rules and sense of purpose, they hold themselves accountable. They hold themselves accountable even if it causes them pain. They become steadfast in their resolve and their actions are not who they are. Reinforcing a higher standard which they are demanding of themselves. Setting the bar high and taking full responsibility for their actions, choices and decisions in order to stay on track.

The sixth thing that these people who win have in common is the knowledge that everybody in life has different rules. Forging relationships in life are crucial to success and happiness. People who succeed understand the need for strong relationships, and as they are cultivating those partnerships they are also learning the rules by which they live their lives. Knowing what is important to the other person and the rules by which they live helps to understand them and resolve any conflicts before they cause pain. Lastly, Successful people understand life has a purpose, but they also recognize the importance to never take life and more importantly themselves to seriously. Why do angels fly? Because they take themselves lightly. Flexibility allows us the advantage to see life in many different ways, it becomes the difference between succeeding and failing.

Right now, we are going to find a way to develop a greater sense of meaning for ourselves. First, relax by letting out a big sigh of release. I'm not telling you to go and create some grandiose purpose, or author pages and pages describing what your purpose is. I will be sticking with simplicity as our guide, because the simplest things can be the most dynamic things. So, take a moment and close your eyes. Think about what is it you wanted to be, growing up as a kid? Think back to when you were a little kid, still curious about the world and a time when all things were still possible. What did you want to be, when you grew up? I doubt you need to think considerably hard, you probably have an plethora of ideas. What were you inspired to become, who were your role models at the time? Why did you want to become that person growing up? Maybe take a moment and write some of these thoughts down and let's work on this together.

Back to our question. What did you want to be, when you grew up? Well, I remember one of the first things I wanted to be was a fighter pilot. Once you remember what you wanted to be, then think about why you wanted to be that? Another way of asking is, what is the feeling you were hoping to get from that profession?

As a kid when you thought about what you wanted your dream profession to be can you describe why you chose that idea? What were the sensations it would bring you, or what kind of feeling? Taking a magical carpet ride back into time, I can vividly describe the reasons I wanted to be a fighter pilot. I started out as a kid with a toy musket and you never saw me without my official Davy Crocket Coon Skin Cap. I built forts near and far searching for enemies throughout our neighborhood's woods and creeks.

After a couple years I graduated out of the Davy Crocket cap, and I would march up and down the street with a towel tied to a long tree limb, also known as my flag or banner of honor. I wanted to be the hero, I wanted to have new adventures everyday, while facing the giants of the world, and by faith knowing good would always conquer evil.

What's intriguing is I'm still seeking adventure today. I have a unwavering faith that the good in people will always subdue the bad guys, and I strive to empower the good in all people. Today, many of those things I loved about being a fighter pilot I am already doing every day. Resulting in my primary goal of what being a fighter pilot would mean to me, I'm just not sitting in the cockpit of an F-22 Raptor. I have been able to create that feeling of adventure, today, just in a new and unique way. So, I challenge you to discover what you actually wanted if you would have grown up to be that person but on a deeper level rather than the superficial. What is it that excited you? What feelings did you think it would allow you to experience? After you finish this exercise repeat it. Recall another person you wanted to be when you were a kid, and rework the same questions. I was rather consistent growing up, If it wasn't a fighter pilot then it was always some kind of front line soldier, I wanted to be in the action, traveling far and abroad. I wanted to be living a life of adventure every day. I wanted to uncover what some of the deeper reasons I had were, so I came up with a few I want to share.

In my Boy Scout troop we had two of the most incredible men I ever met, and I wanted to be what they were. Their names we Col. Donahue and his subordinate Capt. Solgare of the United States Marine Corp. Both men were in the top five of their graduating classes from The United States Naval Academy, they have traveled all over the world, led men in battle and commanded in theaters of war. They were fearless and there was no man or threat on earth which could shake their resolve. They stood for those who could not stand for themselves.

The Purpose of Life

They spoke in a foreign language made up of: YES SIR! TAKEN CARE OF SIR! DONE SIR! They spoke with the absence of any excuses, blame, or general reasons why something could not be accomplished, instead it was always completed.

Their stories would began with, We were in the middle of nowhere... when we asked why they seemed to always be in a land of nowhere, the answer was simple:

"We are Marines, they don't want us around people or places, we blow things up, we get the job done!"

As a kid, and even today, when I think of the definition of a Real Man, I automatically think of these men.

When I received my Eagle Award in Scouting, the greatest honor came from the attendance by both these men. Standing at attention donning the iconic Marine Corp full dress blues uniform. Top to bottom every crease was perfect, every medal, insignia meticulously displayed, it was perfection even including their Naval Academy Sabers attached to their sides. I believe the feeling is obvious, one look at the Col., or Capt., in their full Dress Blue's it was a feeling of honor, respect, strength, tradition, values, character, selflessness, pride, ego, greatness, vitality, and the list goes on.

You throw many of those qualities into a box, you would come up with an underlying theme of their character and values which is service to others. This was the foundational feeling I wanted, and I have found a way to that create in my life. Sure, it's much different then my original scope, yet the purpose is the same. Now, in your case maybe it's not the same purpose, it could be they have some commonalities to what you initially wanted to be, or as far apart as California to New York.

Now that we indulged in another, Story Time with Tollie, let's get back to YOU. What else did you want to be when you were growing up, and why did you want to be that? Detail the feelings you expected to receive from that profession, tell me your story. Allow your story to become real to you, wake up that little kid still inside of you. This needs to become real and vivid, as real as strapping a towel onto a tree limb and marching through your neighborhood standing watch against all evil. Now, of course I highly recommend you forgo actually marching the streets with a towel as your flag. I have a feeling your future would involve a room with padded wall paper, wearing a helmet at all times for good measure. All and all, this is how you get excited and feel your mojo flowing. Discover what you want and what is your purpose in life. What is it that will give meaning to your life? You have learned of your purpose before, as a kid you gave your life purpose, you just had no idea what purpose, was. This is why staying curious will lead to an overwhelming expansion of possibilities and happiness in your life. Pretend I'm there with you, share with me one other person you wanted to be? I'll help trigger your brain while I share one more of mine. Aside from being G.I. Joe incarnate, the only other thing I dreamed of becoming was an entertainer. I wanted to create a feeling while captivating the audience. I wanted to affect people's emotions and state, anytime by being up on stage or on the screen. I wanted to feed off of their energy, creating an escape creating a feeling so they would leave inspired, open to all possibilities. I wanted to be a true all around entertainer. I aspired to follow the legends, such as James Cagney, Bob Hope, Sammy Davis Jr., Cary Grant, Charlie Chaplin, and the list goes on. Because, these were the gentlemen of entertainment, versatile in their skills and craft.

Whether it be on screen or off, singing or dancing, dramatic or comedic they could do it all. They could give a toast in honor of, or roast you with a slip of the tongue and a devilish smile, with charm and a canny wit. They were actors, singers, dancers, speakers, producers, they were the all in all, one size fits all, legendary men of the silver screen and stage. It was their ability to create so many emotions, and feelings by controlling the environment, setting life to music and directing once again, a film called LIFE. So, I was able to take my natural talents and use those theatrical aspects in order to promote empowering messages, challenge the dreamers across the world while showing what's possible if you will choose to believe.

Maybe your not doing what you originally envisioned, but that doesn't stop you from finding a way to do it even better. I may not sing or dance all that well, yet put me in front of any crowd and I guarantee you I will make an impact, I will inspire change. First off, just have faith in yourself, your dreams, your abilities, and in knowing it's through the process and journey you find answers, achieve success, feel passion and YES even ask more questions. If you at least know the emotion you want and how you will contribute to others, by developing yourself I am certain you will find an even better way, to create those same feelings. Besides, what was once considered cool, might not be so Super Duper, or even Groovy, today. Are you still wanting to become the next member of the New Kids on the Block, or go solo like Sinead O'Connor? If you answered yes to either of those questions, then WOW.... thats all I can say! What I know is you can magnify your original desire as long as you continue to develop yourself. It is through faith you will uncover the answer. First off, before you find the way, you must find the essence of what you really want, or purpose?

Now with your eyes closed again, think about a situation in your life where you felt on a roll completely unstoppable. You were a square peg in a square hole kind of world. You know those type of days where you feel untouchable. Those days where every word spoken by others is one of agreement, accolades, and jolly cheer. A day where you drive down the road and cars merge to allow you a direct unobstructed path to your destiny! The day where all the lights are green, streets are lined with well wishers, waving as you pass by. Yes, this is a time of ultimate fantasy, a slightly exaggerated story depicting just another day in my life. I know you followed along with where I was going, you catch my drift, you pick up what I'm putting down.

It's the feelings, confidence, faith, and courage you feel on those days. As far out and absurd as what I just wrote sounded, on those days we can feel like that. As cliche as it may sound, we do walk around with a spring in our step. These were the days when everything was effortless. You would exclaim to the whole world, This is it! This is what life is all about! Can you remember a time like that? Young or old it's when you are in that flow, and playing in your head is the same song, *"This is it! This is what life's all about!"*

Think of a situation like that. Right now! It's time for the ultimate throwback, step back into your mind, jump back into your body from that time period. Just get back to your funky self! Seriously, it's ok. I can kick it old school with you. Look through your own eyes as you were then. You were emboldened with the excitement and you felt like this is what life's all about! Take a moment and creep on yourself, this is the only time I give anyone permission to do this. Now your back in the day, you are back in your old body. Seeing what you saw, hearing what you heard. Now, what were you doing and feeling? What kinds of states were you in at the time, and what were you experiencing?

Go back to that time, hear the music in your head. The same music that was playing on the radio that day, tell me all the details. While you relive the perfect day, recognize any similarities between this day and the ideas of what you wanted to grow up to be. Take a moment because I have a suspicion if nothing else, you have a song playing in your head. Don't shake your head like I'm crazy, because I know you do. In fact, you are probably even bobbing your head up and down right now, as the beats hit. Yes, yes and now your body is swaying a little bit, swaying from side to side.

See, it doesn't matter if it's Kris Kross making you wanna, jump, Jump, or even little Michael and his brother's singing to you, I'll be there... It's through stepping back, and into these perfect moments, when you find yourself with that perfect jam playing in your head, as your moving your body to the beat. You feel all the emotions of that perfect moment. In that moment, all was GOOD! You were the BOMB! Let me tell you how, we can recreate this.

The more times you can recall different experiences, everything was flowing perfectly. At least through your perception, everything was perfect. The more times you can feel every feeling, encompass all the emotions, see the faces, the details of each event, and move to the music while you relive conversations,and say the words just as you did, at the time. These exercises allow you to discover the links between all of them. There are common threads, you just never have taken the time, to consciously see what they are.

The exercise we just used allows you to be emerged in the moment, the time, the place, the people, and the event. You can discover what it was, in those specific events, that produced the result of a perfect day. You'll find the common thread which was present in each event. Maybe, in each instance you took a chance, and allowed your faith to put you into a state of confidence and you made it happen.

When is the last time you took a chance in your life, any chances that pertain to any and all aspects of your life? So when you are trying to discover the purpose of your life, the discovery will be known, by understanding the feelings you want and the contributions you gave to others, which resulted in creating an euphoric feeling for you.

The Purpose of Life

Think about the purpose of your life, in the most bare bones simple terms. If you were going to, blurt out the purpose of life in one sentence, one phrase, what would it be? Write it down, The purpose of my life is to... When you do this you need to keep in mind a couple of parameters, I want you to abide by.

First, you must state it in a way that is positive. We don't need to write down how the purpose of your life is to stop all the horrible things happening in your life, nope wrong answer. Keep your answer positive.

Second it needs to be brief and concise. Use words that have an emotionally charged meaning to you. Also, it must include how you are going to be as a person, and what are you going to do.

What's Your Purpose?

You need to make sure you are personally in your Purpose of Life statement, and of course other people.

So write it down now, what is the purpose of your life? Not the right answer. Not the perfect answer. Just the answer, the purpose of your life is to be and do what for yourself and others? When you write it down, each time it becomes clearer.

It will only improve and help you really discover the absolute truth of what your purpose in life is.

The Purpose of Life

"The purpose of my life, Tollie Schmidt is to serve God and my fellow man. Being an Inspired Unbreakable, passionate, loving, outrageous, and courageous, strong, playful, eccentric, crazy, and dorky example of the never ending possibilities that God gives when you commit your life to service."

When I hone in on contribution being at the core the overall essence of my purpose, which it is, then I can change the words and use other meanings. I know what my purpose is, which is service to others. And you need to know what that is for yourself and your life. Knowing what the overall theme is of your purpose will allow you to make decisions while it feeds your motivation to get up early and stay up late. Allowing you to connect with people in ways you haven't done before. It has to be more than just you, it must include others and include emotions and be intense to compel your soul. So stop now, and write it down, let you pen go crazy on the page.

When you write down the first thing, then keep going and write another thing. Keep the flow in rhythm and allow all your thoughts feelings, ideas, and dreams to began the process of authoring the story of your life.

I hope you wrote them down, and allowed yourself the opportunity to decide on a purpose. Your job is not to be perfect, it's to be excellent. Perfection can never really be achieved anyways, if you are truly a perfectionist then it's never perfect, but it's getting better all the time. So what is the purpose of your life? Also how does it feel when you think about, This is the purpose of my life!

One more small guideline I haven't mentioned yet. Did you write your purpose in a way, which requires you to die, before it's complete? If so, change it. We want to have purpose for your living life, and not your Legacy after your life. Let me reiterate, you purpose is not some massive pie in the sky, end all, be all. It's not your bodacious, Super Duper Groovy, in a far out kind of way objective. No. Your purpose, is something you should experience and create every single day, so you can be groovy every day. In fact I encourage it, so get down with your funky self, as long as it aligns with your purpose in life and is lived each and every day.

The Purpose of Life

Over the next month take this purpose statement and keep it in front of you. Inject it into a system that you use for managing your time and your to do list. Put it up on your wall, or next to the mirror in the bathroom, so you see it every morning as you are getting ready for the day. Don't just look at it. Think about how you can live your purpose, more each and every day. When you need to make a decision about doing something in your life, and your not sure why your doing it. You can reference your purpose. You now have a guiding principle, no matter what happens these principles never waver.

Principles are the essence of who you are, and your principles are impenetrable. Those inner values will never change, and although your environment may change, the vehicles in which you achieve your goals may change, your character will always be pointing North, allowing you to compensate and reset your compass.

One thing I'd like to say, is that if you want to send me your mission statement to Tollie International Inc., I would love to receive it. I would love to see the language you used, describing the purpose of your life. So if you feel like doing that, please do and address it to me personally.

Failed Dream? or Destiny?

Not Getting Your Dream | Gives You Your Destiny.

It's like I was saying earlier, sometimes people set out to achieve a particular goal and they don't achieve it. They take that disappointment and turn it into frustration which turns to resentment towards others and themselves. The truth of the matter is, whatever happens you must look to find an empowering meaning in any situation. Remember to ask yourself the right questions, ask yourself how you could use the event to serve a higher purpose. Ask if the situation was going to make you more, then how would it make you more.

Often in life you look back and see how the worst situations in your life ended up being your best, if you were willing to trust that it happened for a reason. Maybe there was a situation in your past that hurt you, yet because of that situation your kids will never be hurt the same as when you were a child. It could be that you went through a tough time in your life, but by going through the situation you have the opportunity to help someone else, so they never feel the pain you did. Maybe the pain forced you to make a new decision, casting you into a brand new direction, which brought you to this destiny. I truly believe deep within my heart we must be willing to trust and have faith. We need to look for answers, as we actively pursue those answers, and if we do all these things then every human experience supports us.

In this day and age some of the best examples and metaphors are directed by Hollywood, so let's use a movie reference which I really like. Im sure you remember the movie Field of Dreams.

THE FAMOUS QUOTE WHICH HAS BECOME TIMELESS:

"If you build it, they will come."

In the film Kevin Costner seeks out an old man, by the name of Doc Graham. Doc was played by Burt Lancaster. The first time he meets this man he was telling him about a field of dreams. It was a field created so these old men could come back and play again, to feel young and play the game they love so much.

WHEN HE MET WITH DOC GRAHAM, HE SAID TO THE OLD MAN:

"I understand you were only able to play one inning in your life."

DOC REPLIED:

"Yeah, and my whole life I had one dream, which was to play baseball professionally. Every single day I would get up and give my all, I lived my passion. I practiced non-stop, fielding ground balls, and batting practice, I pushed myself and gave my all. Finally, I made it to the big leagues."

DOC CONTINUED TO TELL HIM:

"I never got my chance to play all season, until the final game. It was the eight inning, when the coach looked over at me and told me to get in right field. I ran out there, so excited to be living my dream, I couldn't wait for someone to hit the ball in my direction, so I could show what I was made of, and nothing happened."

Doc, was so upset because after that game they sent him back to the minor leagues, without ever having another chance, in an instant his opportunity came and went. Doc, told him how at that point he was a broken man, and he couldn't go through that again, so he just quit.

Kevin Costner, was very sympathetic to Doc's story. He couldn't imagine how it felt, being so close to the opportunity to live your dream, to live your passion only to have it snuffed out in minutes. He was telling Doc, how that must have been the most dramatic and painful experience to ever go through.

DOC REPLIED:

"No son, playing baseball for only five minutes was not a disaster, what would have been a real disaster is if I would have only been a doctor for five minutes."

KEVIN COSTNER LISTENED INTENTLY AS DOC CONTINUED TO EXPLAIN:

"If I would have hit that baseball, that might have been the bigger disaster. Because then I never would have come to this little town. I would have never saved this man's life or deliver that little girl, or got to know the people who are now my best friends in the world."

It is a powerful message, because sometimes not getting your dream, gives you what you really want and are destined for.

The moral is very simple. Inside each of us, we have our desires, the things we want that will bring us pleasure and avoid any pain. Yet, also within all of us, we have our moral needs. These needs go beyond ourselves, and on to something greater. It propels us into giving more of ourselves in way that we have never given before. Maybe it will be something that will never be recognized, still it will give us the most awe inspiring sense of fulfillment we never knew was possible. All your past trials and tribulations are merely preparation for a time in your life, when opportunity is unfolding and you recognize your gift and rise, you rise Inspired!

Don't sit back waiting for your moment of greatness, go out and do the small things. Go out and enjoy all the small things today, so you will appreciate the bigger things even more. In essence, do as my Granny did, be a person who loves people, animals, and all beings. Be a person when other people can't love you as you might deserve, you share with twice as much love. Be a person who gives more than anybody else gives, and you will be living your purpose. Stand in the gap, holding yourself to a higher standard and be prepared for that day, when you recognize that ominous moment and rise to meet the opportunity.

Gertie May Daniels

Granny Daniels "Legacy"

Granddaddy Tollie Daniels "Legacy"

Joe Swindell's World Championship

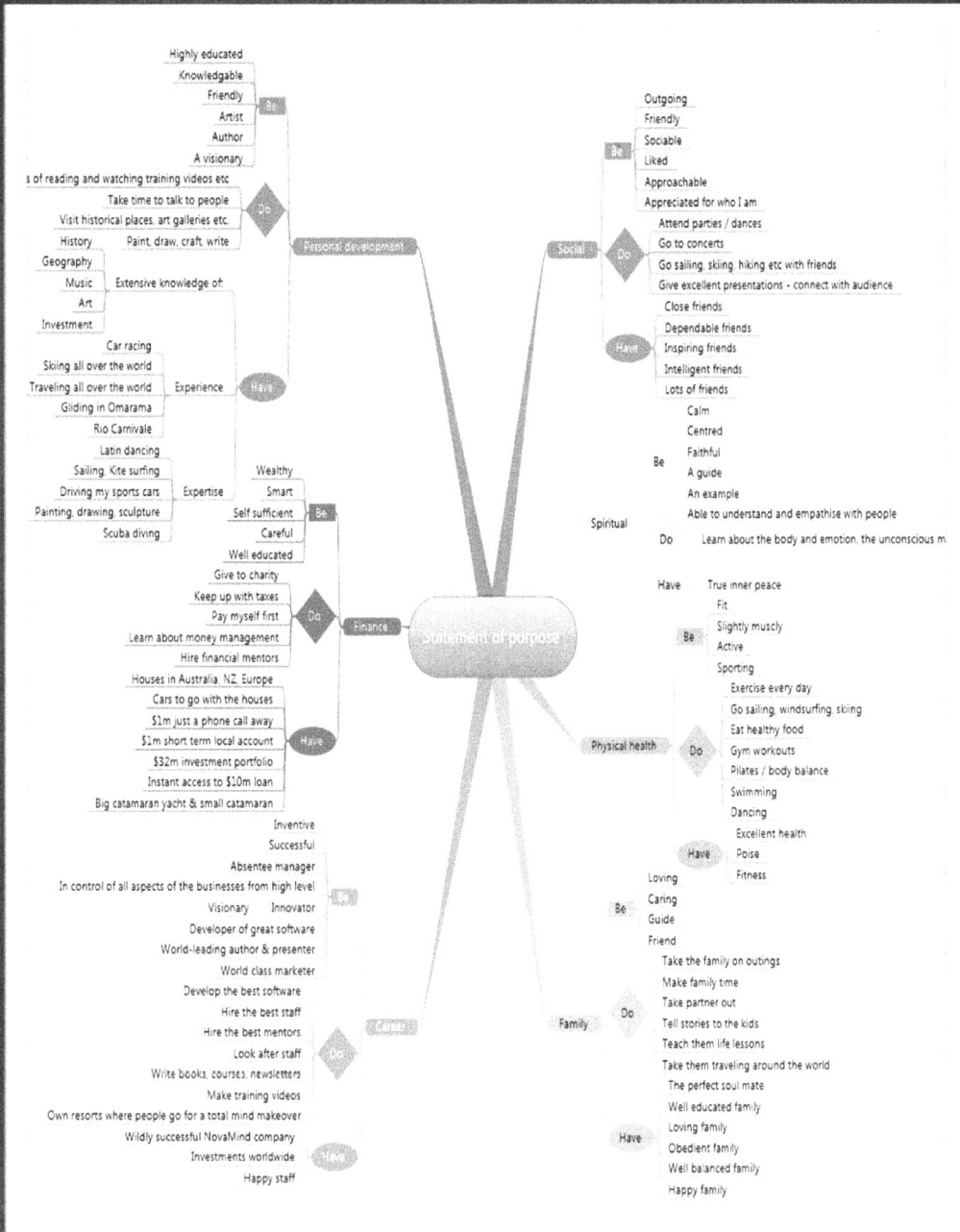

Statement of purpose

Personal development

Be
- Highly educated
- Knowledgable
- Friendly
- Artist
- Author
- A visionary

Do
- s of reading and watching training videos etc
- Take time to talk to people
- Visit historical places, art galleries etc.
- Paint, draw, craft, write

Extensive knowledge of:
- History
- Geography
- Music
- Art
- Investment

Have

Experience
- Car racing
- Skiing all over the world
- Traveling all over the world
- Gliding in Omarama
- Rio Carnivale
- Latin dancing

Expertise
- Sailing, Kite surfing
- Driving my sports cars
- Painting, drawing, sculpture
- Scuba diving

Finance

Be
- Wealthy
- Smart
- Self sufficient
- Careful
- Well educated

Do
- Give to charity
- Keep up with taxes
- Pay myself first
- Learn about money management
- Hire financial mentors

Have
- Houses in Australia, NZ, Europe
- Cars to go with the houses
- $1m just a phone call away
- $1m short term local account
- $32m investment portfolio
- Instant access to $10m loan
- Big catamaran yacht & small catamaran

Career

Do
- Inventive
- Successful
- Absentee manager
- In control of all aspects of the businesses from high level
- Visionary   Innovator
- Developer of great software
- World-leading author & presenter
- World class marketer
- Develop the best software
- Hire the best staff
- Hire the best mentors
- Look after staff
- Write books, courses, newsletters
- Make training videos
- Own resorts where people go for a total mind makeover

Have
- Wildly successful NovaMind company
- Investments worldwide
- Happy staff

Social

Be
- Outgoing
- Friendly
- Sociable
- Liked
- Approachable
- Appreciated for who I am

Do
- Attend parties / dances
- Go to concerts
- Go sailing, skiing, hiking etc with friends
- Give excellent presentations - connect with audience

Have
- Close friends
- Dependable friends
- Inspiring friends
- Intelligent friends
- Lots of friends

Spiritual

Be
- Calm
- Centred
- Faithful
- A guide
- An example
- Able to understand and empathise with people

Do
- Learn about the body and emotion, the unconscious m

Have
- True inner peace

Physical health

Be
- Fit
- Slightly muscly
- Active
- Sporting

Do
- Exercise every day
- Go sailing, windsurfing, skiing
- Eat healthy food
- Gym workouts
- Pilates / body balance
- Swimming
- Dancing

Have
- Excellent health
- Poise
- Fitness

Family

Be
- Loving
- Caring
- Guide
- Friend

Do
- Take the family on outings
- Make family time
- Take partner out
- Tell stories to the kids
- Teach them life lessons
- Take them traveling around the world

Have
- The perfect soul mate
- Well educated family
- Loving family
- Obedient family
- Well balanced family
- Happy family

Statement of Life Purpose

Purpose of Life Mind Map

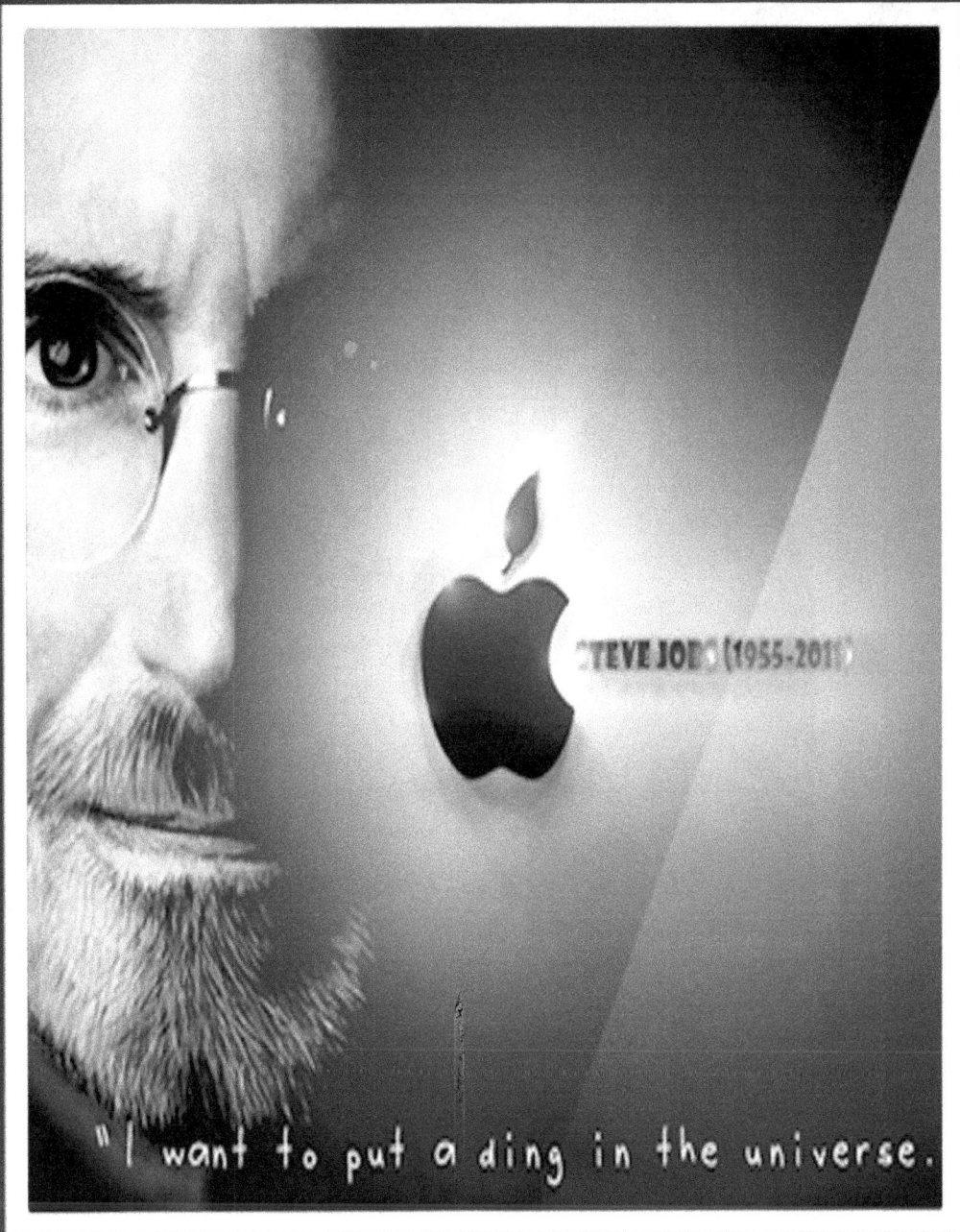

STEVE JOBS (1955-2011)

"I want to put a ding in the universe.

What's your Legacy?

Chapter IX

The Art of Influence

"MOVIES CAN AND DO HAVE TREMENDOUS INFLUENCE IN SHAPING
YOUNG LIVES IN THE REALM OF ENTERTAINMENT TOWARDS THE IDEALS
AND OBJECTIVES OF NORMAL ADULTHOOD" -WALT DISNEY

As we discussed, we know that when it comes to control, we have absolute authority over our own minds and body's. What about the entire outside world? Unlike having full control over every aspect within our body's, we cannot control all events that take place in the outside world. But, we can utilize many tools we have discussed, especially Neuro Linguistic Programming (NLP) to direct events in our lives. This is crucial considering the world today has many aspects that revolve around change happening on a multiplying level. It's now in history we can look directly to all the powerful vehicles directly influencing large groups across the globe. This ability to utilize influence world wide on large sectors of our population can be used to buy more iPads, wear the latest fashions, or watch a specific television show. Same is true when it comes to influencing the hearts and minds of people around the world in an empowering way.

It comes down to who is soliciting the influence and why. In this chapter we will look at changes taking place on a bulk system, understand how they take place, and what this influence means. Then, we will give you some of the most powerful tools you will ever have at your disposal. You will learn how to inspire, through influence and how you can direct many aspects of your life, through your abilities.

We constantly hear how today's world is overflowing with stimulation, as I said it has become the preferred treatment to drug people when they have to much stimulation. In earlier times the people also had plenty of stimuli in their world, although there were some differences. Consider the early explorers, they were always surrounded by sights and sounds and smells, all which could mean the difference between life and death, or between food, and no food.

Here's the difference between then and now. The early explorers who traveled the unknown lands, sought to discover all the bounty. The world had to offer. The stimuli they encountered on a daily basis became their motivation. It was by their own choice and desired to discover new places, animals, vegetation, etc., The early explorers ultimately decided what meaning they gave to their findings. If they saw gold at the bottom of a stream, the motivation to go and pan the gold was their decision, no outside forces were dictating their behavior. Early explorers didn't discover gold laying at the bottom of a stream, and before they felt the motivation to start panning for gold, they needed a commercial to entice them even further.

Today's world is a sharp contrast to the days of old. Nowadays we are bombarded, nonstop by ads, and media pushing us to take an action of their chosen desire. They will stimulate us to buy a car, even instigate influence to direct how we vote for a political candidate. Maybe it's exhorting influence through strategically planned campaigns to support efforts to feed the hungry children of the world. Or as simple as half-naked models inviting you to join them, and all you need is X product. It is through focus group tested influence that surrounds us today in our world. This influence can make us feel good about having something or make us feel bad that we don't have something. What was known as propaganda in the previous century, became known as persuasion. Today has begun the era of influence. Today, we are engulfed by people with the knowledge and skills coupled with the latest technology to influence all aspects of our lives. What can be felt across the world yet has no physical being to it? It is influencing my friend. Consider the same catchy commercial being infused directly into us can also be infused across the world at the same exact time.

Consider any high fat, exuberant calorie busting fast food restaurant in the United States. Years ago people could claim ignorance about the health implications of fatty meats, and high sugar drinks. Also, in that time the average family didn't consume these types of foods regularly, it was still a culture norm to prepare meals at home. Fast forward to today, and over the past several years the Fast Food industry on a while has been under siege. Through activists, health organizations, medical research and studies, a rise in diabetes and overall obesity in our nation with a direct link to high fat diets. We have seen new Government regulations hoping to curb the epidemic of expanding waistlines in America, especially our youth. Yet, unless you have been living under a rock, you fully understand the health concerns with Fast Food Restaurants. Yet, have seen any decline in their sales, or a decline of new fast food joints opening up, the answer is no. Let's look at a few reasons why?

People on average love the convenience and taste of their favorite fast food joint, but is that enough to keep them coming? People had to be taught how to use fast food as a trigger to create a meaning of convenience and value for the busy mom, feeding the family.

You can drive thru, feed your whole family and be healthy. You can substitute apples for fries. You can order a fresh salad, just ignore the label of the small packet of ranch dressing where it says, 40 Grams of Fat Per Serving, SALAD! That's all you need to know, and salad equals healthy! Right? So why does mom or dad

The Art of Influence

head for the drive thru window with the kids, statistically as frequently as 4-5 times a week, knowing the health concerns and overwhelming facts?

They do it because they have been reframed of what a Fast Food restaurant means, and then that new representation and state have been anchored into place. People and focus groups with specialized knowledge in influence has spent millions upon millions of dollars to convince the public that eating at your local fast food restaurant is as American as Apple Pie.

Through skillful restaurant designs offering parents a FREE place for kids to play, or offering FREE Wi-Fi, just for entering their doors.

Precision Targeted Advertising

Precision Advertising, clever images and sounds were used to put us in positive-feeling states.

After focus group testing those desired states were associated with or linked to a Family Friendly Economical Restaurant called Fast food joints. McDonalds extra value meals, put a smile on your family's faces tonight!

I'M LOVIN' IT, FEED YOUR HUNGRY FAMILY AND GET MORE FOR LESS.

"Mom's you have enough to worry about, we know what your kids like, so come on in, and we'll do the cooking."

Great way to anchor all the emotions a mom wants to feel, and is how the Fast Food Kings have linked several happy states to direct your behavior. There's no added value or social need to a fast food joint on every corner, of every street, in every town, and every city, in every state, across these United States.

Yet, we have been influenced to eat at fast food restaurant because they are economical while being fast and easy. Throw a toy in with a burger and fries, and you sold the kids. Families can share quality time together in a safe well lit, inviting environment and have FREE use of the indoor and outdoor play areas. Don't worry most families don't visit fast food restaurants very often, and they offer a huge assortment of delicious, chef inspired, healthy food choices, with vibrant colors picked for their emotional feeling they represent.

Besides, have you ever seen a fast food commercial with someone overweight? No, depending on the time of the day, commercials are run showcasing happy meals, toys, and fun loving characters. Other times of the day, your teens can grab a quick bite, for only a dollar, or two with their friends, and they are Lovin It!

Consider my list for a moment. Now being completely honest with yourself, answer the following question. If you were driving home and just wanted to get something quick for dinner, what's the first option that pops into your mind? Probably the same as 99.5% of everyone else who answered that question. I have a feeling it is a place offering, great value, warm smiles, freshly cooked 100% this, and 100% that. With crisp this on top of a succulent that. Words evoke emotions, colors evoke emotions, design evokes emotions; the list goes on. There is a reason why most of the pictures on the menu board are of plastic, or a man made material. It is to entice your sense of taste through visually vibrant, bold, succulent colors.

Sorry, for my little detour and unscheduled tangent, we now continue with our regularly scheduled program now in progress. But, many specifics I pointed out are not product or industry specific, they are

The Art of Influence

used on a large scale globally. As we have already discussed, advertisers put out images that put you in a receptive, elevated state. At the hight of the experience, they anchor you with their message. Once it has been finely tuned, and run through focus groups to ensure proper saturation they hit the public.

They repeat the messages on TV, online, magazines, radio, billboards, busses, schools, anywhere and everywhere so that the anchor gets constantly reinforced and triggered.

- Why does Nike pay Tiger Woods or Priceline pays William Shatner to sell its products?

- Why do politicians wrap themselves in the Flag?

- Why is Miller brewed the American way?

- Why is Apple products packaged as though they came from a high end boutique or Art Gallery?

- Why do we love hot dogs, baseball, apple pie, and Chevrolet?

These people and symbols are already powerful anchors in our culture, and the advertisers are simply transferring the feeling we have for these people or symbols to their products. They use them to entice you to be more open to their message, since someone you trust is telling you about it.

Why back in the Reagan era, did the TV ads he ran to play off the hostile symbol of the bear in the woods? The bear, symbolized Communist Russia, it was a powerful negative anchor that reinforced the image of the need for strong leadership, something Reagan proposed he would continue to provide. What ever happened to the fuzzy Wuzzy cuddly bears we used to have run around in the woods? Why did this ad effect people in such a threatening way? Simply through the setting, lighting and the words and music used.

Any effective ad or political campaign can be dissected so you can see the same precise framework we have set up in this book. First, they set the emotion they are trying to evoke, through stimulating visuals and sound to enhance the desired feeling. Then, it anchors your state to a product or service they are trying to sell. Also, the same is true if they are trying to get you to act, do an action they want done. Through repetition, they saturate the target market place until your nervous system effectively links the state with their product or directed behavior. Now, a good ad will use images and sounds attracting and effecting all three major representational systems, sight, sound and kinesthetic.

Network television is still king, when it comes to the best bang for your buck in advertising. Also, TV has always been the most influential form of delivering messages. The reason TV is the most effective is simply because it uses the big three: you get your beautiful pictures, you can tie in music or a jingle, and it can provide a message with passion to inspire. Think of the most effective ads we have seen for soft drinks, the polar bear ads for Coke during the Christmas Season. We all can think of iconic beer commercials, and you can easily spot who their target market is with each ad. Now consider an ad for axe deodorant, where the marketing campaign all revolves around, average man, uses axe deodorant then gets freaky with above average hot girl. Was the ad used by axe effective? You bet!

Sex Sells

No Matter How Far We Think We Might Have Come, Sex Still Sells.

This is one of the reason's people urged me to start my own advertising and marketing firm instead of only serve a few select clients. People want to be Inspired and empowered thru Hi-Impact dream infused advertising. Sex may sell, yet we breathe life, into dreams and ideas. Yes, we have those ads that are infamous for effecting the opposite images. They are your shock and awe, type ads. They break your state abruptly, to rattle you, and put emphasis on something negative. Think of the animal cruelty ads. Have you ever seen the one featuring Sarah McLachlan, and her song playing in the background softly, as images of cattle are being plowed over with a bulldozer? The Anti Abortion ad running in Texas, showing bloody fetus's and body parts over and over?

These ads are effective when the purpose is to interrupt a pattern, when they show a very real and barbaric reality to their cause. It causes such a disruption to the viewers pattern; it almost horrifies them.

We live in a world of power and influence, you can learn to influence others, develop a stronger report instantly with strangers. You can either influence and inspire, or you can be the person who is easily persuaded. Choose to set your own course in life, or someone will fill the gap and redirect you. The essence of this entire book has been about influence. It's shown you how to become inspired and the tools to achieve your life's purpose. All these tools are so you can cast your vision, set your compass, and chart your path in life, so you can influence others. Influence others as a role model for your kids, or a commanding presence in the workplace.

Influence wields power; we all know this. The most successful and powerful people in the world are also those who can influence others with direct results. Those who cannot influence others, simply do what they are directed to do. Sadly, even if you point out the reality to them, they will blow you off and say your crazy.

Social Media and The Art of Communication Becoming a Commodity

Today Like No Other Time in History Communication is Crucial, and Will Become More Powerful in the Years Ahead.

I truly believe, that the art of communication has become a specialized skill. Master the art of communication, and you will have boundless opportunities. There has been no other time in our history, where the ability to avoid simple conversation between two people ever existed. Resulting from the popularity of text messages, instant messaging, twitter, Facebook, and many other personal device messaging applications, many have turned to typed messages over a conversation.

Frequently I have been asked by someone to help them out and give guidance or even discussed business. Yet, when I try to communicate with them they will avoid a conversation at all costs. Meaning gets lost in the land of, OMG, LOL, :) XD. How can you gauge your ability to connect with the other person without having as many tools at your disposal to determine if your message is being received as you intended it? What I mean is, when you have a conversation over the phone, you can determine jokes, sarcasm, concern, you can listen to dips in their voice, special emphasis on particular words which they are attaching stronger meaning to.

None of these tools are available to you through a text message, or instant messenger, and many people cannot write a coherent and direct email or letter. I am a person who struggles with grammar, and I must take extra care when communicating through a letter or email. I have been taking lessons to increase my effectiveness through proper grammar and word choices. Still, nothing compares to a face to face communication. It is through a personal connection you can build an instant report, or as they say, press the flesh.

Because so much of how we communicate is with our body. We use facial expressions, eye movements, body language, hand gestures to add validity to our words. As you will learn soon, this is also how you can read a person and determine many facets of their life, character, values, experiences, and if they are speaking the truth or leading you on. You can also tell whether a person believes their own words, or if they are merely searching to tell you what they think you want to hear.

The Art of Influence

Sadly, I can almost say with certainty as I am writing this that maybe the greatest influence you can learn is the art of a simple conversation. Because people who can actually carry on a coherent, witty, and playful chat with someone is become a rare commodity.

Nothing is more annoying than speaking with someone on the phone and after you hang up, you realize that the only message you received from the conversation had something to do with Ummmm, ummmm, and You Know, So you know... and that is not worth remembering.

So to truly influence you must first champion the art of a conversation, then the power comes from your ability to influence.

- If you're influential and have no arms, you'll influence someone to carry your load.

- If you're influential and have no money, you will influence someone to lend you some.

- Influence is the greatest artful which leads to inspiring change and creating opportunity.

We all know someone who can talk your ear off; they could carry on a conversation with a brick wall. For me, that person is my dad, the gift-of-gab serves him well and made him extremely successful in sales and onto management. I would sometimes joke, that the reason he could easily sell so was if a potential customer became a client because he felt a positive report with my father then that's a win-win situation.

However, he also had needed to find out how many people were buying just as a white flag, to get him to shut up and go away. In the end, guess it really didn't matter.

However, because of his unique gift for gab, then just like other people who can influence, if they ever felt alone in the world it will be easy for them to find a relationship.

You can have the next big idea, or life saving invention, but without the ability to influence you are still empty handed.

Remember how we spoke about Steve Jobs and his imprint on our world. It was not only his ability to dream up products that people would love to use, and enriched their lives, but it was his ability to influence the world through his presentations, and speeches, is what made people inspired to buy.

The ability to communicate what you have to offer is what life is all about. Like we have discussed in depth; it is the ability to connect with another human being on a deeper level. There is nothing with a higher value than the ability to communicate and connect to others.

Nothing But the Clothes on Your Back | The NLP Experiment

NLP Can Alter Your State & Change How You Communicate With Others.

We have discussed the value of using NLP in our lives, so we can alter our state and change how we communicate with ourselves. Here's an example of how to use the power of NLP to influence. When I created our first 7-day Neuro-Linguistic Infusion Program, I needed an exercise that would force participants to use their new tools. In the course one of the first things, I reinforce over and over is the power in confidence and stature. I told them, that they could go anywhere, do anything, be anybody, and accomplish all their dreams, if they could first walk the walk and talk the talk. I told them about a few of the places I have been, where I was not supposed to be. All I did was look as if I belonged there. It's the confidence to walk purposefully in a backstage setting, or the employees only corridors.

If you walk with confidence, acknowledging those around you, and are always approachable with a smile people will assume you belong. It's the ability to blend in and be a chameleon in all situations. It is when you try to avoid, hide, or lack confidence and become nervous that people start to notice you.

So here's what I did. I got everyone in the program together, at midnight. I handed them one gallon zip lock bags and asked for them to give me their keys, their cash, their credit cards, their wallets, their cell phones - everything but the clothes off their backs. (*Because then it just is called hazing, and that's a no-no.*)

I told them that to achieve anything in life, they didn't need anything but their personal greatness and the ability to influence others. I explained that all the tools you needed to fill the needs of others they already had, and they didn't need money, status, an iPhone, or even their car. Because these are merely items which our society teaches us, we need to achieve our dreams in life.

We were in Houston, TX at the time. Their first task was to find a way to get to Austin, about two hours away by car. I said, take extreme care of yourselves, and use the tools you have available to you to arrive safe in Austin, and they'd need to find a fine place to stay, and to eat. Also, I told them that one of the greatest freedoms they could ever experience in life is the freedom of losing everything. I said you now have the gift of losing it all, which means your free to be, free to do, free to go, free to say, free to become absolutely anything.

Because you have nothing to lose, and everything to gain. The result was mind blowing! Let's just say that all of them arrived in Austin. All of them had a fine place to stay, a few had built such amazing rapports inside the hotels they found themselves staying on concierge floors, and one in the Presidential Suite. One of the guys, walked into a restaurant kitchen and started inspecting all the food, and when the Angry Chef approached him he modeled the movements, mannerisms, lingo and attitude of a food critic he once had dealt with. So, the chef prepared a dish especially for him, pairing it with wines, and desert.

However, he didn't stop there. Since the restaurant was inside a five star hotel, and you had all the amenities, he decided to accidentally spill the last of his desert on himself. The Chef not going to allow a small mess to ruin his review made sure he was provided new clothes from the Hotel stores, and a room to cleanup and stay for the night. There were so many amazing and crazy stories of their accomplishments.

Yet, the most inspiring of the stories was a common theme among them all, and that was how all of them, each and everyone made a significant contribution to a stranger or a gaggle of strangers. A slew of resourceful individuals cleared up people's phobias and other emotional dysfunctions.

The man who dined with the chef and scored a gourmet meal, new digs and the swanky room to top it all off, returned the favor. By trade he was a producer and director of documentaries, and has traveled all over the world doing freelance for studios, networks and news agencies. He returned to the hotel with his crew and did a phenomenal one hour feature story about his adventure. However, he made he made it news worthy by creating a back story. He said what he did was to do a story on the power of the human spirit. He talked about how the chef fed him when he was hungry, the Hotel staff clothes him when he was cold, and provided shelter when he had nowhere to go. And they ate it up, and that kind of free inspiring publicity cannot be bought.

The whole idea behind this was to prove to them. The kind of power they wield at anytime when they choose to call upon it. Also, the importance of their complete faith in the process, and their own abilities. When you have no other option, it makes it much easier to really put your all into your focus so that determination creates results.

Sadly, as I am writing this and remembering the event I am also reminded that I have not been doing as much as I am capable of. The reason I chose this exercise, which many might find as drastic, is that I have been there.

First, those who see the exercise as drastic, can't make an objective observation. They have no idea what tools they learned, the opportunities and possibilities using the NLP techniques, and the overwhelming success it brings forth.

Few years ago I have been stuck in cities and towns where I ran out of money, out of gas, and knew no one in town. Often, it became the greatest blessing that I could ever ask for, and it shows you the real underlying good nature and caring hearts and souls we share this earth with. They learned they needed nothing more than their own resourceful states, and skills to get around. They didn't need all the usual vehicles we rely on in our daily lives. They didn't need a car, money, reputation, contacts, credit, and so on. The consensus was the participants never felt a feeling of confidence as that night, and all had the most euphoric and inspiring challenges ever.

They walked away with new friends, and helped hundreds of people. Yes, even without physical money, you can contribute in a significant way to others. Do you recall how we discussed the different ways people perceived power in the first chapter? You might recall, or commonsense tells us there are those who attach negative connotations to the word, power. The choose to see power in only a conquering, oppressed negative way always hurting the common good. Let's be honest with each other, and truth-be-told, in today's global environment influence is not a choice.

Influence is a constant in the world. Someone is always injecting influence. Remember, millions upon billions of dollars are being pumped into the influence machine, to get out their messages, and shape the conversation in a way it becomes more favorable to their interests. And to say how unfair it is that people use their influence, to secure special curry with decision makers or any other sphere of influence is only burying your head in the sand and ignoring history and the fact everyone are culpable. So either you choose to influence and inspire for empowering choices, or someone else will influence for their agenda.

A New Vision Cast for Empowering Advertising

Tollie International Inc. Breathing Life Into Ideas & Dreams.

Because of this fact, we have invested considerable time and resources into building Tollie International Marketing & Advertising Firm. Because it is our resolve to create empowering change, embrace the dreams of others, breathe life into businesses, and ideas. While we prove that advertising through the lens of curiosity, wonder, dreams and creating the belief that all is possible is right. We know our ability to create truly inspiring campaigns, concepts, brands, and to market new visions to inspire and create possibilities while we promote values, determination, competition, and stand in the gap of the human spirit that strives to do more, be more, and looks for opportunity not pity.

See, our marketing and advertising services are not meant for the masses. We pride ourselves on being the absolute incomparable best at what we do. We create a feeling, we inspire action, and we always believe in the individual.

Our curiosity spurs ideas infused into dynamic concepts. Our standard has created unsurpassed value in our brand. We breathe life into ideas & dreams. A larger vision must be cast, a strategy developed and deployed with faith thru confidence we create a feeling compelling the hearts & minds of the individual spirit Bypassing conventional competition to impact markets and exceed expectations. Because the one truth we know will always hold true is this; In every market, in all demographics and behind all the unique backgrounds making up this world we all have a binding desire. We all have the desire to become more, to dream bigger and the faith that everyday can and should be something more. We concede that influence with sex, body image, self gratification, misleading facts, repetition and market saturation will always be an effective form of advertising.

The Art of Influence

However, history has proved time and time again that when people are provided a choice. When influence is taken from the masses and directed to the spirit of the individual, then hands down inspired influence through curiosity and possibility creating true opportunities. People choose to ask, What Can be... we are creatures of wonder and adventure where dreams-infused thru vision will trump sex by dissolution. In the end, it is the spirit of the individual with faith that will choose to believe in what can be. The world is ready to dream again. Our bar is set higher as we stand for something bigger, we stand to empower the weak, challenge the strong, and unleash the passion, drive and ambitions for all, creating opportunity as we build up and magnify the human spirit.

If knowledge of influence is an issue for you, consider this. The difference in your kids behavior comes down to who bears the greater influence over them, is that you, or maybe the influence of the gangs or drug dealer? If your goal is to gain control over your life, while becoming an elegant, effective model to those you care for most, then it is crucial you learn to influence. To be blunt, if you do not step up, the bench is deep with plenty of people ready to step in and fill that void. We understand the value of using NLP to enhance our ability to influence. When we step back and look at all the problems of the world it can be quite daunting. But, there's good news, all the problems of the world are caused in one form or fashion to man. Stay with me, All human problems are behavioral problems! Another viewpoint is for example, a gun is not the problem - it's people's behavior that creates this thing we call gun violence.

Look I am the last person who should be giving any lessons on the English Language and grammar; however, no one else is here, so here we go. It's common practice that we take sets of actions and turn them into nouns as if they were objects, when actually they are processes. If we continue to substitute human problems as if they were things, then we continue to shoot ourselves in the foot, by blowing them out of control and creating the perception they are beyond control. Weapons of mass destruction are not the problem in and of itself. The way human beings behave is what create or prevents catastrophic consequences and war. Famine is not the problem in Africa. Human behavior is the problem. Ravaging the lands, will never create a sustainable food source.

In basic terms can we agree that human behavior is at the core of all human problems or that new human behaviors can also be the solution to those problems. So now we can do a little happy dance, because we

The Art of Influence

know all these behaviors are results of the states these individuals are in, which becomes their model of how to respond, when they find themselves in these states.

We also discussed the fact that the states that project these behaviors are all based on how the communicated the specific meaning of the event or situation. It's just like the example we used earlier, which is people have linked swinging thru the drive-thru to a particular state. They don't visit the local fast food drive thru every minute of every day, only when they are is a fast inexpensive meal state. People don't horde food every minute of every day, only when they are in a state they have linked to overeating. So once you can change those meanings or the linked response, you change the emotion, and change the behavior.

Today there is an abundance of technology available that sends a multitude of different forms of communication across the globe in seconds. Look at all the forms of communication we use today to spread the word, project our messages, and expand out influence. We have media, radio, television, movies, print, computers, internet, satellite, cell phones, iPads, iPods, and the list are expanding faster than even the average American's waist line, and that is Super Freak'n fast.

How the Internet Has Shaped the Use of Influence

The Internet Has Become the Ultimate Equalizer.

Because of the internet, the abilities to communicate through all medians of media have an instant ability to hit people in all parts of the world simultaneously. Imagine the movies or books or television shows, and all the forms of media we have today, if they can change people's internal representations and states for the better, then it means that they can also change the world for the better, too.

Today, the media has immense influence over our entire culture, not just influence on the products we buy. Media can affectively change the world for the better, some of the examples are: Live Aid concerts, Awareness to local issues that can attract a global response. Consider the massive response and money that are raised for natural disasters. When Haiti was hit with a hurricane causing catastrophic damage and, plight there was a message of urgency sent out immediately and the response was felt worldwide. Same is true from the tragic Tsunami that hit Japan wreaking havoc on their Nuclear Power Plant and capturing the lives of thousands of loved ones pulled into the seas and never recovered. It was automatic, and the system was in place as people worldwide opened their hearts and wallets to support our fellow man.

Also it's important to point out the differences between the internal representations of these disasters on the people of Haiti, Japan and America's last catastrophic natural disaster which were Katrina hitting the New Orleans area. For the people of Haiti it was complete and uttered disaster, and loss. The Haitian people depend on each other, their family, neighbors and local villages for their support system. Because in Haiti they live under a corrupt Government, and the country lacks the basic infrastructure most countries take for granted. The Haitians lost their entire support system. They lost family members, neighbors, their homes, their villages, all was gone. The basic necessities of food, water, clothing, shelter, and medical care did not exist. Until foreign aid arrived and then they were at the complete mercy and dependency of strangers, and in fear of their Government stealing the much needed supplies and care.

Hurricane Katrina devastated not only New Orleans but much of the bottom parts of Louisiana, Mississippi, along the Southern States reaching into Texas were dealt a catastrophic blow. Not only were the local Governments ill prepared for the disaster, many areas hit the hardest were poverty stricken areas. Most victims entire means of living and surviving are relied upon by the Government. So in the aftermath their internal representations of the event went into basic humanistic survival mode, every man, women and child is on their own. They have lived their lives solely dependent on Government, they have no internal representations to care for themselves, nor their neighbors since they too were dependents on Government. So, when Government was not there to care for them, it became violent, and everyone was out for themselves, stealing, looting, harming their fellow man, because they had no other meaning for what their behavior should have been.

Now in Japan in the days following their disaster we saw a completely different scene unfold. In Japan, their internal representations were much different. Historically the Japanese live by a code of honor, and respect. In times of great strife they look to one another for support, and all necessities. So after the storm, you saw the Japanese people who lost everything, thousands of loved ones perished, many of their bodies were never recovered. Yet, as they have always done throughout history, in times of disaster they comfort each other; they all work for the common good, with respect to their fellow man. See, it's not the disasters that caused violence in two nations and not the third. It is their internal representation of the event that caused human behaviors to cause the violence. Just imagine what could be if we could change those internal representations on a global level through empowering influence.

So what does all this mean? It means the ability to change people's internal representations, change people's states, and the ability to change people's behavior on a large global scale is already possible today, because of technology. By expertly deploying our knowledge of the triggers to human behavior coupled with the internet and other forms of media and communication, we can change the future of our world.

Back in the late 1970's there were a documentary film, and television series called Scared Straight, which recently has had a resurrection on the A&E channel called Beyond Scared Straight. This is an excellent example of the ways we can effectively change someone's internal representations, which in return transforms their behaviors through the power of the media. It's a program where they take teens who are at risk or acting out in destructive ways, or their overall behavior is on a collision course in crime and takes them to a prison. At the Prison inmate volunteers help to change the teens internal representations by taking the reality of prison life and making it very real to them. The teens were interviewed in advance. Most had a, I'm a badass, demeanor, and protrude a tough exterior and attitude. They also said how going to prison wouldn't be that big of a deal. Their internal representations changed real fast, when the reality was up close and personal. They were welcomed by large, tatted inmates screaming at them, threatening them, using every vulgar, outrageous metaphor and curse word to describe what they were going to do when they came to play in their house. When advice was rendered by a mass murderer showcasing the truths of prison life, relating the details in such a vivid horrific form that would change anyone's physiology!

The Art of Influence

Scared Straight was initially extremely effective in altering the internal representations of the teens. However, what I have seen from the revamped Beyond Scared Straight is a less effective method, mainly because the initial idea has been used as sketch comedy by Saturday Night Live, and so many teens go into the prison with a confidence that this is all a show.

Still, the proof is still evident from the initial documentary Scared Straight, which is we can change impressive numbers of people's behaviors if we can create a compelling new representation appealing to people in the most effective illustrating strategies.

By creating an environment, which force the teens to reevaluate how their minds perceive the event or situation. If they now link only pain, fear, torment and horror to prison, it's going to create new behaviors, just by their nervous systems need to avoid pain. So the theory is viable to suggest when we create a way to change behaviors of the majority; we can change the course of history.

Politics, Focus Groups, Play on Words and It's Game Time

Here's a Great Example, and is Relevant Today in Our Current Political Climate.

As I have made references to before, how many arguments, and terminology we hear in the political arena is used by design, and has been tested with focus groups to determine the effectiveness. Once these concepts, and platforms have been developed and terminology tested, they are then deployed along party lines as they're new mantra's and talking points, to saturate the target demographics and anchor their agenda by linking the desired feelings to the argument.

Here are a few examples. If the political agenda must influence the public to give them more money to spend, then they must create a compelling narrative to influence the people at large. Stripping away all the rhetoric, this is what they are saying to you as a taxpayer. We want you to give us more money to spend. Well they know just from preliminary polls, and study that an argument based on their primary objective would never achieve the result they need.

So to influence people to give them their desired objective of more money to spend. However, if you have worked in a nonprofit, or have had to be a fundraiser, the first thing you quickly learn is to ask for people who have money. Then, you ask for people who have lots of money to give you a lot more than the others. It's common sense, you need money, you to someone who has it.

It's like kindergarten, and we needed to learn the concept of sharing with others. We needed to learn the value in playing well with others. If you have a handful of animal crackers and I want one, then I need to influence you to share one with me. Because, I didn't give you those animal crackers. The teacher didn't give you a bunch of animal crackers but chose to give me none. So, at some point you acquired the animal crackers, maybe you did something for another kid and he gave you some animal crackers. Maybe you gave your crayons to someone, and they exchanged their animal crackers for your crayons. How you got the animal crackers is irrelevant, because I didn't give them to you, and I didn't earn any on my own. Still, I need you to give me an animal cracker, so I influence you so you give me one. Well that didn't fill me up or quench my desire, so I need more animal crackers. I look around the room, and everyone else only has a couple animal crackers, except for little Timmy, he has a pile of animal crackers. But, if I go and ask for Little Timmy for another animal cracker, he may say no, since he's already given me one. I guess I can understand, since he already gave me one, and I still didn't do anything to earn them; they are his after all. But, I still really really want them.

The Art of Influence

I need a way to influence him to give me more, and my best strategy is to get the other kids to help me. But, when I ask for them to please go and tell Timmy to give me another animal cracker they said no. Ugh, now what? Ooh, I'll ask for the other kids if they could ask for Little Timmy to share another cracker with me. Well, a couple kids asked for him to share another with me, but that punk Little Timmy said, NO! Said he already gave me one, and he doesn't need to give me anymore. He earned his animal crackers and said I need to do the same, and not just keep coming to him when I want stuff. Need a new strategy.

So I take another look around the room, and it's frustrating, all I want is another lousy animal cracker, and that punk, Little Timmy won't give it to me, and he has plenty! Seriously, Little Timmy has a bunch of animal crackers, everyone else has a couple, and I already ate mine, that's not fair! I go to Suzy to vent, telling her how I don't see how it's fair that I don't have any animal crackers and Little Timmy has a bunch and won't SHARE one with me. What makes him so special that he has a bunch and, Suzy you have only a couple. You work so hard around here, picking up toys, getting gum out of people's hair.

I mean why does Little Timmy deserve so much when we work so hard. Suzy starts agreeing with me; this is great! I asked her earlier to tell Timmy to give me another cracker, and she said no. Now, she is agreeing with me, what have I done different? A wait that's it, now I have an idea; I'll ask for Suzy if she would agree with me that asking Little Timmy to share just another animal cracker is only fair. I mean I'd ask for you Suzy, but you have only a couple, and you work so hard already. Honestly, I don't understand how Little Timmy got so many animal crackers; we all work hard here. How is it fair that he has so much and we don't, and all I am asking for is such a small percentage compared to what he has. Seriously, is it good for us to be around someone so selfish or greedy? Am I asking to much from other hard working kids here to say, Little Timmy, you need to give your fair share.

Fair share, BINGO! See when a focus group was asked, if they would agree that wealthy Americans need to pay more taxes, and the overwhelming response was no. As we have discussed, change the words and you change the meaning. So they formed a new focus group and rephrased the question. This time they asked for participants if they would agree that the wealthiest Americans among us, need to pair their fair share? Now, the overwhelming response was yes. So, what changed?

The Art of Influence

The question is exactly the same, only the words changed, therefor the entire meaning changed and how the participants perceived the question. So what changed? First off, the word wealthy was changed to wealthiest, this simple change gives a whole new meaning to people. When you hear someone is wealthy it can mean a very broad spectrum of people, so you don't really link wealthy with rich. Envy is much higher with the rich, than with someone who is merely wealthy. But, when you use the word, wealthiest, now I am Jack on the Titanic stuck in steerage as the wealthiest among us are wined and dined, drinking champagne, and being showered in a life of luxury, and I can't even find a girl who will share a floating door in the middle of a cold ocean with me.

Life's not fair!

Just changing the ending of a word changed the entire meaning according to several focus group studies.

Even Americans who were polled and consider themselves wealthy, still do not feel they are apart of the wealthiest class. Although, no dollar amount was ever affixed to what we consider wealthy or the wealthiest. It is only a word, then we changed the negative connotation of taxes, and softened it with a term our society sees as an American Value. Americans believe in fairness, it's taught starting in preschool and is a core American Value. People hate taxes, so to say you want to raise taxes; you have a non starter. So you call it a share, and we come up with fair share, Perfect! Because asking whether someone should be paying their fair share, is the same as sating someone is NOT paying.

It is a trigger to most people that they have been not paying their taxes; they have been cheating on their taxes. So, they found a winning combination asking Americans to ask the Wealthiest, among us to pay their fair share. Now, all they need to do is create the narrative, get other people in the party to anchor this phrase to anything related to wealth, business, or success. Broadcast nonstop messages through commercials, speeches, and media. Now, you have effectively influenced the majority in a country that there are some Rich Fat Cats not paying their fair share. And it works perfectly, no one asks why you need more money. No one asks, why do only some people need to pay more when half of the people pay nothing. No one asks to clarify what it is meant by the word wealthiest?

How does a movie like The Patriot make you feel about war? It makes killing and brutality seem like the ultimate show of Patriotism, there is a sense of romanticism intertwined, doesn't it? Does that make us more or less receptive to fighting in a war? Obviously, one movie would have difficulty in changing the behaviors of a country. It's also important to note that Mel Gibson is not trying to promote killing people. Quite the opposite, his movies are all about overcoming great limitation through hard work and discipline. They are models of the possibility of winning despite great odds. It is crucial we recognize the effect of the majority culture we consistently effect. It's important for us to be mindful of what our brains are soaking up and make sure those messages support us in achieving our goals in life. Imagine what could be if we changed the world's internal representation of war? What is the same influence used to get volumes of individuals to fight could be focused on the pursuit of bridging differences, values, and create a global respect and unity for the individuals rights and liberty. If you look at current hot spots around the world, what is one of the biggest similarities in those places? It is the lack of information and access to technology for the common man. Even in Afghanistan, most all the men and women are illiterate.

Where do their beliefs come from? How are their internal representations formed? Simple, by the people or group who can give them the most compelling meanings and beliefs. Yet does the technology exist that could support this kind of change? I believe it does. However, please don't misrepresent my over optimism, I'm not suggesting this would be a cake walk at all, we can't just make a couple quick flicks and show them worldwide and then walk outside light a candle and join hands across the world singing Kumbaya. I am just saying; we have the same technology and capabilities to create change just as we have the tools for destruction. I believe we need to be cautious of the things we see, hear, and experience on a ritual basis and take note of how we represent experiences to ourselves on an individual basis and as a whole. What we want to see in our families, communities, countries, and the world at large, requires we stay astutely to our environment and situations before we give them meaning. The power to show an event online within minutes of the event taking places can be powerful and destructive. Imagine the hit dictators and oppressive rulers felt, watching the demise of Gaddafi live and in real time streaming on the internet at the time of the rebels capture. How did they internally represent that situation?

Maybe it provided a trigger to create a change to give more rights and freedoms to their people, trying to avoid the same result. Maybe, it emboldened they're resolving to seize even more power and to strip more rights from their citizens. And the worst case scenario that is being played out in Syria right now, and who's result is yet to be told. Where a man is holding onto power, and if he feels that a collapse is imminent, instead of face the same fate as he saw with Gaddafi he unleashes thousands of chemical weapons on his own people, the classic go out in a blaze of Glory.

Using NLP to Shape and Lead the Conversation

I look at our current philosophy and strategy when it comes to working with a leader like Vladimir Putin, in Russia, and feel some concern.

I recall the time I met Putin, it was at an informal gathering and my impression of the man is skewed. Because of the unique situation I just happened to be in, living in Russia, I was accepted and embraced simply by my associations. So, President Putin, was pleasant, engaging and I loved talking with him about history, cars, and pop culture. However, I am also very astute to how he came to power, his grasp on industry throughout all of Russia. I knew his background and had no false notions about what this man is capable of. I am very aware of the sharp contrast there would have been if meeting under different circumstances. This is where more influence would come into play, and putting myself in a matched state as he. Their style of communication and talks still utilizes intimidation, deceit, threats, and an overly masculine, bold, assertive, loud demeanor.

Not matching this state would leave him with a sense that he overpowered you and discover a weakness he can exploit later. Because of his KGB background you would be aware that he has more in depth knowledge about your life, and your mental state, he will have a preconceived conclusion and have already measured you up. So, you can't break his pattern very easily, you can't pretend with him it will be seen as disingenuous and you will lose ground for any kind of trust to be developed. Things you would focus on to influence him is posture, gestures, direct unwavering eye contact, staying true to whom you are, while projecting a confidence and unwavering physiology no matter what he says, or insinuates, and even threatens. It is just one example of influence, also understand where they are coming from, and don't have any preconceived notions about the kind of information they already have on you.

However, the ultimate form of influence is through sheer numbers. You can live your life in a couple different ways. You can follow the latest trending topics, tabloids, and gossip show, jumping to all the latest trends and messages that are funneled to you. You can be romanced by war, hooked by junk food, or salivating over every trend being fed to you through the boob tube.

STEPHEN LEACOCK HAD THIS TO SAY ABOUT ADVERTISING:

"Advertising: the science of arresting the human intelligence long enough to get money from it."

Some of us live in a world where are intelligence is dictated to us through endorsements and Hollywood. Our society today, seeks out celebrities, actors, actresses, singers etc., and will give their comments and ideas the weight of an intellectual expert and authority. Who could ever imagine that to understand the situation in the Middle East we need to go to the Jersey Shores for guidance and wisdom?

The alternative is to live a life of your design. You can learn the power through the control your brain allows you to wield over all internal functions and nervous system. You can link new empowering representations to events and situations, so you can change your state and behavior. You can be aware when you are being manipulated or coerced. You can affirm when behaviors and meanings are being forced on you truly align with your values and when they don't. Then, you can cut straight through the crud and act on those things that have real value to you, blocking out those that don't.

The Art of Influence

Trends change on a weekly basis, and there is no shortage of experts, out there to tell us how to live every aspect of our lives. If you can influence, you become a trend creator instead of a lapdog to the latest IT personality telling us to jump or when to bark. It's important to set a course when you cast your vision, nothing is worse then finding yourself on the edge of Niagara Falls and then looking for your compass. Influence is to lead and blaze a path, cast a vision, and chart a course that leads to exceptional outcomes.

It always comes back to the spirit of the individual. It wasn't until Sarah Joseph Hale urged for a National holiday of Thanksgiving. She had a goal to bring a unity to our country on this day. She succeeded in a task that others had failed at for over 250 years. Although many of us believe that the Thanksgiving Holiday has been an American Tradition since the Pilgrims first gave thanks in October of 1621, yet it was not for another 155 years till there was a consistent or unified Thanksgiving celebration within the Colonies.

Even after The War of Independence marking a momentous victory and celebrated throughout the country, and still the tradition was not upheld. Actually, the third Thanksgiving was held after successfully drafting the United States Constitution, when President George Washington proclaimed November 26, 1789, a day of national Thanksgiving. Still, it failed to become a recurring event.

It wasn't until 1,827 when Sarah Joseph Hale, a determined, and persistent force to be reckoned with pushed to make it all happen. She was the mother of five, supported her family as a writer, during a time in our Country that few women had a profession of their own. She was the editor of a ladies' magazine, her hard worked made that magazine a huge success nationwide with a circulation of 150,000. Best known for her expos on behalf of women's colleges, free public playgrounds, and daycares. And she also is the lady who wrote a little nursery rhyme you might have heard before titled, Mary Had a Little Lamb. Sarah's most important cause was the creation of a permanent national Thanksgiving Day.

Even with a long list of success in business and charitable work within her community. It was through the magazine that gave her a platform to influence those with the power to act. Over thirty-six years she gave the voice to her cause, she wrote letters on a ritual basis to presidents and governors. She was the squeaky wheel that would only get louder until the oil arrived. She influenced the hearts and minds of women by

The Art of Influence

publishing tempting Thanksgiving menus, heartfelt stories, and poetry focused on Thanksgiving themes, and she wrote column after column for an annual Thanksgiving Day.

It was after the Civil War when Hale saw the opportunity to influence the nation and capture a feeling which she could anchor to Thanksgiving Day.

SHE WROTE:

"Would it not be a great advantage socially, nationally, and religiously to have the day of our American Thanksgiving positively settled?"

IN OCTOBER 1863, SHE PUBLISHED:

"Putting aside the sectional feelings and local incidents that might be urged by any single state or isolated territory that desired to choose its own time, would it not be more noble, more truly American, to become national in unity when we offer to God our tribute of joy and gratitude for the blessings of the year?"

Her letter to then Secretary of State William Seward was shown to President Abraham Lincoln who felt a day of national unity was perfect. In only four days, the president issued a proclamation setting the last Thursday in November 1863 as a national Thanksgiving Day. And in the wise words of Forest Gump, That's all I gotta say about that. One person, one woman with persistence, and influence effectively used the power of the media to communicate her message and influence changes.

The Art of Influence

Here are a couple systems to create lasting trends. I try to instill a powerful and empowering difference through educating others. If we want a lasting effect on the future, it is up to us to give our students the tools that create the most powerful changes in life, and all those come from within. My organization brings possibilities to life in our programs we offer through, Tollie's Out of the Darkness Project. In these programs, we teach kids to utilize their natural curiosity coupled with tools we teach so they can understand and run their own brains.

They learn the concepts and proactive directing their own behaviors creating fun and exciting new results in their life. They learn how to communicate and feel a real connection with all types of people and backgrounds. They role-play scenarios learning how to break through limiting beliefs, and to shoot for the moon with new perceptions of what is possible. Also, teaching the importance of choices and decisions, taking responsibility for every aspect of their life and how to achieve measurable results in the process. At they end the kids, a rattle off ideas, and dreams at over a hundred miles an hour.

One parent emailed me a day after, saying how her son would not shut up all night long, life was endless possibilities, and was making lists of things to do, steps to take to make his goals viable.

SHE ENDED HER EMAIL BY SAYING ONE OF THE BEST LINES:

"Thank you! Nothing is worse than your son coming home, and all they will say about their day was, it was fine. Yesterday, he came home, and he was full of LIFE! I felt like a kid again, and it's the best feeling in the world..."

When I read that, I said the most profound, poetic expression ever to pass my lips, How Freak'n Cool is THAT! Working with students has been one of the greatest privileges in my life, and they will always be a constant focus of mine.

The Art of Influence

Yet, I'm just one person, and our partners can reach out to only so many kids. So we have developed Rise Beyond, systems to provide teachers, and mentors with the possibilities that only NLP can provide for these students. That was a great platform heading in the right direction to affect change within our future leaders. However, it was not on a large enough scale to truly create a shift in the possibilities in education. Now, we are in the first stages of mind mapping a new project, our idream Project.

Tollie's idream Project removes the barriers and opens the doors to teens and young adults worldwide to showcase creative talents, while encouraging growth through competition. Tollie's idream Project is the first online social network to provide a safe and unbiased platform to showcase talents, and create intense competition. Discovering talent, has just gone viral, allowing Tollie International to be poised to launch a full production online HD Network with new talent and a vast audience. Simply put the idream Project is the product of Passion + Opportunity + Talent... Collide! If you have input about this project, I invite your letters and comments.

Many people in today's society don't give a second thought to the quality of knowledge and meanings being absorbed each day. According to the latest statistics published by the A.C. Nielsen Co., the average American watches four hours of television a day and 32 hours online a month. More alarming is according to parentstv.org 66% of children (ages ten to 16) surveyed say that their peers are influenced by TV shows. And when it comes to the influence of sex 62% say that sex on TV shows and movies influences kids to have sex when they are too young.

TELEVISION ALONE IS RESPONSIBLE FOR 10% OF YOUTH VIOLENCE. - LEONARD ERON, SENIOR RESEARCH SCIENTIST AT THE UNIVERSITY OF MICHIGAN.

I am not a person who is big on stats, or even surveys. I don't put much weight into their meaning I use them as a barometer to gauge a situation. Yet, These stats to me are more than mere numbers; this is a wake up call! It's imperative we examine what is being absorbed into our brains, especially if we expect them to grow and continue to be curious and challenge themselves and unleash their full ability to create a dream infused life experience. Guys, our brains function much like a computer, and if we continue to communicate to ourselves a meaning that says blowing up villages with a machine gun are awesome or that unhealthy junk food is brain food, then those new meanings will direct our behavior.

We have more opportunity today than ever before to mold how we communicate and represent events so we can direct all our behaviors. We have a daunting challenge facing not only our country but all civilization, and that is to deal with the disempowering kinds of images and mass meanings we produce. When you focus more on self esteem without criticism and challenge we will lose our innovation. When we focus on making people feel good about mediocrity, you lose the passion to become more. When you focus on everyone feeling good about being comfortable you lose your mojo and lose purpose in life.

Vision creation is what leadership is about; it's the heart and soul of this book.

You now have the tools to create state, develop a strategy, act and control your internal communication with your brain to determine meaning, and changing behaviors.

You know how to filter out all the noise and distractions, and you know how to resolve conflict and create deep and significant relationships with others. But, if you really want to create change, you need to cast a vision and have the faith and courage to rise and lead.

To lead, you must know how to communicate and influence you must become inspired to create an unflinching power inside to lead with passion.

Remember, the world is led by those who can influence.

The Art of Influence

If you can harness the curiosity, talent, and passion of those around you to implement a strategy to success then you expand your infinite possibilities. I know this is true we do it everyday at Tollie International; we breathe life into your ideas and dreams.

Our faith and ability to influence the majority while casting possibilities into a world of dreams. Just as a stone creates a ripple atop the water of a still pond, the extent of change we will create has only just begun to be felt.

Precision Marketing Examples

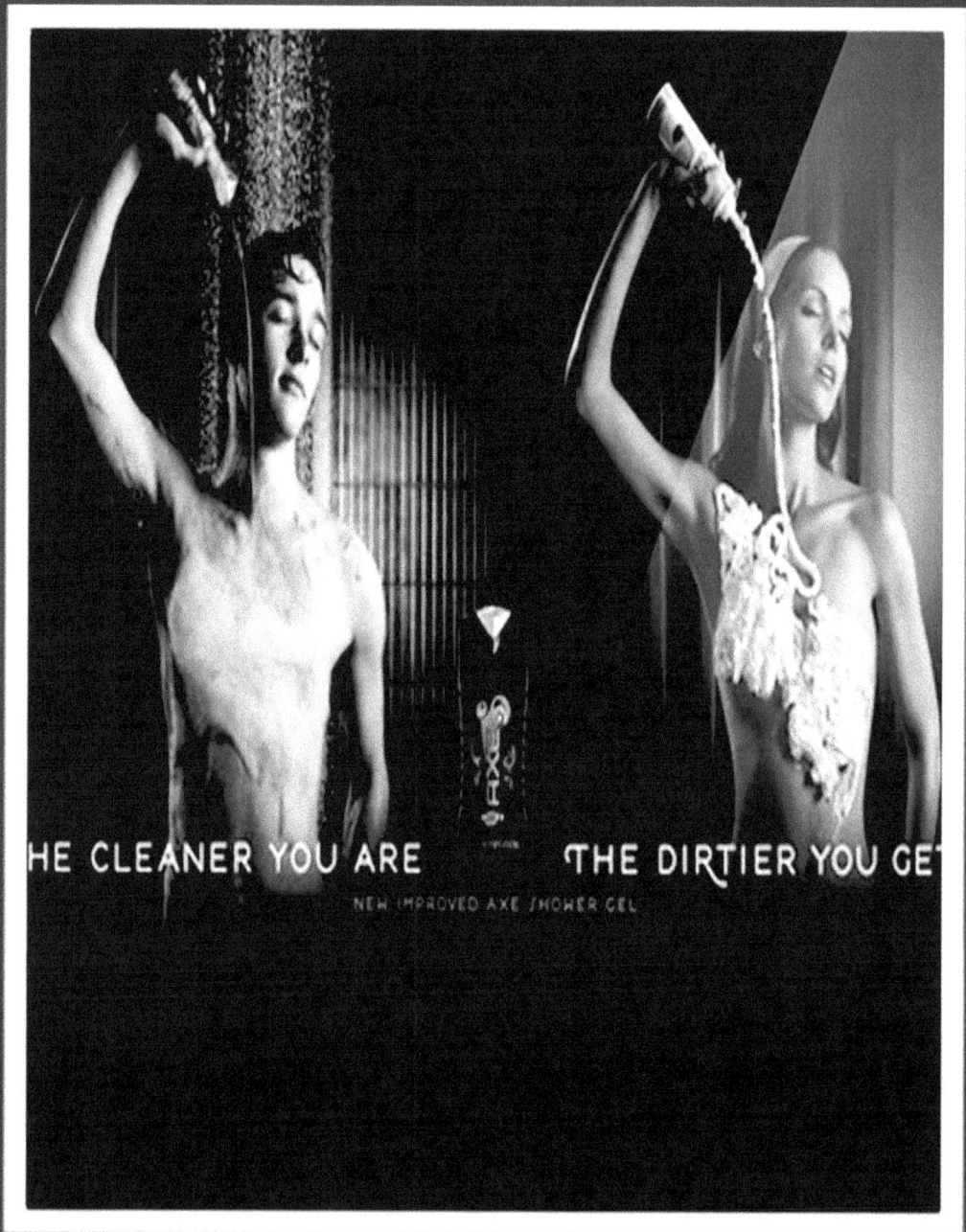

THE CLEANER YOU ARE   THE DIRTIER YOU GET

NEW IMPROVED AXE SHOWER GEL

Sex Sells Advertising AXE Body Wash

Retro YouTube Advertising Artwork

Twitter

The sublime, mighty community with just 140 letters!

A VIRTUAL locality with a wide assortment of people. That's Twitter! A notorious new mechanism that lets you maintain virtual contact with family and friends no matter where they are. By following or being followed, you will enjoy previously unimagined experiences like sharing incredible amounts of information including videos, photographs, etc. Twitter is a truly magnificent tool!

TWITTER®

Retro Twitter Advertising Artwork

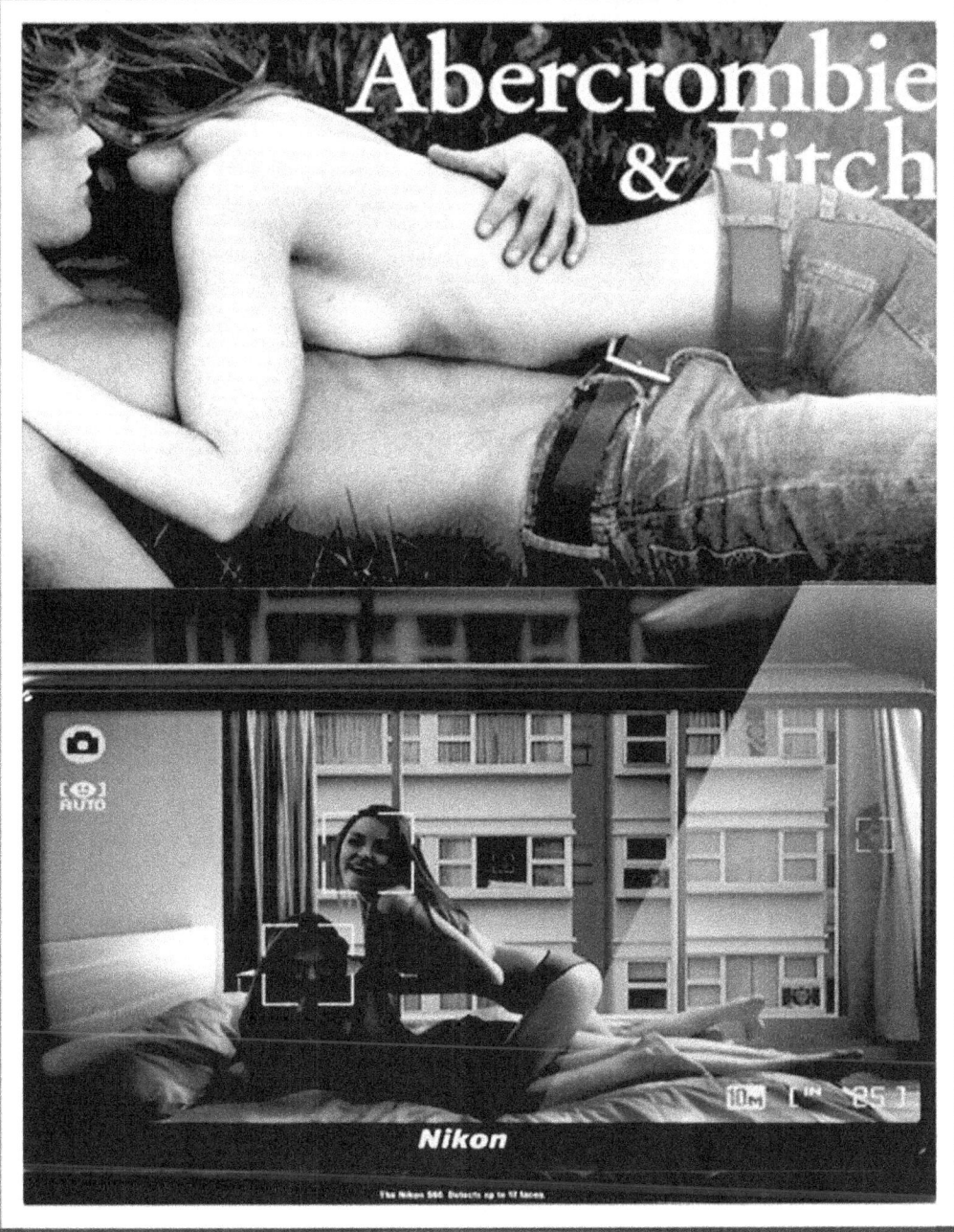

Abercrombie & Fitch

Nikon

Sex Sells Advertising Nikon & A&F

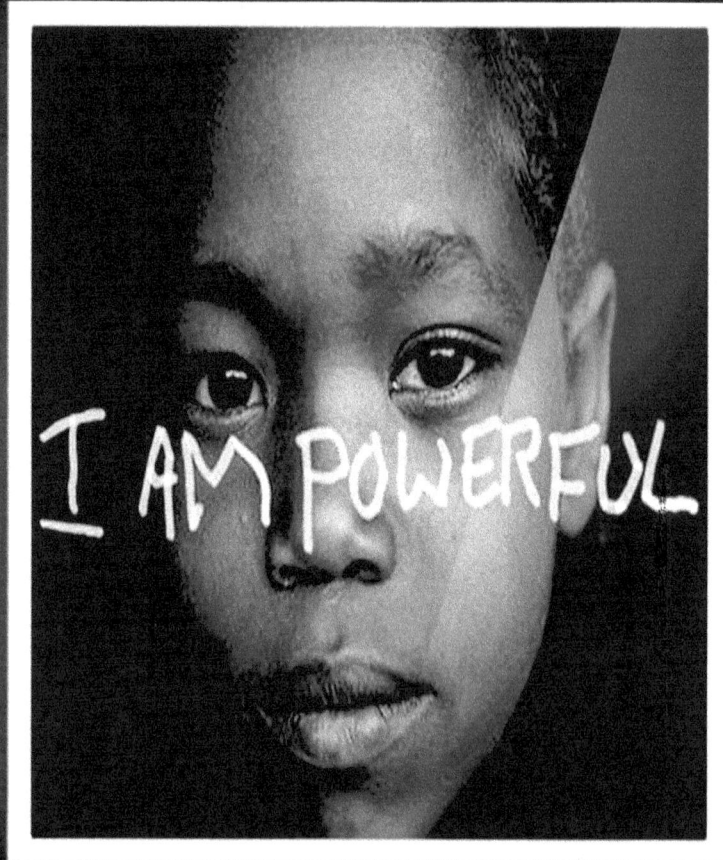

I AM POWERFUL

Chapter X

The Challenge

"MY EXPERIENCE HAS BEEN THAT WORK IS ALMOST THE BEST WAY TO PULL ONESELF OUT OF THE DEPTHS" -ELEANOR ROOSEVELT

We Have Journeyed an Exciting Path Together.

Yet, the distance you travel, how far you'll allow the path to lead you, is ultimately your decision. This book has been a source of tools to allow you the opportunity to Rise to an Inspired state. You can easily put this book down and feel happy, for at least a while. Maybe you can even achieve a sense of stronger self esteem. As we discussed early on, the idea of being happy, with a great self esteem is an illusion. You now know that the power to change, is the power to be. All change is possible once you get honest with yourself. I hope you take purposeful steps everyday taking control of your life and your brain. You can live an extraordinary life, creating the inspired powerful beliefs and states to achieve that everyday. It happens only by you taking the action to do so.

Let's take a look back at the main things you have learned.

You know now that the most incredible tool on the planet is the bio computer between them two ears of yours! The capability of what is possible has never even been within a fraction of what the brain can actually accomplish and process. This is it! Apple has nothing on what you can accomplish within your nervous system, utilizing the most resourceful states, crating inspired powerful behaviors. Well run, your brain can make life more tremendous than any dream you've ever cast before.

You learned the difference between a daydreamer and a dreamer who achieves their goals. You know the difference is action! Dream big, cast your vision and then develop the strategy and immediately take action, be flexible and work your plan consistently till you hit your target. We can never say enough times, the difference between a successful person and a not very successful person is many times the one who succeeds takes action. Education, knowledge, and skills are important, but it's not enough. Tons of people had the same information as a Steve Jobs or a Glenn Beck. But, those who took action achieved enormous success which left an imprint on the world.

The Challenge

You've learned the significance of modeling. You can always learn by the process, the old trial, and error method. You can speed up that process vastly by learning how to pace. Success leaves clues, those who achieve great things have a specific process they use in order to succeed, and an ultimate psychology. So learning to model those footsteps allows us to recreate the success by following their proven formula. Drastically cut the time it takes to master something by modeling the internal processes (*mental*) and external actions (*physical*) of those who achieve momentous outcomes.

Like the saying goes, work smarter not harder.

In a matter of hours, days, or maybe a few years, depending on your vision, you have the ability to learn what took them months or years to discover.

Remember the 10,000th hour rule, many times the success we know of with the iconic high achievers club came after the 10,000th hour.

You've learned that in order to be inspired and ultimately live a life of tremendous passion, its through communication. How we communicate with ourselves, as in the stories we tell ourselves, those excuses, and most importantly the meaning of any event is the meaning you give it.

Remember, you can communicate with your brain empowering signals allowing you to be in the most resourceful state to call upon only the most pleasurable and powerful emotions to create the most desirable behaviors at any moment.

Also, swinging the pendulum in the completely opposite direction, you can communicate to your brain everything you can't do, you can't accomplish, you don't have, you can even make yourself depressed, EVEN certifiably, clinically depressed. Two choices, where the pendulum swings is in your control and this is your

The Challenge

destiny. Those who DO and people of distinction can take any situation and make it work for them. People like Dick & (*son*) Rick Hoyt, Garth Brooks, Chris Williams who can take unimaginable tragedy and loss to find peace and goodness in all situations.

We can't hop in our Delorean and fire up the flux capacitor and go Back to the Future. We can't change the events of the moment. But, we can control how we process the event, to find the good and ultimately give us something positive in the future.

THE SECOND FORM OF COMMUNICATION | OUR RELATIONSHIPS WITH OTHERS.

THOSE WHO MASTERED THE ART OF COMMUNICATION, YIELDED TO INFLUENCE WHICH SHAPED OUR WORLD.

You can use everything in this book to uncover the true desires or others, allowing you to be more effective, precise, and influential, and not to mention allowing you to connect with others on a deeper level.

Life is GOOD!

You Create Positive Change | Don't Wish or Think Happy Thoughts | Create Positive Empowering Beliefs

You've learned the huge difference between the concept of simply wishing happy thoughts, or positive thinking and the power of creating positive empowering beliefs.

Empowering beliefs, empower you to develop a strategy, act and stay in an empowering resourceful state to be flexible in order to achieve your dreams.

The best part is, you learned specific tools in order to change your beliefs so they work for you. You learned what your mojo is. The power of your state and physiology when combined is the source of free flowing abundant mojo! It's from this mojo we can simply say, Life is GOOD!

You know now strategies people use, and you know how to build an instant rapport with anyone you meet. You've learned how to reframe events in your life and how to anchor those events to empowering feelings and emotions. You've learned how to communicate with confidence and influence, and how to communicate with others in order to develop long lasting relationships. You have learned the seven inspired character virtues, the seven attributes that allow successful people the juice to do whatever it takes to achieve.

I have no false preconceived notions that you will find yourself completely transformed after you put this book down. I can't have you run onto a stage, have me put my hand on your forehead and as I am sweating Protrusively under the revival tent lights to yell out, You're Healed! I mean we CAN do that, it just will lack the actual effect. Some of the things we've talked about in this book will be easier for you to absorb than others. But, as I continually said, the best things in life don't come from the achievement of the goal, it comes from the experiences and learning along the way.

This is not the last book you read in order to feed your thirst of knowledge, enhance your capacity for different and effective ideas and resources. Changes lead to more changes. Growth leads to more growth. Success leads to more success. Small changes will bring small growth; massive changes will bring about

The Challenge

tremendous growth. It's the ripple effect, your first step in life's pond of possibilities will cause a small ripple. But, when you decide you are ALL IN, full steam ahead and jump with the intensity and impact of a cannon ball, then when you hit the ponds still surface splashing thru doubt and fear, your ripple grows with intensity displacing the ponds bounty causing an overflow of life's potential.

Life's successes and failures can be measured by a millimeter many times. Think about it, if you hit a gold ball and it flies straight and true all day long, then you are on track for success. On the other hand, your partner hits the ball and it flies off far to the right, every time. Yet, both of you are using the same clubs, same technique, have the same skills and background, so what is the difference?

An outside observer points out, that both men are hitting the ball perfectly, yet the friend is slightly off by merely half a millimeter. Hitting that golf ball slightly off center begins as such a minuscule mistake, yet as that ball travels it never corrects the course and that slight mistake is now off in the woods. See success and the systems you put in place will always be changing and adjusting. If you start off on the wrong track and never learn and adjust you will never hit your target.

That's what you can use this book for. You can't change overnight (*you could start working on yourself tonight!*). Yet, when you understand how to communicate with your brain, and how you can communicate internally the representations of events. Give new meaning to events in order to create empowering emotions so you will change your behaviors. You learn to know your values, learn your purpose, get specific and disturbed. Then using your daily mojo time to start your day in a perfect state! Then the changes over a few weeks, four or five months, and even ten years into the future will change your entire life!

There are things in this book you already do; one of them is pacing or modeling others. Others are new. Keep in mind everything in life is advancing. Just using one of the tools in this book is moving you forward. You have taken that first step and in doing so have thrown your life into motion, through motion you enhance your emotions which then change your behaviors. Your behaviors move you towards achieving your goals, and you are now in full motion in a direction to achieve life's dreams. Every direction bears with it an inspired haven.

"Every day you may make progress. Every step may be fruitful. Yet there will stretch out before you an ever-lengthening, ever-ascending, ever-improving path. You know you will never get to the end of the journey. But this, so far from discouraging, adds only to the joy and glory of the climb." - Sir Winston Churchill

HERE'S A NEW QUESTION TO CONSIDER.

- What direction is your present course taking you?

- Can you say the direction of your current course where you will be in five years or ten years?

- Are you happy where your course will take you in five years or ten years?

It's as I have said a few times throughout this book, who you are today, magnifies in the future. All the things in your life today, all the feelings you have on a consistent basis today, all the events and challenges you experience today will only multiply down the road. Are you excited about that future? If not, you now have the tools and skills to make changes and reset your compass and the course of your life, so cast a compelling vision and become that person you need to in order to reach your extraordinary life ahead of you.

The one thing this book has taught you, is the ability to change rise inspired in no time at all, both on a personal basis and globally. Inspired power is the ability to change, to adapt, to expand, and to transcend. Inspired power doesn't mean you will always succeed or that you will never fail. Inspired power just means you grow and expand from all of life's experiences and make every experience work in your favor in some way. It is inspired power to transform your perceptions, to transform your actions, and to transform the results you're creating. It's your inspired power to love and serve that can make the greatest difference in your life's experiences.

Here's another suggestion to set yourself up to win in the game of life. Find the right team to play on. We have discussed power in terms of what we can do with others. Inspired power is the strength in numbers working for a common goal, adding fuel to the fire so it grows and expands. It could be your family, also your close friends. It can also be your partners in business or people your partner with and care for. Your work intensifies if you're working for others as well as for yourself. You contribute more, and you receive more.

Remember when we were talking about the importance of relationships, and how as human beings they are a necessity to have close relationships. Just ask for someone to tell you one of their greatest experiences in life, and usually it will involve something they did as part of a team. A memory of days went by, and that perfect moment under the Friday Night Lights when together their high school football team rallied and won against all odds.

Sometimes it's that team at work who landed the big account. Many times the team is your loved ones or your spouse. Being on a team makes you push harder, makes you expand as a person.

- PEOPLE CAN CHALLENGE YOU IN WAYS YOU CAN'T DO FOR YOURSELF.

- RISE INSPIRED AND GET IN THE GAME

- PEOPLE WILL ALWAYS GIVE MORE OF THEMSELVES TO OTHERS THAN THEY WILL GIVE TO THEMSELVES.

By contributing to others they receive experiences which adds to their human experience. If your breathing, you're on a team of some kind. Your team could be your family, a relationship, your businesses, your town, your country, your world. You can be the bench warmer, or getting in the game.

My hope for you is you get off that bench, rise inspired and get in the game and play with passion, because life should be lived with passion. Because the more you contribute to others, the more you give of yourself, the more human experiences you get back, which add to your own life's experience. They more you use the lessons and skills from this book for yourself and for others; the more they will give back to you.

Make sure the team you are on will challenge you. It's easy to stray off course. It's easy to know what to do and still do nothing. For many that just seems to be the way life is. The conventional pull of life is gravity, pulling you down. We all experience off days. All of us have times we don't do what we know we should. But, if we choose our environment by surrounding ourselves with champions who don't exercise excuses, they are always moving forward, they are focused on achieving their goals, they support us, it pushes us to be more and do more and give more.

If you can be around those individuals who will never let you settle for less than you can be, then you have the ultimate gift and blessing in life. An environment plays a monumental role in who you are and who you will become in life. Be sure those you surround yourself with make you a better person by having them in your life.

Becoming more each and everyday are a great purpose in life. Because to become a better person, to challenge yourself and strive for more means that you have a pattern of taking action. Taking action requires accepting responsibility for decisions and outcomes. Yet, its this pattern of taking action and creating results.

There are times in life. A difficult situation is present, and you decide to help and give of yourself. After the difficult situation, you look back to give meaning to what took place. Then that night as you are lying in bed, your lover looks at you and says how proud they are of what you did in that situation to help in a difficult time.

The Challenge

You look back at her, after spending time reflecting on the meaning of the event, and you conclude as you say to her:

"Yea, but the thing is anyone could have done the exact thing!"

LOVINGLY, THEY ANSWER:

"Anybody could have, but you did."

"Love begins at home, and it is not how much we do... but how much love we put in that action." -Mother Teresa

So that's the key to being inspired that is the greatest theme running through this book. Just do it! Take the lead, take action. Take what you have learned here, and use it now. It's not just abut doing things for yourself, it's about your contribution to others as well.

Gifts from the unselfish acts will always be grander than can be imagined.

There's no shortage of talking heads in the world, but talk is cheap; actions speak louder than words. There are tons of people who have all the answers, they have all the skill and knowledge, yet they achieve nothing, produce no measurable results. It's never going to be enough to talk the talk, you must walk the walk.

That's what inspired power is all about. Inspired to rise and take action, effect changes, produce results, and serve others with all your heart! Muhammad Ali had a philosophy on training that I think sums up the philosophy of someone who will do.

IT'S WORTHY OF PACING. HE SAID:

"I hated every minute of training, but I said, 'Don't quit. Do it now and live the rest of your life as a champion'."

THAT'S WHY HE WILL ALWAYS BE THE GREATEST.

Impossible is Nothing

At a Time, There Were Two Great Orators of Antiquity. One Was Cicero, the Other Demosthenes.

When Cicero was done speaking, people always stood and cheered, What a great speech! On the other hand, when Demosthenes concluded, people would rise and say, Let us march, and march they did. That's the contrast between presentation and influence. I hope to be remembered as being in the latter category.

If you read this book and say to yourself, Wow, great book; excellent insight, tools and knowledge, and you don't do anything with those tools, then we would have wasted our time together. Instead, if you take that first step right now and goes back through the book and utilize it as a handbook for creating change,

The Challenge

controlling your brain, and nervous system to lead your body and mind and with a steadfast resolve to rise, rise inspired and take that first step. Use this book as a guide to changing any aspect of your life, if you do this for yourself, you might have embarked on a life journey that will make the dreams of your past seem like child's play.

I KNOW THAT IT HAPPENED TO ME, AND NOW I ONLY SAY:

"Dream Big, Nothing is Impossible!"

I challenge you to rise inspired, become the artist as you stroke the canvas breathing life into your vision, with bold colors, fine lines, and noticing all the little details life's journey allows us along the way. As you stroke the emotions of love, joy, fulfillment, passion, purpose, and service to others then as you stand back from your creation a smile comes across your face as you stare at your life's experience your life's eternal masterpiece.

I give you a sincere thanks for your commitment to learning and growing in order to develop yourself and for letting me share with you some of the differences that made the difference in my life.

I pray God blesses you with all his love and affection as he smiles down upon your journey. No one can tell you what to do next, you can tell yourself all the stories you want, in the end they are still excuses.

IT COMES DOWN TO A VERY SIMPLE QUESTION:

* Why is it the hardest thing for people to believe in; is themselves?

Believe, believe in you, believe when I say, you deserve only the best for yourself, and do NOT except anything less. Expect more, be more, and give more. Finally, I'm going to leave you with one last message from the greatest champion. The world has ever known, the great Ali!

"Impossible is just a big word thrown around by small men, who Find it easier to live in the world they've been given than to explore the power they have to change it. Impossible is not a fact It's an opinion Impossible is not a declaration It's a dare Impossible is potential Impossible is temporary Impossible is nothing." -Muhammad Ali

The Challenge

www.ingramcontent.com/pod-product-compliance
Lightning Source LLC
Chambersburg PA
CBHW081422090426
42740CB00017B/3155